DIES ILLA

DEATH IN THE MIDDLE AGES

VINAVER STUDIES IN FRENCH

GENERAL EDITORS: A R W JAMES & JANE H M TAYLOR

ISSN 0264-5564

I

DIES ILLA

DEATH IN THE MIDDLE AGES

PROCEEDINGS OF THE 1983 MANCHESTER COLLOQUIUM

EDITOR: JANE H M TAYLOR

X

FRANCIS CAIRNS

Published by
Francis Cairns
The University, P.O. Box 147, Liverpool L69 3BX
Great Britain

First published 1984

Copyright © Francis Cairns, 1984

British Library Cataloguing in Publication Data

Dies illa.—(Vinaver studies in French,
 ISSN 0264-5564; v.1)
 1. Death—Social aspects—France
 I. Taylor, Jane H.M.
 306.9'0944   HQ1073.5.F7

 ISBN 0-905205-18-9

Phototypeset by I.M.R. Ltd, Manchester

Printed in Great Britain by
Redwood Burn Ltd, Trowbridge, Wiltshire

CONTENTS

FOREWORD

To choose the title *Dies illa* for a celebration may not seem at first sight at all appropriate. The phrase is linked, indissolubly it seems, with what precedes it: *Dies irae*, the terror and foreboding attendant on the Day of Judgement. Set in our minds is that image of an end of the Middle Ages peopled by bands of penitents and flagellants intoning the anthem which a popular mythology attributes to them: *Dies irae, dies illa* ...

Yet this image of apocalyptic despair is misleading. Certainly, detached from its context, the phrase suggests fear of the divine wrath, but the context is revelatory: the Day of Judgement will be a day not of terror but of salvation. *Dies illa*, long awaited, will be a day of consolation, of salvation, of entry into the bliss of eternity, a day of looking not backward in despair and penitence, but forward in hope and confidence.[1]

It was in this spirit that the Department of French Studies at the University of Manchester chose to celebrate the man who for thirty-three years, from 1933-1966, was its guiding hand. When Professor Eugène Vinaver died in 1979, it was the wish of the Department that a fund should be collected, on the one hand to enable the Department to keep alive his memory for future generations of scholars and students, but on the other hand to reflect, as he would have wished, the present and future of French studies. A man who at seventy-eight could introduce a seminar by promising his audience "a few new ideas I am trying out"[2] would, the Department felt confident, have wished *colloquia* established in his name not to indulge in easy nostalgia, but rather to welcome diversity and challenge.

Professor Vinaver's career was itself diverse. He was educated in three cultures, in St. Petersburg, Paris and Oxford; he worked on *Tristan* and Malory, Béroul and *Roland*; he inaugurated and edited the Manchester French Classics series; after his "retirement", he spent some fifteen years lecturing in the United States and in Sussex; he was passionately interested in music and drama and painting. An outstanding medieval scholar, who yet made his mark also with work on Racine and Flaubert; the moving spirit behind the vast and highly successful International Arthurian Society, who yet had time to spare for young and insignificant research-students; an academic the embodiment of a more elegant old world who yet adapted, at seventy-seven and as to the manner born, to the demands of the television interview; for such a man, the only appropriate tribute was the creation of something new and dynamic.

It was perhaps for this reason, among others, that the Department chose, as theme for the first *Eugène Vinaver International Colloquium, Death in the Middle Ages*. Again, the topic may seem retrospective or gloomy, but the consensus among those who took part in the *Colloquium* was that the occasion was one of pleasure in scholarship and delight in the exchange of ideas. And the theme itself is that of a branch of scholarship which is energetic and prolific.

The field of study which the French know as *Histoire des Mentalités* has recently concentrated, and particularly in France, on the history of attitudes towards death. The tip of the iceberg is perhaps the studies devoted to the subject by the brilliant historian and popularist Philippe Ariès: his two major works, *Essais sur l'histoire de la mort en Occident du Moyen Age à nos jours* and *L'Homme devant la mort*[3] have focussed the attention of a wide audience on the subject, and recent highly important studies of attitudes towards death and dying, such as those of Chaunu,[4] Lebrun[5] and Vovelle,[6] have produced a wealth of minutely-researched archival detail. Studies of demography, pin-pointing individual cities or regions in narrowly-defined periods,[7] have enabled the reader to replace broad and perhaps ill-founded generalisations with accurate statement. Philosophers[8] and anthropologists,[9] theologians[10] and psychologists[11] and sociologists[12] have taken part in a veritable explosion of activity around a subject not long ago considered virtually taboo.

In all this, the, Middle Ages and especially the later Middle Ages have been a focus of particular attention. Scholars, and the general public, have long conceived what Huizinga called the Waning Middle Ages as marked by a morbid concentration on death, judgement and bodily decay.[13] Huizinga's own chapter on the fascination of death and Émile Mâle's long disquistion on funerary monuments and macabre paintings and woodcuts[14] are illustrative of attitudes long held and perhaps insufficiently examined. References to the Black Death and the Schism, the *transi* tomb and the *Danse Macabré*, seemed for long to justify a picture of the late Middle Ages as morbidly bent on the contemplation of death.

More recent scholarship has enabled critics and historians to provide a much more nuanced picture, and to submit such generalisations to exhaustive and critical scrutiny. Some indication of the urgency with which the question is now invested is given by the fact that the present *colloquium* is the fifth on the subject in recent years,[15] that an entire number of *Annales* was devoted to the subject in 1976,[16] and that to look in the check-lists of the *Cahiers de Civilisation Médiévale* is to find a bibliography of truly alarming dimensions. A telling example of this proliferating activity is provided by studies devoted to the Black Death which for the first time allow accurate estimates of death-rates, and accurate description of the effects of plague on population. A mass of detailed and highly documented research, concentrating on individual towns or provinces,[17] finally permits the grand syntheses, for example, of Biraben[18] and of Delumeau.[19]

These studies are of course demographically and statistically based, and it is demography and statistics which interest both social and economic historians.[20] What Chaunu calls "l'histoire sérielle"[21] is at the base also of research into attitudes towards death. Thus careful studies of testaments have led on the one hand to Chiffoleau's masterly *La Comptabilité de l'au-delà*,[22] and on the other to a clearer understanding of medieval popular beliefs in relation to the after-life.[23] This, in conjunction with careful study of parishional life and beliefs in the Middle Ages,[24] and with new surveys of the Schism[25] and of medieval spirituality,[26] have done much to transform scholarly understanding of medieval religious life and attitudes to death.

Such attitudes are naturally reflected in the literature of the Middle Ages. Four major studies have been devoted in recent years to the subject of death in medieval poetry and literature,[27] and quite apart from these, there is a flood of articles on individual literary genres or works. There have been important studies of the *Artes Moriendi*[28] and of the *Danse Macabré*[29]; there have also been papers on the theme of death in, for instance, the *chanson de geste*.[30] Particular interest is currently centred around the *planctus*,[31] and around depiction of the deaths of individual characters in the romances and epics of the Middle Ages.

In the plastic arts, too, there has been a wave of interest in death and its iconography. Alberto Tenenti's study of 1952 seems to point the way,[33] and several tendencies are discernible thereafter. One centre of interest is tombs and funerary art and ceremony: the *transi* tomb, the royal monument.[34] Another is the link between the erotic and death: a major exhibition was staged in Michigan in 1975-6,[35] and there has since been the important study by Jean Wirth.[36] And a final category is that of the plague: accurate studies of work directly inspired by the Black Death, rather than easy generalisation.[37]

★

In this burgeoning activity the present volume will, it is hoped, play a modest but worthy part. It is the reflection and culmination of a project long meditated and which could never have come to fruition without the help and contribution of many. It is my pleasure to offer the thanks of the Department of French Studies and the Eugène Vinaver Memorial Fund to Barbara Orr whose patience in transferring complex texts into complex lay-outs on the word-processor made the whole technical process pleasurable; to the anonymous scholars who produced the summaries and résumés for which the editor assumes full responsibility; to the British Academy, to the French Cultural

Delegation and to the Elie Auguste Bretey Fund of the University of Manchester for their generous financial help; to Dr. A.R.W. James in particular, without whose help and support the project would have foundered; and finally, with greatest appreciation, to the contributors to the Eugène Vinaver Memorial Fund, listed in this volume, whose generosity made the vision of memorial *colloquia* a reality. To all these, to the Eugène Vinaver Memorial Committe, and to other colleagues and friends whose contributions have been of such support, I offer, on my own behalf and on that of the Department, my most heartfelt gratitude.

Jane H.M. Taylor

NOTES

1. I am extremely grateful to Dom Jean Leclercq, who supplied my colleague Dr. A.R.W. James with the following details which he kindly allows me to quote: "En réalité, les formes *dies haec, ista* (ou *iste*), *illa* (ou *ille*) sont fréquentes dans la Bible, en particulier dans l'Ancien Testament, surtout en des formules prophétiques, c'est-à-dire annoncant l'avenir. Le caractère de celui-ci – événement ou période – est parfois précisé par un terme évoquant la vengeance (Ier 30,7), la fureur (Is 13,13). Mais la perspective du bonheur ne manque point non plus, en ce contexte; *dies consolationis, retributionis, visitationis, redemptionis, ostensionis Israel, dies Christi, dies aeternitatis* (....) C'est surtout avec cette signification prophétique, d'attente joyeuse d'une manifestation glorieuse de Dieu, que de telles expressions ont été adoptées par la liturgie."

2. For the details which follow, I am grateful to Professor Brian Woledge whose portrait of Vinaver introduced the Manchester *Colloquium*, and to the late Professor Cedric Pickford (see particularly his tribute, published in the *Sewanee Mediaeval Colloquium Occasional Papers*, number I, Spring 1982).

3. The first Paris, 1975, the second Paris, 1977. The latter has now been translated into English and published by Penguin Books under the title *The Hour of Our Death* (London, 1982).

4. *La Mort à Paris, XVI ͤ, XVII ͤ et XVIII ͤ siècles* (Paris, 1978).

5. François Lebrun, *Les Hommes et la mort en Anjou aux XVII ͤ et XVIII ͤ siècles* (Paris, 1971).

6. Michel Vovelle, *Mourir autrefois: attitudes collectives devant la mort aux XVII ͤ et XVIII ͤ siècles* (Paris, 1974).

7. Pierre Chaunu's notes and references (*op.cit.* pp. 194-6, 237-8) give some idea of the seething activity in the field. There were at one time fifty or more students working under his direction on studies of this kind.

8. e.g. Vladimir Jankélévitch, *La Mort* (Paris, 1965), and Jacques Choron, *La Mort et la pensée occidentale* (Paris, 1969).

9. v. for example, L.V. Thomas, *Anthropologie de la mort* (Paris, 1975).

10. v. for example, G. Martelet, *L'Au-delà retrouvé: Christologie des fins dernières* (Paris, 1975) and cf. also Mircea Eliade, *Histoire des croyances et des idées religieuses* (Paris, 1976), t.I.

11. v. for example, M. Charlot, *Vivre avec la mort* (Paris, 1976).

12. v. for example, Geoffrey Gorer, *Death, Grief and Mourning in Contemporary Britain* (New York, 1963), and Edgar Morin, *L'Homme et la mort* (Paris, 1970).

13. Johann Huizinga, *Le Déclin du Moyen Age* (Paris, 1967) (published in English as *The Waning of the Middle Ages*, London, 1955).

14. *L'Art religieux de la fin du Moyen Age en France. Etude sur l'iconographie du Moyen Age et sur ses sources d'inspiration* (Paris, 1969) (first published Paris,1908).

15. *La Mort au Moyen Age*, Colloque de la Société des Historiens Médiévistes de l'Enseignement Supérieur (Strasbourg, 1977); *Death in the Middle Ages*, ed. H. Braet en W. Verbeke (Louvain, 1982) (Mediaevalia Lovaniensia, Series I – Studia

IX); *Il Dolore e la Morte nella spiritualità dei secoli XII e XIII*, Convegni del Centro di Studi sulla Spiritualità medievale V, 7-10 Oct. 1962; *Le sentiment de la mort au moyen âge. Etudes présentées au Ve Colloque de l'Inst. d'Etudes médiévales de l'Univ. de Montréal*, ed. Claude Sutto (Saint-Denis (Montréal), 1979).

16. *Annales: Economies, Sociétés, Civilisations*, XXXI.i (1976).

17. The best-known of these is perhaps Elisabeth Carpentier's *Une Ville Devant la Peste: Orvieto et la Peste Noire de 1348* (Paris, 1962) (Ecole pratique des Hautes Etudes – VIe section, centre de recherches historiques: Démographie et sociétés VII), but it is only one of a mass of similar studies; v. for example H. Dubled, "Conséquences économiques et sociales des mortalités du XIVe siècle, essentiellement en Alsace," *Revue d'Histoire Economique et Sociale* XXXVII (1959); R.W. Emery, "The Black Death of 1348 in Perpignan," *Speculum* XLII (1967); D. Herlihy, "Population, plague and social change in rural Pistoia 1201-1403," *Economic History Revue* XVIII (1965); M. Mollat, "Notes sur la mortalité à Paris au temps de la Peste Noire d'après les comptes de l'oeuvre de Saint-Germain l'Auxerrois," *Le Moyen Age* XIX (1963); G. Prat, "Albi et la Peste Noire," *Annales du Midi* LXIV (1952); G. Sivery, "Le Hainaut et la Peste Noire," *Mémoires et Publications de la Société des Sciences, des Arts et des Lettres du Hainaut* LXXIX (1965); Ch. Verlinden, "La Grande Peste de 1348 en Espagne," *Revue belge de Philosophie et d'Histoire* XVII (1938); Raymond Williamson, "The Plague in Cambridge," *Medieval History* I (1957); Michael W. Dols, *The Black Death in the Middle East* (Princeton, 1977). This is merely a very small sample of the available literature; a complete bibliography can be found in the *Cahiers de Civilisation Médiévale*, under the key-word Peste.

18. Jean-Noël Biraben, *Les hommes et la peste en France et dans les pays européens et méditerranéens, I: La peste dans l'histoire* (Paris/The Hague, 1975) (E.H.E.S.S., Centre de recherches historiques, Civilisations et Sociétés). c.f. also J. Grimm, *Die Literarische Darstellung der Pest in der Antike und in der Romania* (Munich, 1965).

19. Jean Delumeau, *La Peur en Occident, XIVe-XVIIIe siècles: une cité assiégée* (Paris, 1978).

20. For a useful *mise au point*, see E. Carpentier et J. Glénisson, "Bilans et méthodes: la démographie française au XIVe siècle," *Annales: Economies, Sociétés, Civilisations* XVII.i. (1962). Other valuable recent studies include W. Abel, *Agrarkrisen und Agrarkonjunktur: eine Geschichte der Land- und Ernährungswirtschaft Mitteleuropas seit dem hohen Mittelalter*, revised edition (Hamburg, 1966); G. Bois, *Crise du féodalisme, économie rurale et démographie en Normandie orientale du début du XIVe siècle au milieu du XVIe siècle* (Paris, 1976); J.C. Russel, *Late Ancient and Medieval Population (Philadelphia, 1958); Edmond Baratier, La démographie provençale du XIII^{e}au XVI^{e}siècle* (Paris, 1961) (Ecole pratique des hautes études, VIe section, Centre de Recherches Historiques).

21. v. particularly *Histoire science sociale* (Paris, 1974), Chapter II: *Histoire et sciences humaines – L'Histoire sérielle*.

22. Jacques Chiffoleau, *La Comptabilité de l'au-delà: Les hommes, la mort et la religion dans la région d'Avignon à la fin du Moyen Age (vers 1320-vers 1480)* (Rome, 1980) (Collection de l'Ecole Française de Rome XLVII). Chiffoleau includes (pp.24-25) an exhaustive bibliography of recent testamentary research.

23. See for example, Jacques Le Goff, *La Naissance du Purgatoire* (Paris, 1981); H. Neveux, "Les lendemains de la mort dans les croyances occidentales (1250-1300)," *Annales: Economies, Sociétés, Civilisations* XXXIV.i. (1979); G. and M. Vovelle, *Vision de la mort et de l'au-delà en Provence, d'après les autels des âmes du Purgatoire, XVe-XXe siècles* (Paris, 1970) (Cahiers des Annales XXIX).

24. P. Adam, *La vie paroissiale en France au XIVe siècle* (Paris, 1964); E. Delaruelle, *La piété populaire au Moyen Age* (Turin, 1975); F. Rapp, *L'Eglise et la vie religieuse en Occident à la fin du Moyen Age* (Paris, 1971); J. Toussaert, *Le sentiment religieux en Flandre à la fin du Moyen Age* (Paris, 1963); D. Rosenthal, *Tod, Semantische und wörtgeographische Untersuchungen auf Grund germanischer Evangelien- und Rechtstexte* (Göteborg, 1974).

25. See for example, E. Delaruelle, P. Ourliac, E. R. Labande, *Le Grand Schisme d'Occident et la crise conciliaire*, in *Histoire de l'Eglise*, ed. A. Fliche et V. Martin (Paris, 1962-4).

26. See for example, A. Vauchez, *La spiritualité du Moyen Age occidental, XIIe-XIIIe

siècle (Paris, 1975); G. Dumoutet, *Aux sources de la piété eucharistique médiévale* (Paris, 1942).

27. Edelgard DuBruck, *The Theme of Death in French Poetry of the Middle Ages and the Renaissance* (The Hague, 1964) (Studies in French Literature I); Christine Martineau-Génieys, *Le Thème de la mort dans la poésie francaise de 1450 à 1550* (Paris, 1978) (Nouvelle Bibliothèque du Moyen Age VI); Philippa Tristram, *Figures of Life and Death in Medieval English Literature* (London, 1976); Alberto Tenenti, *Il senso della morte e l'amore della vita nel Rinascimento* (Turin, 1957).

28. R. Chartier, "Les Arts de Mourir, 1450-1600," *Annales: Economies, Sociétés, Civilisations* XXXI (1976); M.C. O'Connor, *The Art of Dying Well: The Development of the Ars Moriendi* (New York, 1942); R. Rudolf, *Ars Moriendi* (Cologne, 1970).

29. S. Cosacchi, *Makabertanz: der Totentanz in Kunst, Poesie und Brauchtum des Mittelalters* (Meisenheim am Glan, 1965) (first published in Budapest, 1935-44, when the author's name was spelt *Kozaky*); see also H. Rosenfeld, *Der mittelälterliche Totentanz: Entstehung – Entwicklung – Bedeutung* (Munster/Cologne, 1954); K. Meyer-Baer, *The Music of the Spheres and the Dance of Death: Studies in Musical Iconology* (Princeton, 1970).

30. Claude Blum, "L'espace imaginaire de la mort dans les chansons de geste, des origines à 1250," *La chanson de geste et le mythe carolingien, Mélanges René Louis, publiés par ses collègues, ses amis et ses élèves à l'occasion de son 75 ᵉ anniversaire* (Saint-Père-sous-Vézelay, 1982); J.-C. Payen, "Une poétique du génocide joyeux: devoir de violence et plaisir de tuer dans la 'Chanson de Roland'," *Olifant* VI (1978-9).

31. P. Zumthor, "Etude typologique des *planctus* contenus dans la *Chanson de Roland*," *La technique littéraire des chansons de geste* (Colloque international tenu à l'Univ. de Liège, septembre 1957) (Liège, 1959); V.B. Richmond, *Laments for the Dead in Medieval Narrative* (Pittsburgh, 1966)(Duquesne Studies/Philological Series VIII); E. Schulze-Busacker, "Etude typologique de la complainte des morts dans le roman arthurien en vers du XII ᵉ au XIVᵉ siècle," *An Arthurian Tapestry. Essays in Memory of Lewis Thorpe*, ed. K. Varty (Glasgow 1981); C. Thiry, *La plainte funèbre* (Turnhout, 1978) (Typologie des sources du Moyen Age occidental, XXX).

32. See for example, Joel H. Grisward, "Les morts de Roland," *La chanson de geste et le mythe carolingien: Mélanges René Louis publiés par ses collègues, ses amis et ses élèves à l'occasion de sa 75ᵉ anniversaire* (Saint-Père-sous-Vézelay, 1982); J. Frappier, "La douleur et la mort dans la littérature francaise des XIIᵉ et XIIIᵉ siècles," *V Convegno di Studi, sul tema: il dolore e la morte nella spiritualità dei seccoli XII e XIII* (Todi, 1962); M.N. Lefay-Toury, *La tentation de suicide dans le roman francais du XII ᵉ siècle française médiévale (des origines à 1230)* (Geneva, 1967) (Publications Romanes et Francaises XCVIII); P.B. Taylor, "The Theme of Death in *Beowulf*," in *Old English Poetry*, ed. R.P. Creed (Providence, 1967); E.C. Schweitzer, "Tradition and originality in the narrative of Siegfried's death in the *Niebelungenlied*," *Euphorion* LXVI (1972).

33. *La vie et la mort à travers l'art du XV ᵉ siècle* (Paris, 1952).

34. Kathleen Cohen, *Metamorphosis of a Death Symbol: the transi tomb in the late Middle Ages and the Renaissance* (Berkeley, 1973); A. Erlande-Brandenburg, *Le Roi est mort. Etudes sur les funérailles, les sépultures et les tombeaux des rois de France jusqu'à la fin du XIII ᵉ siècle* (Paris, 1975) (Arts et Métiers Graphiques: Bibliothèque de la Société francaise d'archéologie); Henriette s'Jacob, *Idealism and Realism: A Study of Sepulchral Symbolism* (Leiden, 1954) (contains an extensive bibliography); E. Panofsky, *Tomb Sculpture: Aspects from Ancient Egypt to Bernini* (London, 1964).

35. v. W.R. Levin, *Michigan, Museum of Art. Images of Love and Death in Late Medieval and Renaissance Art* (Ann Arbor, 1976).

36. *La Jeune fille et la mort: recherches sur les thèmes macabres dans l'art germanique de la Renaissance* (Geneva, 1979) (Hautes Etudes Médiévales et Modernes XXXVI, du Centre de recherche d'histoire et de philologie de l'Ecole pratique des Hautes Etudes).

37. H. Mollaret et J.-B. Brossollet, "La peste, source méconnue d'inspiration artistique," *Jaarboek 1965: Koninklijk Museum voor schone Kunsten, Anvers*; M. Meiss, *Painting in Florence and Siena after the Black Death* (Princeton, 1951).

★

11

HISTORY AND SOCIETY

LES "DANSES MACABRE": UNE IMAGE EN NEGATIF DU FONCTIONNALISME SOCIAL

★

Jean Batany

Les "danses des morts" sont nées de la fusion du thème des "estats du monde" avec celui de la mort inéluctable.[1] Passer en revue la société par catégories, du Pape aux mendiants, en prêtant plus ou moins à chacune une fonction dans l'organisme social, c'était un petit jeu auquel étaient rompus les moralistes de France, d'Allemagne et d'Angleterre depuis le XIIe siècle.[2] Parler de la mort, c'était aussi un sujet familier aux sermonnaires, et même aux trouvères qui se piquaient de quelque "sérieux". La rencontre de ces deux thèmes nous paraît toute naturelle. Mais que signifiait-elle?

Le titre du présent exposé suggère une réponse, plus évidente qu'originale, et qu'il ne s'agira pas ici de contester pour l'essentiel. La mise en valeur des fonctions propres à chaque catégorie sociale, clergé, chevaliers, marchands, paysans, etc., aboutissait à mettre en valeur la hiérarchie de la société; or, pour qu'un ordre social se maintienne, il faut que la hiérarchie y soit quelque peu occultée, afin d'éviter les révoltes et les contestations. Quel meilleur moyen de l'occulter que de montrer que tous les hommes sont égaux devant la mort? Les différences entre les catégories sociales vont paraître alors secondaires au public, et il les acceptera plus facilement. Ce processus, bien sûr, n'est pas un savant calcul conscient de la part des auteurs, mais un phénomène préconscient du type de ceux qu'identifie couramment, de nos jours, l'analyse des idéologies. Les *Danses Macabré* peuvent donc avoir eu pour base un mécanisme idéologique de type classique, assurant le maintien de l'ordre social, en donnant une contre-image de la hiérarchie, que cette contre-image justifie par une dialectique élémentaire.

Mais la mise en place historique de ce jeu dialectique soulève des problèmes, que je n'ai pas la prétention de résoudre aujourd'hui: je voudrais simplement poser quelques jalons à partir desquels on pourra réfléchir.

A la fin du XIIe siècle et au début du XIIIe, la revue des "manières de gens" a pour perspective essentielle la problématique des devoirs et des vices. Quand on présente une catégorie sociale sous un jour plutôt positif, c'est parce qu'on met en valeur sa haute fonction dans la société et qu'on la croit assez bien remplie. Quand on en présente une sous un jour négatif, c'est en soulignant que tel ou tel vice l'a envahie: simonie, hypocrisie, brutalité, etc. Mais il s'agit toujours principalement des devoirs de chaque type social et du jugement que ses représentants peuvent attendre dans l'au-delà. Il y a quelquefois une certaine confusion entre le vice et le malheur, entre le bonheur et la vertu, mais c'est tout de même le point de vue du jugement moral qui domine. Dans ces conditions, la mort ne peut apparaître dans les "revues d'états" qu'à titre de passage vers une sanction définitive de la conduite des hommes pendant leur vie.

On le voit, par exemple, dans les *Vers* de Thibaud de Marly.[3] Un ouvrage récent sur les *Danses Macabré*[4] cite cette oeuvre distraitement, dans sa bibliographie, sous le titre: *Vers de la mort*, sans doute par confusion avec la vieille édition du poème d'Hélinand où Méon l'attribuait à Thibaud, mais aussi, je pense, parce que la mort est présente à chaque instant chez Thibaud de Marly, et en particulier après la mention des vices de chaque catégorie évoquée: avocats, prélats, religieux, rois et seigneurs, usuriers. Mais sous quelle forme est-elle présente? En fait, pour chaque type social, le poète-prédicateur cite brièvement la mort et passe aussitôt à une description circonstanciée des tourments de l'Enfer – et des joies du Paradis pour quelques justes, mais ceci n'intervient que pour les deux catégories les plus élevées! En somme, il ne s'agit pas de la mort: il s'agit du salut, et du salut mis en rapport avec une vie présente dont on ne pense guère à envisager les douleurs ni les joies, mais seulement les bonnes et les mauvaises actions. Chez les moralistes de cette époque, ni la vertu ni le vice n'apparaît comme une joie; le vice peut même résulter d'une angoisse.[5] Et, au fond, même et surtout quand il les condamne, le moraliste se sent confusément solidaire des "états" dont il parle: il ne les considère jamais avec le détachement de l'objectivité.

Ce détachement commence à s'esquisser dans les premiers "Vers de la mort" portant réellement ce titre, ceux d'Hélinand, dans les dernières années du XIIe siècle.[6] Le procédé rhétorique de l'apostrophe anaphorique ("Mort ..." en tête de chaque strophe) y donne une réalité éprouvante à un personnage allégorique dont la littérature morale n'avait pas abusé jusqu'alors, sans doute parce qu'il ne pouvait représenter qu'une circonstance nécessaire, mais sans valeur par elle-même dans le processus du salut. Chez Thibaud de Marly, cette circonstance ne créait pas une rupture radicale dans la typologie sociale, puisque le salut était envisagé en fonction de chaque "état". Chez Hélinand, au contraire, l'existence de la mort semble détruire dès ce monde le système des "états", pour l'occulter derrière l'écrasante individualité des personnages et des lieux: il ne parle pas de la mort des princes ou de celle des évêques en général, mais de celle de quelques-uns qu'il désigne nommément, parfois après leur ville de résidence. Parmi les groupes à statut fonctionnel, il n'y en a guère que deux qui apparaissent en tant que groupes. L'un est représenté par le nom de *Rome*, qui donne aux papes et aux cardinaux une délimitation géographique escamotant leur rôle hiérarchique. L'autre est celui auquel appartient l'auteur, l'"ordre" des "moines blancs", mais il apparaît à la faveur d'un raisonnement par l'absurde: les Cisterciens ont choisi la pire des vies s'il n'y a plus rien après la mort.[7] L'idée même qu'une catégorie sociale ait une fonction en ce monde est abolie: les ascètes ne représentent quelque chose que par leur rôle négatif ici-bas; les autres sont ramenés à l'individualité ou à la contingence géographique: De la structure sociale d'ensemble, on ne voit surnager que l'opposition des riches et des pauvres, ceux-là "humant le sang" de ceux-ci, et la mort retournant leur relation.[8]

Une perspective aussi désocialisante a pu valoir à Hélinand des accusations de valdéisme, et il ne faut pas s'étonner si le Reclus de Molliens, reprenant peu après certaines de ses idées dans le même modèle strophique, a tenu à souligner lourdement son orthodoxie et son attachement à la tradition.[9]

Hélinand annonce les *Danses Macabré* par certains aspects: place imaginative donnée à la Mort-personnage, tendance (encore faible) au détachement objectif, glissement vers la problématique du bonheur. Mais la vision de la société est toute différente, et c'est pourquoi j'hésite à suivre ceux qui voudraient attribuer au même auteur la plus ancienne version du poème latin *Vado Mori*[10], ainsi nommé parce que chacun de ses 34 distiques commence et finit par ces mots, procédé rhétorique qui contribue à orienter de moins en moins la réflexion vers l'idée du Jugement et à la focaliser de plus en plus vers la mort elle-même. Sur ces 34 distiques, treize font parler des types sociaux: "Vado mori, rex sum ... ", puis *papa, praesul, miles, pugiles, medicus, logicus, juvenis, senior, dives, judex, pauper.* Cette liste ne constitue pas encore un tableau complet de la société, comme celui des *Danses Macabré.* Les types sociaux qui y sont présentés sont choisis: par hypothèse, ils ont une certaine relation pragmatique avec la mort, en général une relation de résistance présupposée, et qui s'avère inefficace (ou, par contraste, une relation de facilité, pour le *senior* et le *pauper*). Cette première vraie rencontre entre la typologie sociale et le thème de la mort est déjà liée à une certaine mise en sourdine du problème du salut, car il n'est aucunement question d'enfer ni de paradis dans ce poème.

Alors que les *Vers* d'Hélinand opposent nettement et longuement l'hypothèse d'une mort sans jugement (mise dans la bouche d'une sorte d'"esprit fort") et celle d'une mort suivie de la restauration de la justice pour chacun, le *Vado mori* ne parle que par allusion de la hiérarchie morale rétablie par Dieu dans l'autre monde, si bien que le tableau qu'il esquisse de la hiérarchie de ce monde-ci fait d'elle la seule échelle de valeurs à laquelle l'imagination peut s'accrocher; certes, la fonction de chaque statut social est finalement démentie par la mort, mais la phrase qui souligne ce démenti le présente à chaque fois comme un paradoxe, sous une forme qui présuppose que ce statut a une valeur, provisoire mais réelle. Par exemple, le *judicium* n'est évoqué qu'à propos du *judex*, dont l'activité prend le sens d'un modèle, même si ce modèle se retourne contre lui.[11]

Dans l'évolution vers les *Danses Macabré*, le XIIIe siècle me paraît une sorte de palier d'arrêt. Les *Vers de la mort* de Robert Le Clerc[12], malgré leur imitation formelle d'Hélinand, sont plus près du point de vue moral de Thibaud de Marly: les comtes et les rois, les ordres mendiants et les officiaux y apparaissent au passage, mais par référence à leurs vices, en fonction du problème du jugement; et ces types sociaux ne sont pas détachés en galerie de pantins comme dans le *Vado mori*, mais noyés dans une masse d'idées générales convenant pour tous les hommes. Chez Rutebeuf, les évocations de la mort, que nous a si bien analysées Jean Dufournet, sont généralement distinctes des revues systématiques de la société. Le rapprochement des deux thèmes littéraires, fortement esquissé en latin dans les *Vado mori*, ne va s'imposer en français que dans le courant du XIVe siècle.

Reprenons donc les choses vers 1330-1340, et jetons un coup d'oeil sur ces traditions littéraires en France, de cette date jusqu'au début du XVe siècle où l'on situe la *Danse des Innocents*. On peut tenter, pour cette période, une classification grossière des "revues d'états" selon le principe qui détermine le choix de leur nomenclature sociale. Il y a les textes qui analysent la société comme un organisme administratif à base politique. Il y a ceux qui suivent directement le schéma des "trois ordres"; il y a ceux qui alignent des chapitres "des Papes", "des prélats", "des marchands", etc., sans avoir une structure d'ensemble nette; et il y a ceux qui présentent une certaine mise en scène narrative. En principe, suivant le type de texte, on est plus ou moins loin de la *Danse Macabré*.

Ce qui en est le plus loin, c'est sans doute l'analyse de la société comme un organisme politique, appuyée sur l'image du corps social[13] ou sans elle.[14] La diversité des catégories sociales est alors expliquée par la diversité des fonctions dans ce monde, où la société forme un organisme cohérent: ni la mort, ni ses suites ne sont généralement envisagées. La nomenclature proposée est sous la dépendance de ce fonctionnalisme plus ou moins administratif et économique: une place importante est donnée aux fonctionnaires royaux, ou bien à certaines professions urbaines comme les changeurs.

On est un peu moins loin des *Danses Macabré* dans deux autres types de "revues d'états", celui qui se fonde sur les "trois ordres", et celui qui énumère un catalogue peu structuré. En général, au XIVe siècle, les textes fondés sur le schéma ternaire sont assez brefs[15]: seul Philippe de Mézières développe longuement le thème dans le *Songe du Vieil Pélerin*, mais en distinguant quatre "hiérarchies" au lieu de trois, et en se rapprochant beaucoup des textes politiques. Le plus souvent, au contraire, ce sont des oeuvres de longue haleine qui présentent les "états" en chapitres séparés suivant une liste apparemment arbitraire.[16] Dans ces deux catégories, la morale générale l'emporte sur la pragmatique sociale, et la vie n'a pas toujours le dernier mot: mais l'accent est mis sur le problème des devoirs et des vices, donc du salut, bien plus que sur la brutalité de la mort individuelle. Il est frappant, du reste, que les pièces d'Eustache Deschamps sur la mort soient nettement distinctes de celles où il propose une liste de catégories sociales.

On sent déjà pourtant, dans les grands catalogues de la société par chapitres, une atmosphère légèrement différente de celle des "revues d'états" des XIIe et XIIIe siècles. Le simple fait de présenter brusquement chaque état par une rubrique hors-texte, "des officiers de Sainte Eglise", "des chevaliers", c'est déjà le signe d'une tendance à la froideur objective qu'on ne trouvait pas chez Guiot de Provins et chez Rutebeuf, et le détail du texte confirme souvent cette tendance.

Mais surtout, on commence à trouver, dans les oeuvres de cette époque, de nettes apparitions du problème du bonheur, en marge de celui des devoirs et des vices. Par exemple, dans *Renart le Contrefait*, l'Epicier de Troyes nous explique, par la bouche de Renart, que les bourgeois ont plus de chance que les nobles, parce qu'ils peuvent se livrer à une activité manuelle sans crainte de déroger quand ils ont des difficultés financières.[17] Jean Dupin ne présente plus la pauvreté comme un destin rapprochant l'homme du Christ et l'aidant pour son salut, mais comme un revers de fortune contre lequel on peut lutter.[18] On trouve même parfois ce problème du bonheur à propos des "trois ordres": Geoffroy de Charny affirme que ce sont les chevaliers, et non les moines comme le disait la tradition, qui ont le plus à souffrir dans la vie.[19] Eustache Deschamps, dans sa ballade 184, dit que le peuple a une vie plus tranquille et plus longue que les princes et les prélats, qui ont bien du mal "pour leurs estats, pour maintenir leurs noms".[20]

Ce problème du bonheur respectif des diverses catégories sociales, nous le rencontrons encore dans les "revues d'états" qui utilisent la forme narrative. C'est déjà vrai avec l'apologue "Dui chevalier vont chevauchant"[21], où il semble bien que les vilains, malgré la condamnation morale explicite que l'auteur lance contre eux, apparaissent comme privilégiés en ce monde par la faculté qu'ils ont d'assouvir immédiatement leurs besoins les plus vifs. C'est peut-être vrai aussi, malgré les apparences, pour le *Blanquerna* de Raymond Lulle,[22] où l'orientation extrêmement religieuse de la pensée n'empêche pas un souci constant d'assurer à l'homme un certain bonheur dès le monde d'ici-bas. Et c'est vrai surtout pour l'histoire du "filz non estable", insérée par Renaud de Louhans dans sa traduction de Boèce en 1336, et inspirée d'un passage du *De Disciplina scholarium*. Il s'agit alors du choix d'un métier, et l'on voit un jeune homme essayer successivement les divers "états": clergé, marchandise, "cultivage", état de chevalier, d'avocat, d'homme marié, d'étudiant en astronomie; non pas pour y pratiquer des devoirs particuliers ni pour y tomber dans des vices spécifiques, mais pour y chercher un bonheur impossible et finir, après tous ces échecs, par souhaiter devenir un âne.[23]

Et quarante ans plus tard, ce thème du bonheur impossible dans chaque état est lié à celui du trépas par Jehan Le Fèvre de Ressons, dans son *Respit de la mort*.[24] Le sujet de ce poème est une sorte de jeu rhétorique, qui justifierait peut-être une étude orientée dans le sens des réflexions proposées par Rolf Max Kully sur l'*Ackermann aus Böhmer* au colloque de Montréal.[25] Jean Le Fèvre, procureur au parlement de Paris, est gravement malade, et il tente, suivant les procédures juridiques qu'il connaît bien, d'obtenir un sursis pour sa mort. Dans son débat avec ses collègues du Parlement, qui s'opposent à sa demande, il en vient à préciser sa pensée: il admet très bien que la mort est naturelle et que le monde ne vaut pas la peine d'y rester, mais il demande un répit pour avoir le temps de s'amender. L'exposé qu'il fait à ce propos sur la vanité du monde passe en revue les parties du corps de l'homme, puis les différents états: marins, marchands, riches, gens mariés, étudiants; chacune de ces catégories croit avoir trouvé le bonheur, mais tombe dans toutes sortes de malheurs. Parmi ces malheurs, le risque de damnation tient peu de place; il s'agit plutôt des malheurs de la vie présente: *la* tempête pour le marin, les brigands pour les marchands, etc. C'est donc la première fois, en francais, qu'un tableau assez général des "états du monde" est tracé en même temps selon la problématique du bonheur et en fonction du risque de la mort.

En fait, le lien entre ces deux problèmes, dans le *Respit de la Mort*, n'est pas exactement celui qui apparaîtra au Cimetière des Innocents quarante ans plus tard, et qui était sans doute déjà apparu en Espagne dans la *Dança general de la Muerte*[26]; pour Jean Le Fèvre, la mort n'est pas ce qui rend illusoire le bonheur des divers "états", mais, au contraire, c'est parce que leur bonheur est illusoire que la mort n'est pas un mal absolu. Le raisonnement est différent, mais il repose des deux côtés sur l'articulation des mêmes concepts: la mort, les statuts sociaux, le bonheur illusoire. Cette inspiration commune me paraît suffisante pour permettre de dire que Jean Le Fèvre, d'une certaine façon, a fait ainsi, dans cette oeuvre, une sorte de "Danse Macabré". Mais il est peu vraisemblable, en raison de la différence de perspective que nous venons de noter, qu'il ait écrit par ailleurs une *Danse Macabré* proprement dite, qui serait perdue

C'est pourtant ce que l'on soutient bien souvent, à cause d'un vers situé un peu plus loin dans le *Respit de la mort*: *Je fis de Macabré la danse*. Depuis longtemps, on discute sur ce vers: est-ce une image, ou une déclaration de paternité littéraire, comme les auteurs médiévaux aiment à en insérer dans leurs oeuvres? Gaston Paris avait déclaré brutalement que cette expression n'avait pu signifier au figuré que "mourir" et non "manquer de mourir", et que, cette valeur étant impossible ici, l'auteur avait voulu dire: "j'ai écrit une *Danse Macabré*". Ce point de vue est repris tel quel par Geneviève Hasenohr-Esnos dans son édition de 1969. Mais cette interprétation n'est-elle pas influencée par la connaissance que nous avons de textes qui porteront ce titre à l'imitation de la Danse des Innocents, alors que ni la Danse espagnole, ni la Danse latine de Wurzburg ne s'appellent ainsi? Au temps de Gaston Paris, on aimait rêver d'un "prototype perdu" pour chaque "genre" ou "thème" du Moyen Age... Mais le passage où se situe le vers en question permet-il cette interprétation? Ce n'est absolument pas le genre de contexte où un auteur de Moyen Age rappelle ses oeuvres antérieures: ici, Jean Le Fèvre est en train d'expliquer qu'il reconnaît la nécessité de la mort, et qu'il demande un sursis et non pas une dispense (on est en plein dans le "texte" et non dans le "métatexte"):

Mon crediteur est souvrain maistre,
souverain roi, souverain prestre.
Se je li dois de mort treuage,
bien say que c'est commun usage:
toutez gens, toutez nacions,
par toutez obligacions
y sont liés de leur naissance.

(3078)   Je fis de Macabré la danse
           qui toutes gens maine a sa tresche
           et a la fosse les adresche
           qui est leur derraine maison.
           Il fait bon en toute saison
           penser a sa fin derrieniere
           pour muer en mieulx sa maniere.[27]

Et une anecdote vient à l'appui, celle de l'homme qui se fait dire tous les matins par son valet pour le réveiller: "Sire, vous morrés".

Il me semble hors de doute, dans ce contexte, que: *je fis de Macabré la danse* ne peut signifier qu'une chose: non pas "j'ai écrit un texte intitulé *Danse Macabré*", ni "je suis mort", ni "j'ai failli mourir", ni même "j'ai pris conscience de la mort comme inéluctable" comme le propose Mme Legry-Rosier dans son édition dactylographiée[28], mais tout simplement: "j'ai suivi avec tout le monde le chemin de la vie, où nous nous agitons comme dans une danse, et qui mène à la mort". Que cette expression soit née spontanément à partir du rôle des textes des *Macchabées* dans le rituel des funérailles[29], ou bien qu'elle ait été inspirée par des peintures dont l'existence avant 1376 est assez vraisemblable, ou même par un texte littéraire autre que la *Dança general* espagnole où le mot *Macabré* ne figure pas, cela reste à préciser; mais il me paraît difficile de ne pas admettre que l'expression existait (pour dire à peu près: "j'ai vécu"!) à l'époque où écrit notre auteur. Qu'elle ait été employée beaucoup plus tard au sens de "mourir", après la diffusion de la Danse des Innocents, ne prouve aucunement qu'elle n'ait pu avoir que ce sens, du reste absurde à la première personne, et, finalement, bien moins naturel même en fonction des textes du XVe siècle, car, dans les *Danses Macabré*, les personnages *vont* mourir, mais ils sont encore en vie, et ce que l'auteur veut dire, ce n'est pas tellement qu'ils vont mourir par hasard, mais que *toute vie* mène à la mort. Il est donc tout à fait arbitraire, lorsqu'on trace des tableaux généalogiques des danses des morts, d'y caser une "danse Macabré de Jean Le Fèvre" avant la date de 1376. Même si on tient absolument à faire de ce vers une déclaration de paternité littéraire, rien ne prouverait que l'oeuvre perdue ainsi désignée avait le même type de contenu que celle qui apparaît sous ce titre quarante ou cinquante ans plus tard.[30]

Cependant, la poésie de la mort, en France, continuait à évoluer, et à se rapprocher des "revues d'états". Deux oeuvres caractéristiques à cet égard se situent dans la première moitié du XIVe siècle. L'une est le *Mireuer du Monde*, adaptation française des poèmes latins *Vado mori*, expression traduite littéralement par *Je vais mourir* au début et à la fin de chaque strophe.[31] Comme dans les poèmes latins, on y voit apparaître, au milieu de considérations très générales, quelques strophes qui constituent l'ébauche d'une revue d'états de type scénique, chaque type social prenant lui-même la parole: le pape; les cardinaux; patriarches et légats; les autres membres du clergé; les savants en droit et en théologie; les savants en logique et en médecine; les rois et empereurs; les princes et les ducs; les riches bourgeois; les marchands; les gens de grand lignage; les chevaliers et la "chevaleresse" (premier exemple du personnage féminin dans ce type de texte). On est plus près d'une revue d'ensemble de la société que dans les premiers *Vado mori* latins, mais il s'agit uniquement de types sociaux que leur puissance semblerait mettre à l'abri du malheur: le pauvre n'est pas mis sur le même plan que le riche, c'est-à-dire que son absence, ici, lui laisse une sorte de privilège.

Mais l'atmosphère morale s'orientait encore vers le problème du bonheur, qui ramenait toujours à une *auctoritas* fondamentale, la *Consolatio Philosophiae* de Boèce. Il ne faut donc pas s'étonner si Renaud de Louhans, traduisant cette oeuvre, après y avoir inséré l'histoire du "filz non estable" citée plus haut, y insère des "vers de la mort" qui ont échappé à la plupart des historiens du thème macabre.[32] Chez lui, ce ne sont pas les types sociaux eux-mêmes qui parlent; on reste plus près d'Hélinand avec une dramatisation du personnage allégorique au début et à la fin de chaque strophe: "La Mort prend ..."; moins intégré à la situation de communication que dans le prototype du genre, où il était interpellé, ce personnage allégorique reste donc dominant, du point de vue rhétorique et scénique, par rapport aux personnages sociaux, désignés, du reste, par une pluralité trop abstraite[33]: cardinaux et papes, prélats, chanoines, moines, nonnains, empereurs et autres princes, chevaliers, jeunes damoiseaux, dames et damoiselles, riches vilains, avocats.

Voilà pourtant une nomenclature dont la tendance à l'exhaustivité est assez nouvelle, par rapport aux poèmes sur la mort des cent cinquante ans précédents. Et si l'on peut la comparer à celle de l'autre digression du même auteur, il ne faut pas s'en tenir à l'idée superficielle que le "choix d'un métier" limitait les possibilités du "filz non estable": ce serait confondre le texte et le prétexte. Au fond, les deux digressions de Renaud de Louhans ont quelque chose de commun: la nécessité fonctionnelle des statuts sociaux y est oubliée, et ils sont énumérés en fonction du problème du bonheur. Cependant, les deux nomenclatures ne se recoupent clairement qu'en distinguant l'état de l'"avocat", mais avec des détails très différents; l'état de "cultivage" et celui de "marchandise", distincts pour le "filz non estable", sont réunis cette fois-ci dans la catégorie des "riches vilains"; et pour le reste, nous avons le sentiment d'un contraste entre un système qui voyait la société par le bas, du point de vue de celui qui cherche à gagner sa vie, et un système qui la voit par le haut, du point de vue de ceux qui détiennent la puissance. Le même auteur inverse sa perspective, mais avec une même présupposition valorisant les cadres sociaux de l'existence. Et on se demande, devant l'exemple de Renaud de Louhans, si l'abandon du fonctionnalisme axé sur les devoirs au profit du problème du bonheur n'amène pas à une dislocation de la nomenclature des "états": pour un même auteur, cette nomenclature peut, on le voit ici, prendre des formes très différentes. Peut-être faudra-t-il la restauration de l'autorité royale, après 1460, pour que l'ordre social retrouve plus constamment sa vieille structure ternaire ...

On peut rattacher encore au modèle du *Mireuer du Monde* le *Miroir de bonne vie* attribué à Gerson, où chaque strophe commence par "Mirez-vous ..." et où sept strophes sur dix-neuf s'adressent à des types sociaux: haut clergé, princes, savants, nobles dames, curés, bourgeoises, avocats.[34] Ce poème est beaucoup plus orienté vers le vieux problème du salut, et la comparaison avec les sermons de Gerson (où l'on voit la société bien autrement structurée) me fait douter de son authenticité.

Avec le *Mors de la pommé*[35], texte difficile à dater et probablement antérieur à la Danse des Innocents, on est beaucoup plus près de l'esprit de celle-ci. D'abord parce que les vers y commentent constamment des illustrations, et se présentent comme une série de dialogues où parlent, sous chaque image, la Mort, le personnage qui mourra, et un personnage témoin. Les types sociaux y sont mêlés à des noms d'individus pris dans la Bible (Adam, Abel, Jésus ...) et même à des abstractions (l'âme). Ici, le désordre de la nomenclature semble confirmer de façon effarante la remarque faite ci-dessus sur la déstructuration de l'imaginaire social. Le groupement de "celui qui meurt" et du "témoin" aboutit aux curieux couples suivants: la "pucelle" et la "femme", l'"ancien" et la "meschine", le "géant" et l'"écuyer", la princesse et le maître d'hôtel, l'enfant et la mère, le laboureur et le semeur, le chapelain et le chanoine, la demoiselle et la chambrière, la femme et le clerc, le pape et le cardinal, l'homme d'armes et le champion, le changeur et le bourgeois, la reine et le roi, l'empereur et Noblesse. Les "revues d'états" suivaient presque toujours rigoureusement une nomenclature descendante: ici, il n'y a même pas de mouvement ascendant constant; la mort apparaît comme l'installation du désordre.

La jonction est maintenant bien opérée entre le thème des "états du monde" et le thème de la mort, jonction liée à une substitution de la problématique du bonheur à celle du salut, puisque c'est, pour chaque type social, la possibilité du vrai bonheur auquel le faisait aspirer son statut qui est démentie par la nécessité de mourir; mais cette jonction fait voir provisoirement la société comme le lieu d'une confusion démoralisante. Il reste donc à rétablir l'ordre.

Le modèle de l'ordre, c'est la danse, activité ordonnée par excellence, puisque déjà, avant Platon, c'était par la conscience de la chorégraphie que les Grecs avaient élaboré leur notion du *ruthmos*[36]. Nous ne saurons sans doute jamais exactement sous quelle forme première (picturale ou littéraire? latine, française ou espagnole?) la "danse des Morts" est apparue: probablement dès le XIVe siècle, d'après le texte espagnol déjà cité. Mais il est certain que son succès en France, en Angleterre et en Allemagne s'est diffusé surtout en partant de la fresque et des vers qui ornaient le Cimetière parisien des Innocents au début du XVe siècle.[37] Ce texte trop bien connu, j'en rappelle seulement la nomenclature, celle des personnages qui dialoguent avec "le Mort", leur double décharné qui les entraîne en leur montrant le pas: le Pape, l'empereur, le Cardinal, le roi, le patriarche, le connétable, l'archevêque, le chevalier, l'évêque, l'écuyer, l'abbé, le bailli, le "maistre" ("astrologien" dans l'édition de 1486), le bourgeois, le chanoine, le marchand, le chartreux, le sergent, le moine, l'usurier, le médecin, l'amoureux, l'avocat, le ménestrel, le curé, le laboureur, le Cordelier, l'enfant, le clerc, l'ermite, "le roi que vers mengent".

L'ordre est bien revenu. La société est vue suivant sa hiérarchie descendante, avec une savante alternance entre clercs et laïques qui se trouvait déjà dans la Danse espagnole; et cet ordre hiérarchique n'aurait aucune raison d'être, dans un poème sur la mort, si vraiment il s'agissait de montrer que la mort le réduit à néant. Il s'agit donc bien, au contraire, de renforcer cet ordre social, en occultant la notion de devoirs et de fautes spécifiques au profit de la notion de bonheur ou de malheur individuel. Puisque la mort empêche tous les hommes de réaliser pleinement les espoirs impliqués dans leurs statuts sociaux, la hiérarchie de ces statuts est une contingence tolérable, et même rassurante, car la mise entre parenthèses d'une hiérarchie de l'au-delà fait de celle d'ici-bas le seul jeu que l'on puisse jouer.

Il faudrait cependant encore examiner la suite de l'histoire, avec cette première moitié du XVe siècle où le facteur de désordre, dans les "revues d'états" françaises, se présente comme une autre abstraction qui recoupe celle de la Mort: la Guerre. Ce sont des textes sur la guerre et ses méfaits qui posent alors le problème du bonheur respectif des catégories sociales.[38] Partout, dans ces textes, plane l'ombre de la mort; mais le thème nouveau modifie la problématique du bonheur, en introduisant l'idée des responsabilités de tel ou tel "état" dans les malheurs de tel ou tel autre, ce qui rejoint l'atmosphère des "revues d'états" de type politique. D'où les fameux débats entre "états" que constituent les dialogues d'Alain Chartier, et, plus tard, de Robert Gaguin, en attendant que le théâtre s'empare du thème sous Louis XII.[39] Car les différents types sociaux commencent alors à pénétrer sur l'espace de la scène, qui joue pour eux le rôle d'un espace social homogène[40] où ils peuvent dialoguer et se disputer comme ils ne l'avaient jamais fait dans la littérature antérieure.

Mais ceci est une autre histoire, car le théâtre médiéval, dont Henri Rey-Flaud a bien montré l'originalité radicale par rapport au théâtre moderne[41] n'a jamais pu intégrer la "danse Macabré". C'est seulement après 1530 que telle pièce latine d'Anvers[42] ou telle pièce espagnole[43] pourront tenter, de façon très froide, une mise en scène de la danse proprement dite, celle qui présente tour à tour toutes les catégories sociales. En fait, dans la *Danse Macabré*, le dialogue entre les "états" n'est pas possible. Elle représente bien une sorte de théâtre, mais un théâtre de marionnettes, c'est-à-dire exactement l'opposé du théâtre médiéval. Dans celui-ci, l'auteur, les acteurs et le public sont dans une communion confuse où tendent à s'estomper les frontières entre le jeu et le réel; comme nous l'avons déjà vu au cours de ce colloque, la mort y est présente, mais il me semble qu'elle y introduit, au moins dans les *Passions*, une véritable dislocation de l'ordre social. Dans les *Danses Macabré*, le poète et le peintre sont solidaires de la mort et, poussant à bout la tendance à la froideur objective des "revues d'état" du XIVe siècle, ils sont profondément détachés de leurs personnages, qu'ils font tomber brusquement comme des pantins hors de la communauté vivante, mais dans l'ordre. Dans les Mystères, on va et vient selon des règles complexes qui semblent supposer la recherche de quelque ordre nouveau incapable de se dégager, et qui font oublier, au sein d'une socialité exacerbée, si l'on est heureux ou malheureux. Dans la *Danse Macabré* , on tient son voisin par la main de chaque côté et on ne peut pas quitter sa place, mais cette chaîne est liée à une désocialisation profonde, celle qui va peu à peu détruire l'idéologie des "états du monde" pour enfermer chacun dans une individualité fictive et ravageuse.

NOTES

1. Cette rencontre des deux thèmes est à peu près ce que l'on trouve dans la "version kabyle" de *La cigale et la fourmi*, établie il y a quelque trente ans par un chansonnier dont j'ai oublié le nom: "La cigale et la fourmi, c'est tout simple, ti sais. La cigale, l'avait rien a bouffer: l'a crevi. La fourmi, l'avait trop à bouffer: l'a crevi aussi. La moralité: ti bouffes, ti bouffes pas, ti crèves tout pareil ..."

2. Sur ce thème, on peut consulter entre autres l'ouvrage de Ruth Mohl, *The three estates in medieval and Renaissance literature* (New York, 1933), et mon article "La charpente médiévale du discours social," sous presse dans *Europe*, octobre 1983.

3. *Les vers de Thibaud de Marly*, éd. H.K. Stone (Paris, 1932).

4. Joël Saugnieux, *Les danses macabres de France et d'Espagne et leurs prolongements littéraires* (Lyon et Paris, 1972).

5. Voir par exemple *Le Roman des romans* (éd. Tanquerey, *Deux poèmes moraux anglo-français*, (Paris, 1922), str. 154-156, p. 65, développant l'idée que les simoniaques sont des gens qui ont peur de manquer du nécessaire.

6. Hélinand, *Vers de la Mort*, éd. F. Wulff et E. Walberg (Paris, 1905). On peut trouver le texte dans J.M. Paquette, *Poèmes de la mort de Turold à Villon* (Paris, 1979) (10/18), accompagné d'une traduction fantaisiste.

7. "S'après la mort est quite quite/dont ont la pieur vie eslite/tuit cil de l'ordene de Cistiaux" (str. 36): "S'il n'y a pas de comptes à rendre après la mort, alors ils ont choisi la pire des vies, tous ceux de l'Ordre de Cîteaux."

8. Str. 31: "Mort fait franc homme de cuivert/morz acuivertist roi et pape"; str. 42: "Et riche, qui art et escume/sor le povre, cui sanc il hume."

9. *Li Romans de Carité* du Renclus de Moilliens, éd. Van Hamel (Paris, 1885), t.I p. 91, strophe 171.

10. Texte publ. dans H. Rosenfeld, *Die mittelälterliche Totentanz* (Munster, 1954), p. 323-325.

11. "Vado mori, judex: quia jam plures reprehendi/judicium mortis horreo: vado mori" (v. 39-40).

12. Ed. Windahl (Lund, 1887); *cf.* Paquette, *op. cit*, p. 108-135. J. Ch. Payen prépare une édition de ce texte.

13. Comme la traduction française du *Policraticus* par Denis Foulechat, le *Pèlerinage de l'âme* de Guillaume de Digulleville, et, plus tard, le sermon "Vivat rex ..." de Gerson.

14. Par exemple la traduction de la *Politique* d'Aristote par Oresme, ou divers ouvrages de Christine de Pizan.

15. Un passage du *Chapel des fleurs de lis* de Philippe de Vitry, un intermède moralisant interprétant les animaux que l'on chasse dans *Modus et Ratio* (avec le premier exemple de l'expression *tiers état*), plusieurs ballades d'Eustache Deschamps, un passage du *Trésor Amoureux*, et de nombreux passages de sermons de Gerson.

16. Les *Mélancolies* de Jean Dupin, les vers de Gilles li Muisis, le *Livre de l'exemple*, les *Echecs d'Amour*, le *Miroir de l'Omme* de John Gower, la *Mutacion de Fortune* de Christine de Pizan; l'exception est ici constituée par deux pièces brèves d'Eustache Deschamps (309 et 1454).

17. Ed. G. Raynaud et H. Lemaître (Paris, 1914), t. II, v. 38123-38574.

18. Voir mon étude: "Les pauvres et la pauvreté dans les revues des *états du monde*", *Etude sur l'histoire de la pauvreté*, éd. M. Mollat (Paris, 1974), t.II, p. 465-486.

19. *Le livre de chevalerie*, éd. Kervyn de Lettenhove; *Oeuvres de Froissart, Chroniques*, t. I, vol. II, Introd. p. 516-520.

20. Ed. Queux de Saint-Hilaire et G. Raynaud, *Oeuvres complètes d'Eustache Deschamps* t.I (Paris, 1878), p. 320-321.

21. Voir mon étude: "L'apologue social des strates libidinales", *Le récit bref au Moyen Age*, éd. D. Buschinger (Amiens, 1980), p. 133-151.

22. *Le livre d'Evast et de Blaquerne*, trad. fr. de la fin du XIIIe siècle éd. A. Llinarès (Paris, 1970).

23. Texte édité dans mon *Français médiéval*, Bordas 1972, p. 234-237, avec un dossier sur les

"sources". Ce texte avait été publié comme anonyme et mutilé de sa conclusion dans le *Recueil Général des Fabliaux*, et il est encore malheureusement repris tel quel dans le recueil de G.C. Belletti.

24. Ed. Geneviève Hasenohr-Esnos (Paris, 1969).
25. *Le Sentiment de la mort au Moyen Age* ... éd. C. Sutto (Montréal, 1979), p. 139-167.
26. Voir le texte dans le livre de J. Saugnieux (supra note 4).
27. *Ed.citée*, p. 112-113, v. 3071-3084.
28. Paris 1958, consultable à la Sorbonne: W 1958 110, 4°.
29. Le *r* de *Macabré* n'est pas un obstacle à cette étymologie, la plus naturelle: cp. l'apparition d'un *r* explosif après occlusive dans des mots comme *trésor, flétrir, perdrix, encre, pupitre*, etc.
30. A la rigueur, on pourrait supposer que Jean Le Fèvre, dans ce vers, veut comparer le passage précédent du *Respit* à une "danse Macabré" qui aurait déjà existé, par exemple sous forme picturale. Mais c'est peu probable.
31. Ed. Méon, *Les vers de la mort de Thibaud de Marly* ... (Paris, 1835), p.75-79.
32. "Comment la mort prent gens de tous estats", éd. G. Bertoni, *La nouvelle bibliothèque cantonale et universitaire de Fribourg* (Fribourg, 1911), p. 112-115.
33. Voir mon article "Normes, types et individus: la présentation des rôles sociaux au XIIe siècle", *Littérature et société au Moyen Age*, éd. D. Buschinger (Amiens, 1978), p. 177-200.
34. Ed. Mgr Glorieux, *Oeuvres de Gerson*, t.VII, 1ère partie, 1966, p. 281-282.
35. Ed. Schneegans, *Romania* XLVI (1920), p. 560-568.
36. Cette remarque me paraît ressortir des exemples donnés par Emile Benveniste dans son célèbre article "La notion de rythme dans son expression linguistique", *Probl. de linguist. générale* t. I (Paris, 1966), p. 327-335.
37. *Ed.citée* (supra note 34) p. 286-300.
38. Par exemple le discours de Jean de Nielles au nom de Jean Sans Peur conservé par Enguerrand de Monstrelet, le "Veniat pax .." de Gerson, le prologue de la traduction du *De casibus* ... par Laurent de Premierfait, le *Lai de Guerre* de Pierre de Nesson, les *Fortunes et adversités* de Jehan Régnier, etc.
39. Par exemple la *Moralité des trois états réformés par Raison*, du *Recueil Trepperel*.
40. Je m'inspire de la notion de "champ social homogène" utilisée à propos de Machiavel par Claude Lefort (par exemple *Les Formes de l'histoire*, Paris, 1978 p. 134).
41. Henri Rey-Flaud, *Le cercle magique* (Paris, 1973), et *Pour une dramaturgie du Moyen Age* (Paris, 1980).
42. Voir J. Ijsewin, "A Latin death-dance play of 1532", *Humanistica lovaniensia* XVIII (1969), p. 77-94.
43. Voir J. Saugnieux, *op. cit.* (supra note 4).

SUMMARY

This paper starts from the statement that the Dances of Death of fifteenth-century Europe represent a fusion between two themes already prevalent in the literary products of the Middle Ages: the classification of the "estates" on the one hand, and on the other, the image of an inexorable Death. Previous works which appear to operate a similar fusion and which have generally been seen as progenitors of the *Danse Macabré* have however treated the themes differently: Helinand, for instance, makes no pretension to an exhaustive survey of society; Thibaud de Marly concentrates his attention less on the moment of death itself than on the afterlife; surveys of society may deal primarily with the question of earthly happiness, or may offer "sociological" analysis of society's structures; the *Mors de la Pome*, while introducing a confrontation between Death and his victims, nevertheless deals in an unsystematic way both with the fate of "types" and with that of certain individuals (sometimes named), rather than proposing an orderly survey of society as a whole.

The *Danse Macabré* reimposes order precisely through the image of the dance, proposing a rigid hierarchy from highest to lowest, and an ingenious alternation of cleric and layman. It therefore represents an essentially conservative attitude towards social stratifications and constitutes recognition of contemporary reality with no critical undercurrent. For a *critique* of the social structure, we must await the emphasis on individual rather than type which is the fruit of medieval theatre.

★

UN MIROER SALUTAIRE

Jane H M Taylor

The title-page of Guyot Marchant's 1486 edition of the *Danse Macabré* provides, as well as the conventional title by which the text is now generally known, an explanatory sub-title:

> Ce present livre est appellé *Miroer salutaire pour toutes gens et de tous estats*, et est de grant utilité et recreacion pour pleuseurs ensengnemens tant en latin comme en françoys les quelx il contient. Ainsi composé pour ceulx qui desirent acquerir leur salut, et qui le voudront avoir.[1]

This resounding title, with its promise of moral value and even salvation, its pretension to universal relevance, is an echo of the opening stanzas of the poem where it is the author himself who chooses to call his work a *miroir*, proposed for the careful and frequent study of the wise:

> En ce *miroer* chascun peut lire
> Qui le convient ainsi danser;
> Saige est celuy qui bien s'i mire.[2]

Now it might be argued that to labour the mirror metaphor in this context is to attach quite undue importance to what by this time had become no more than a commonplace. Critics agree[3] on the one hand that *mirror* and *speculum* are so widespread in titles in the Middle Ages, and indeed in the Renaissance, that their use almost defies classification and catalogue: my own preliminary check-list[4], although compiled only from published sources, contains as many as forty-six distinct mirror-titles. On the other, it is generally agreed that by the late Middle Ages the verb *se mirer* had lost the special sense of "to look at oneself in a mirror", so that when in the *Renart le Nouvel* we are invited

> Mirons nous où vrai Crucefis,
> C'est où Fil Dieu ki fu en crois,[5]

all that seems implied is *meditation* or *contemplation*, and so that Orr translates the word *mirer* in the *Bible* of Guiot de Provins,

> Li templier se doient mireir
> En la croix et ou bel menteil

simply as "trouver un enseignement dans quelque chose".[6]

It is the contention of this paper, however, that more than mere cliché is involved in the choice of this metaphor: that the use of this image as alternative title for the *Danse Macabré* arouses in the reader precise expectations deriving ultimately from patristic and theological sources but popularised in vernacular moralistic writing; that *mirror* and *death* were associated in literature, folk-lore and art in ways which suggest that the mirror has in this context a well-defined function; and that these two strands unite to make the use of the phrase *miroer salutaire* not a facile opening platitude, but an indication of the overall structure of the poem itself.

First, then, the title. A first common denominator for all mirror titles is the following: that they are works of edification. On the simplest level, the function of these works is purely informative, a function which the mirror itself as household object seems most logically to suggest: the mirror as *summa*, providing an exact reflection of reality. Just as the mirror proper allows the physical eye to encompass in a small area depth and distance, so the metaphorical mirror allows the reader's eye to perceive not merely the particular but the general. Unaided, the reader can apprehend the physical or metaphysical universe only through a lifetime's study of the particular; in a mirror, he can encompass in microcosm the whole spectrum of the theme or subject in question, concentrated in the pages of a treatise and with the advantage that the mirror will have imposed order on what in the particular might well appear confusion.[7] Used in this sense, which I shall term the *mirror as reflector*, in the *Speculum Alchemiae* attributed to Roger Bacon, for instance[8], or in the *Speculum Lapidum* cited by Du Cange[9], the mirror is a purely passive instrument whose function is merely to reproduce, precisely, accurately and in its entirety, what is placed before it; it does not interpret, it provides no message or moral lesson for the reader, and at most its claim is to comprehensiveness.

This most basic of interpretations constantly underpins the metaphor, of course, but it is early overlaid by other and more complex senses not necessarily implicit in the mirror as object, and deriving primarily from biblical and exegetical sources. Vincent de Beauvais' encyclopedic *Speculum Maius* has some claim to have institutionalised the mirror title[10]; its prime purpose is of course universality, a compendium of all that was knowledge, but his general prologue suggests an additional intention:

> Speculum quidem eo quod quicquid fere speculatione, idest admiratione vel imitatione dignum est.[11]

The notion of the mirror as providing a *paragon* or *pattern* for the contemplation and imitation of the reader, which I shall call the *mirror as exemplar*, has a long history which has been studied in detail by Sister Ritamary Bradley.[12] Briefly (for it is clearly not in this sense that the fifteenth-century *Miroer Salutaire* is to be understood), she attaches it to the Pauline statement in I Corinthians, xiii, 12, that "Videmus nunc per speculum in aenigmate: tunc autem facie ad faciem"[13], and credits Saint Augustine with the commentaries which earliest led to the image's popularity and proliferation. For Saint Augustine, it is scripture itself which provides a mirror,

> a mirror of knowledge, when it is said that all which has been written is our mirror; and a paragon for right living, when it is said that God's commands, whether read or recalled to memory, are seen as in a mirror.[14]

This notion had an enthusiastic reception not only among the early Church Fathers, quoted in abundance by Bradley, but also, for obvious reasons, among the twelfth-century platonists.[15] It further encouraged the use of the *speculum* title for works offering a guide to good living, such as the handbook for holy women usually attributed to Saint Augustine himself and commonly known as the *Speculum*.[16] The vernacular moralists of the later Middle Ages and the writers of Latin works for laymen adopted this interpretation with enthusiasm: it is in this light that we must understand the mirror-titles of Durand de Champagne's *Speculum Dominarum*, compiled for Jeanne de France in about 1209[17], with its eulogy of queenly *sagesse*, or Watriquet de Couvin's *Mireoir aus Princes* dating from the 1320s and detailing the characteristics of the perfect prince.[18]

From a very early stage, however, the notion of the mirror had a fundamental ambivalence. For Saint Augustine, scripture as mirror performs two distinct and complementary functions: it provides an

31

ideal, by showing man what he should become, but it also provides a *repoussoir*, by showing man what he is. In the key text which Sister Bradley proposes as demonstrating the notion of mirror as paragon, this essential ambiguity is clearly expressed:

> Et quid intuens, inquis, me videbo? Posuit tibi speculum Scripturam suam; legitur tibi: *Beati mundi corde, quoniam ipsi Deum videbunt* (Matth. v, 8). Speculum in hac lectione propositum est: vide si hoc es quod dixit; si nondum es, geme ut sis (...) Hoc tibi ostendit nitor ille quod es: vide quod es; et si tibi displicet, quaere ut non sis. Si enim cum foeda sis, tibi ipsi adhuc displices, pulchro jam places. Quid ergo? Quoniam displicet tibi foeditas tua, incipis ei in confessione; sicut alibi dicitur: *Incipite Domino in confessione* (*Psal.* cxlvi, 7). Primo accusa foeditatem tuam: foeditas enim animae de peccatis, de iniquitatibus. Accusando foeditatem tuam incipe confiteri a confessione incipis decorari: quo decorante, nisi specioso forma prae filiis hominum?[19]

The mirror here performs yet another function, nonetheless linked to its original sense of place of exact record: it is a gateway to a truth not discernible on a surface level, to a reality deeper than that provided by superficial observation. It is the instrument which enables the spectator to move from the plane of everyday reality, to a plane of profounder reality concealed deep in his heart and soul.[20]

The popularity of this conception of the mirror is evident both from its use as a title and its use as an image within vernacular texts. Eustache Deschamps' appalling *Miroir de Mariage*[21] purports to show the reality of marriage, as opposed to the romanticised, fictitious image to which young men are normally exposed; the *Mirror of Man's Life* (a translation dating from 1576 of Innocent III's *De contemptu mundi*)[22] details the degradation and sordidness of life behind its outwardly pleasant exterior; Ysambart de Saint Leger's *Miroir des Dames* portrays the awfulness of female existence.[23] A similar use of the image informs Jean de Meung's discussion of distorting and true mirrors[24] and lies behind the courtly use of the image, where the eyes are the mirrors of the soul or the heart:

> Mes c'est li mereors au cuer,
> Et par ce mireor trespasse,
> Si qu'il ne blesce ne ne quasse,
> Le san don li cuers est espris.[25]

These texts, in general, while assuming two levels of reality, do not make both levels explicit: Eustache Deschamps, for instance, sees no need to detail the erroneous view of marriage, and confines himself to what I might call the *mirror as repoussoir*. A number of mirror-texts, however, seize on the very notion of duality which enabled them to combine for their readers two models, one admonitory, whose present image and future fate will deter the reader, and one exemplary. Thus Watriquet de Couvin's *Mireoir aus Princes*, previously quoted[26], provides both the image of the paragon and that of his brother, the very image of sin and despotism, and when Ysambart de Saint Leger wrote his continuation of Durand de Champagne's *Speculum Dominarum*, the disquisition on queenly virtues is coupled with a section dwelling on the horrors of human existence in general and the weakness of women in particular.[27] The most dramatic and startling expression of this double-image is provided by Watriquet de Couvin, whose *Mireoir as Dames* epitomises the dualistic structure by combining image and counter-image in one allegorical figure:

> La très plus belle creature
> C'onques peüst fourmer Nature,
> Et la plus blanche au droit costé;
> Rien n'en avoit Nature osté,
> Toute y estoit biautez entiere.
> Mais tant estoit hideuse et fiere,
> Laide, noire, au costé senestre,
> C'on en peüst esbahis estre;
> Plaine de grans plours et de cris,
> Plus iert crieuse qu'antecris;
> Onques chose de mere née
> Ne fu en tel point figurée
> Ne de si hideuse façon.[28]

It is this notion of duality which the *Danse Macabré* particularly adopts. Its conventional English title is misleading: this is not the *Dance of Death*, but the *Dance of the Dead*. This is significant: what is presented to the onlooker is a procession of the living, partnered each by his own *mort*. Although neither the poem nor the iconography states specifically that the dead are the *sosies* or *Doppelgänger* of the living, the suggestion is inescapable: each *mort* knows precisely in what terms best to address his partner[29], and some at least strike attitudes which are ironic reflections of the partner's function: the angle at which *le Mort* holds his spear is a precise echo of his partner the Patriarch's crozier, and the Archbishop's *Mort* raises his hand in a parody of blessing.[30] Guyot himself, or his engraver, was clearly drawn to this possibility: the engravings added by him for the 1486 edition of the *Danse Macabré* proper underline it[31], and those done for Martial d'Auvergne's *Grande Danse Macabré des Femmes*, published in the same volume, with the wisps of hair clinging to the skulls of the dead, make it quite explicit (fig. 1).[32] Each couple may therefore be regarded as representing facets of the same person, and the poem as a whole is constructed around this series of dual images. On the one side stands a procession of types, and it is the particular *trouvaille* of the *Danse Macabré* to present to the onlooker or reader a range of ranks and professions such that each may find his own equivalent and identify himself with one of the speakers; to each of the types corresponds his own *mort*, recognisably the same laid bare, the skull beneath the skin. Thus it becomes the function of the poem and illustrations of the *Danse Macabré* to reveal, as a warning to the living, the essential transience and mortality to which each spectator is subject.

Fig 1:   From the *Danse Macabré des Femmes*, Paris 1491, reproduced by permission of the British Library.

This use of twin images is not, of course, confined to the *Danse Macabré*. Much the same mechanism is at the root of the so-called *transi* tomb, popular at the end of the Middle Ages, which presents the spectator with two distinct images: above, lying on a table-tomb, the effigy of the distinguished departed, serene in his regalia, and below, glimpsed through the fretted stone of a separate compartment, the agonised and contorted cadaver.[33] A similar mirror-metaphor is intrinsic to the *Poèmes des trois morts and des trois vifz*, latent anyway in the numerical correspondence and sometimes actualised, as in the engraving by the Hausbuch Master where the living and the dead wear identical crowns[34], or in the miniature from the *Psalter* of Robert de Lisle in the British Museum, where the attitude of the middle *Mort* is surely a deliberate caricature of the middle *Vif*: same carriage of the head, same hand raised to its breast, same hand clutching its companion, same fall of the draperies (fig. 2).[35]

These, however, still remain (to adopt Ariès' useful phrase)[36] *La Mort de Toi*. The onlooker reacts to Chichele's tomb in Canterbury

34

or to Harcigny's in Avignon with a thrill of disgust, but need not identify himself with Archbishop or king's doctor. And a dramatic confrontation between a royal hunting-party and their dead equivalents would presumably strike a chord mostly in potential hunting-parties. The distinctive *trouvaille* of the *Danse Macabré* is to attach the notion of the dual image firmly to *La Mort de Soi*. The *Poème des trois morts et des trois vifz* is presented as *reportage*, with a plot and characters from whom the reader may remain detached: the living of the *Danse Macabré* are not characters but types, individualised only by externals such as clothes or symbols of office and with their faces carefully anonymous. The mechanism is therefore the following: the spectator looks into the mirror of the *Danse Macabré* and recognises self (the mirror thus once again acting as *reflector*); he next identifies the partner also as self, but as self transformed so that the illusion of youth and immortality is stripped away, leaving the reality of the mortal man. It is precisely this mechanism, that of the *mirror as transformer*, which lies at the root of the mirror metaphor in the *Danse Macabré*: the understanding that within the mirror itself there takes place a metamorphosis of the onlooker, so that he sees not himself, but himself altered. It is my contention that a wealth of association, literary, artistic, traditional, makes the onlooker receptive to this mechanism.

Fig 2:   From the *Psalter* of Robert de Lisle (ms. Arundel 183), reproduced by permission of British Library.

In the elaborate web of medieval allegory and symbol, the mirror was most closely associated with one figure particularly relevant to this investigation: the figure of *Vanitas*, in both the meanings attached to this word by the Middle Ages. If *Vanitas* is taken to imply self-conceit, then a conventional representation of this is a woman with a mirror, as in the Memling painting preserved in Strasbourg.[37] But *Vanitas* in this sense is of course equated with *Superbia*, so that it is not surprising to find in a painting by Bosch, for instance, the mirror being held up by a devil of whose presence the woman is quite unaware, but which has apparently been summoned up by the mere act of looking into the mirror.[38] A woodcut of 1493[39] gives the mirror a more active role. Here the subject is a beautiful young girl combing her hair in a mirror, again quite oblivious of the real presence of the devil behind her. But the mirror here provides a window, as it were, whereby the devil can become visible at least to the spectator: behind her, and presumably invisible to the naked eye, the devil is turning his back on her, and in her mirror is the perfect likeness of the devil's backside (fig. 3). What the mirror represents here, then, is that channel into a different plane of reality of which I spoke earlier: the girl sees not herself, but a visitant from an otherwise invisible world.[40]

Fig 3:   Woodcut from *Der Ritter vom Thurm*, Basel 1493 (a translation of *Le Livre du Chevalier de la Tour Landry*, made by Marquand vom Stein).

Such demonic associations of the mirror were presumably reinforced by the practice of mirror-divining, which suggested corresponding links between prophetic and magic mirrors, and witchcraft and sorcery. That *Specularii* were condemned by the church and by theologians[41] did not prevent "catoptromancy", as it is called, from being widely practised[42]: it was recognised, for instance, as a particularly useful way of finding the location of buried treasure, and of identifying thieves. In general mirrors were faithful reflectors of truth, and could even be beneficial, like Prester John's mirror which enabled him to detect plots hatched against him in any way part of his empire[43], or the useful mirror in Ulrich von Zatzikhoven's *Lanzelet* which detected unfaithful wives and lovers.[44] But they could be used to summon up demons and evil spirits[45], and in unscrupulous hands produced distorted figures and terrifying illusions.[46]

But the associations of the mirror were not only demonic. The theme of *Vanitas* may be associated with pride and self-pride, but it also implies (as in *Ecclesiastes*) the futility and transience of worldly things. The two themes coincide for instance in a woodcut by Daniel Hopfer (fig. 4)[47], which shows two lovely women admiring themselves in a mirror; behind them is firstly a shaggy devil, and secondly the figure of Death holding up a skull and an hour-glass. It is not possible here, however, to see what is reflected in the mirror, and the unperturbed faces of the women suggest that the two terrifying figures are invisible: the message for the onlooker is to be derived not from the women's perception of their own mortality, but from our gloss on the juxtaposition of the two images. The same seems true of Baldung Grien's terrifying images of death where incidentally the devil is not present: here again, the woman stares oblivious into the mirror while the skeletal hands of Death reach for a breast or snatch at a gauzy drape.[48]

In all these, the central message of the painter/moralist is irony: youth and beauty contrasted with the feverish concupiscence of death. The mirror is no more than a pretext, a symbol of worldly oblivion; it is certainly not itself a vehicle for any message.

And yet the mirror itself had, to the medieval mind, a particular association with death and mortality. The most famous of all literary medieval mirrors was itself regarded as an instrument of death,

Fig 4: The Lady, the Devil and Death (copperplate engraving).

37

although (like Ovid) the author of the twelfth-century *Lai de Narcisse*
concentrates more on the theme of self-love and self-absorption as the
source of tragedy, than on the mirror in the pool being in itself
dangerous. Nevertheless, the notion that the *unbres*, 'reflection',
exercises a fatal fascination is implicit in the legend:

> Et voit que c'est unbres qu'il ainme.
> Mout par se blasme et fol se clainme,
> Et neporquant ne set que faire:
> Son corage n'en puet retraire.[49]

and was seized on and explicated by the thirteenth-century *Ovide
Moralisé* which, in its third moralisation, makes the mirror itself the
instrument of destruction and attaches the mirror of Narcissus firmly
to the theme of *Vanitas*:

> C'est li mireoirs perillous
> Ou se mirent li orguillous
> Qui les mondains delis convoitent,
> Que quant plus musent, mains exploitent.[50]

There appears moreover to have been a widespread association in
everyday reality of the mirror and death, of which there is still an echo
in the most common of all mirror superstitions, that to break a mirror
brings at best seven years' bad luck, and at worst death. Popular
superstition supposed that the mirror provided a channel through which
death can enter the individual; this presumably explains the folk belief,
which van Gennep cites as common all over France[51], that mirrors
should be veiled immediately after a death. Frazer[52] equates this
custom with the belief current in some primitive societies that the
reflection in the pool of water is that of one's own soul which is thereby
momentarily separated from the body and vulnerable, and certainly
it was believed that to see oneself in a mirror immediately after a death
might bring about one's own death within a year, and that to let a
child under the age of one see itself in a mirror will mean that it will
always be weakly, and may die. Similar superstitions are cited from
other parts of Europe: in Bohemia, for instance, it was thought that
an infallible sign of death was to see one's double reflected with one
in a mirror[53], and Emile Mâle cites the belief that "en écrivant avec
son sang une formule sur un parchemin, et en se regardant ensuite
dans un miroir, on se voyait tel qu'on serait après sa mort".[54]

It is this widespread folk belief in the mirror as instrument of ill-
omen which combines with the moralist's *Vanitas*-theme to produce
what I have called the *mirror as transformer*, the suggestion that the mirror

is so deeply imbued with the sense of mortality that the spectator looking into it will, ineluctably, see looking back at him his own horrific future self.[55] This is the message, of course, of the grim portrait of Burgkmair and his wife by the fifteenth-century artist Laux Furtenagel[56], where the two are reflected as death's heads in a hand-mirror, under the lugubrious admonition:

Solche Gestalt unser beider was
Im Spiegel aber nix denn das.

It is presumably also the sense, as Hartlaub suggests, of the monument in Bar-le-Duc which shows a grinning and triumphant skeleton holding up a mirror so as to imprint it with his own image.[57]

Everything suggests that this image of the *mirror as transformer* was sufficiently widespread in the Middle Ages to require no gloss, if only, on the most mundane level, because *miroirs de mort* could be bought: René d'Anjou acquired two of them from a painter in Avignon in 1479.[58] Sitters moreover might choose to have their portraits painted doubly: present self and future self juxtaposed as in the double portrait of Hieronymus Tschekkenburlin in Basel, or the serene wedding couple painted opposite two skeletons, recognisably male and female and aggressively wielding cross-bow and scythe, by the so-called Master of the Aachen Wardrobe Doors and preserved in Godesberg.[59] Even where the notion of the mirror-image is not explicit, it may still be understood: René d'Anjou designed his own tomb with what is surely an ironic mirror-image of himself as a dead king, lolling drunkenly on a throne with the orb and sceptre lying on the ground[60], and Paecht suggests that René must at least have sanctioned, and may have commissioned or even painted, the portrait of the dead king with the arms of Anjou which appears in ms. B.M. Egerton 1070 f.53.[61]

It is significant in this context that the popularity of the mirror metaphor as a vehicle for the macabre is widely reflected in the death-literature of the later Middle Ages. No fewer than five macabre works specifically link the concepts of *mirror* and *death*: Robert de l'Omme is responsible for the first, the *Miroir de Vie et de Mort*, which its editor dates to 1266[62]; there is a second *Miroir de Mort* by Jean Castel[63], a third by Chastellain[64], a fourth by Olivier de la Marche[65], a fifth by Philippe de Croy.[66] Moreover every major medieval macabre text makes the connection. For Helinant, death itself is a mirror[67]; *Le Mors de la Pomme* invites its readers to "Mirez vous bien et vous verrez Quele sera vo belle face ...".[68] Jean Castel makes explicit use of the mirror metaphor:

Mirez vous cy, dames et damoiselles,
Mirez vous cy et regardés ma face:
Helas! pensez, se vous estes bien belles,
Comment la Mort toute beauté efface,[69]

and the longest and best known of the *Poèmes des trois morts et des trois vifz*, that by Baudouin de Condé, contains an elaborate and lengthy play on the words *se mirer*, *mireoir*, *mire*, 'doctor', and *mirer*, 'to reward':

Dist li autres [vif]: "Compains, mar voi
Tel mireoir, se ne m'i mire;
Souffrés vous que Diex le vous mire.
Diex, ki le nous a mis en voie
Ce mireoir, le nous envoie
Pour mirer: se nous i mirons
Et certes ci ne se mire hons
Tant orguelleus, s'a droit se mire
Que bien n'ait de cel mehaing mire,
Et pour ce de tant ne m'ires,
K'aveuc moi ne vous i mires.[70]

If the *Danse Macabré*, then, is as I have argued a series of thirty potential self-portraits structured around the notion of image and obverse, the spectator's familiarity with the macabre associations of mirrors was likely to make him able to grasp the message without further explanation. Sermons like those of Savonarola would have invited him to live with "the spectacles of death", to visit death-beds, to keep little skeletons in his pocket, to look at himself frequently in mirrors and recognise his own mortality.[71] Churchmen like Alexander Neckam would have recommended keeping a skull beside him as a speaking mirror of the human condition.[72] Miniaturists like the Master of Mary of Burgundy would have decorated his devotional works with a border of skulls and the macabre motto "Ce sera moy"[73]; his everyday experience would have suggested that mirrors are instruments of ill omen and danger. That special fascination of the mirror which affected Gautier and Cocteau, Lewis Carroll and Rilke, allied with the learned and scholastic *mirrors* that proliferate throughout the Middle Ages, make the mirror a fitting and desirable sub-title for a work of warning and admonition.

NOTES

1. Le Roux de Lincy et L.-M. Tisserand, *Paris et ses historiens au quinzième siècle* (Paris, 1867), pp. 289-290. (N.B. the single existing copy of the *editio princeps* of 1485 does not have this title page).

2. ll. 9-11. All citations will be taken from *La Danse Macabré des charniers des Saints Innocents à Paris,* ed. E.F. Chaney (Manchester, 1945) (Publications of the University of Manchester CCXIII).

3. v. Sister Ritamary Bradley, "Backgrounds of the title *Speculum* in Medieval Literature," *Speculum* XXIX (1954), 100-115; W. Goldin, *The Mirror of Narcissus in the Courtly Love Lyric* (Ithaca (New York), 1967), pp. 3. ff.; Paul Lehmann, "Mittelalterliche Buchertitel," *Sitzungsberichte der Bayerischen Akademie der Wissenschaften, Philosophisch-historische Klasse,* Heft III (Munich 1953).

4. Which it would be excessive to append here, but which I hope to publish at a later date.

5. Ed. M.D.M. Méon, *Le Roman de Renart* (Paris,1826),IV, p. 366, ll. 5834-5.

6. Ed. John Orr, *Les Oeuvres de Guiot de Provins* (Manchester, 1915), ll. 1766-7.

7. v. W. Goldin, *op. cit.,* pp. 77 ff., and cf. G.F. Hartlaub, *Zauber des Spiegels, Geschichte und Bedeutung des Spiegels in der Kunst* (Munich, 1951), pp. 13-15, 87-101.

8. Ed. A Poisson, in *Cinq traités d'alchimie* (Paris, 1890).

9. *Glossarium mediae et infimae latinitatis* (Niort, 1883-7), VII, p. 550, col. 2.

10. Douai 1624. On Vincent de Beauvais, see particularly E. Mâle, *L'Art religieux du XIIIe siècle en France* (Paris, 1925), pp. 23 ff.

11. Vincentius Bellovacensis, *Speculum Quadruplex, sive Speculum Maius* (Graz, 1964), I, p. 3.

12. *Op. cit.,* pp. 101 ff., and cf. J. Frappier, "Variations sur le thème du miroir, de Bernard de Ventadour à Maurice Scève," *Cahiers de l'Association internationale des études francaises* XI (1959), 134-158.

13. Sister R. Bradley, *op. cit.,* p. 102, and cf. W. Goldin, *op. cit.,* p. 8 ff.

14. Sister R. Bradley, *op. cit.,* p. 103.

15. v. especially R. Javelet, *Image et ressemblance au douzième siècle: de saint Anselme à Alain de Lille* (Paris, 1967), and cf. also A. Hunt, "Redating Chrétien de Troyes", *Bulletin Bibliographique de la Société Internationale Arthurienne* XXX (1978), 220-227.

16. *Spechio dei peccatori,* attribuito a S. Agostine, ed. Ugo Antonio Amico (Bologna, 1866). On the doubtful attribution to Saint Augustine, v. A. Mandouze *Saint Augustin: l'aventure de la raison et de la grâce* (Paris, 1968), p. 57 note.

17. v. *Histoire Littéraire de la France,* par des religieux bénédictins de la Congrégation de Saint-Maur (Paris, 1865-1981), XXX, pp. 302-3.

18. Ed. Auguste Scheler in *Dits de Watriquet de Couvin* (Brussels, 1868), pp. 199-230.

19. *Enarratio in Psalmum CIII* (P.L. XXXVII, col. 1338).

20. Frappier, *op. cit.,* p. 134.

21. *Oeuvres complètes,* ed. Le Queux de Saint-Hilaire et G. Raynaud (Paris, 1878-1903), t. IX.

22. English'd by H.K., from the *De contemptu mundi* of Pope Innocent III (London, 1576).

23. Ed. C. Marazza (Lecce, 1978) (Classici Stranieri I).

24. v. Alan M.F. Gunn, *The Mirror of Love: A Reinterpretation of the "Roman de la Rose"* (Lubbock (Texas),1952) (Texas Technological College Research Publications in Literature), pp. 268 ff.

25. Chrétien de Troyes, *Cligès,* ed. A. Micha (Paris, 1975), ll. 704-7.

26. See above note 18.

27. See above note 23.

28. Ed. Auguste Scheler, *op. cit.,* p. 3, ll. 59-71.

29. E.g. *La Danse Macabré,* ed. Chaney (*v.* note 2), ll. 65-72, 113-120, 145-152 etc.

30. v. Le Roux de Lincy et Tisserand, *op. cit.,* pp. 298-9. One objection might be made, though it does not invalidate the argument: the *mort* snatching away the baby is full-grown (*ibid.* p. 312).

31. v. Joël Saugnieux, *Les Danses Macabres de France et d'Espagne et leurs prolongements littéraires* (Paris,1972) (Bibl. de la Fac. des Lettres de Lyon XXX), pp. 22 ff.

32. v. for example E. Mâle, *L'Art religieux de la fin du moyen âge en France* (Paris, 1922), p. 377.

33. E. Panofsky, *Tomb Sculpture: its changing aspects from ancient Egypt to Bernini,* ed.

H.W.Janson (London, 1964), cites the tomb of a mayor of Straubing in Lower Bavaria, which shows him in repulsive detail with the inscription "Sum *speculum* vitae, Johannes Gmainer, et rite/ Tali vos eritis, fueram quandoque quod estis". cf. E.H. Kantorowicz, *The King's Two Bodies: A Study in Medieval Political Theology* (Princeton, 1957), pp. 431-7, figs 28, 30, 31.

34. Reproduced in R. van Marle, *Iconographie de l'art profane au Moyen Age et à la Renaissance* (New York, 1971), II, p. 395, fig. 429.

35. Reproduced in Joan Evans, *The Flowering of the Middle Ages* (London, 1966), p. 241.

36. In *L'Homme devant la mort* (Paris, 1977), Ariès contrasts *la mort de soi,* the agonised experience of one's own mortality, with *la mort de toi,* admiration for the "la belle mort" .

37. v. van Marle, *Iconographie de l'art profane* (New York,1971), II p.81.

38. In the Escurial. Reproduced, for example, in L. von Baldass, *Hieronymous Bosch* (Vienna,1943), plates 11 and 13. Cf. H. Schwarz, "The Mirror in Art," *The Art Quarterly* XV (1952), pp. 97-118.

39. v. J. Boullet, "Le Monde des Miroirs," *Aesculape,* fév.-mars 1962, p. 32.

40. Compare the account given by the Chevalier de la Tour-Landry (quoted Tobler-Lommatsch VI 82-83): "Et si comme il plust a Dieu, si comme par exemplaire, ainsi comme elle se miroit a celle heure, elle vit a rebours l'ennemy ou mirouer qui lui monstroit son derriere, si lait, si orrible, que la damme issy hors de son sens comme demoniacle; si fut un long temps malade". Cf. also the comment of Michaud quoted by Frappier, *op. cit.,* p. 135: "Le miroir est ce qui permet le passage d'un monde à l'autre, et dans chaque monde, d'un plan à l'autre."

41. v. H. Bächthold-Stäubli, *Handwörterbuch des deutschen Aberglaubens* (Berlin and Leipzig, 1927-42), IV pp. 1099 ff.

42. v. L.Thorndike, *A History of Magic and Experimental Science* (New York, 1932-58), II 158 ff., III 505-515, IV 298, 557 etc., and cf. the authorities cited by W. Goldin, *op. cit.,* p. 13, note 22.

43. v. L. Thorndike, *op. cit.,* II p. 243.

44. Ed. K.A. Kahn (Berlin, 1965), ll. 4772 ff.

45. v. A. Delatte, *La Catoptromancie grecque et des dérivés* (Paris, 1952) (Bibl. de la Fac. de Philosophie et Lettres de l'Université de Liège XLVIII).

46. v. L. Thorndike, *op. cit.,* II p. 15.

47. v. Jean Wirth, *La Jeune fille et la mort: recherches sur les thèmes macabres dans l'art germanique de la Renaissance* (Geneva,1979)(Hautes Etudes Médievales et Modernes XXXVI), fig. 75.

48. *ibid,* figs 55, 62, 64-67.

49. Ed. M.Thiry-Stassin et Madeleine Tyssens (Paris,1976)(Bibl. de la Fac. de Philosophie et Lettres, Université de Liège CCXI), ll. 829-832.

50. *Ovide Moralisé,* ed. C. de Boer (Amsterdam, 1915-1936)(Verhandelingen der koninklijke Akademie van Wetenschappen te Amsterdam, Afdeeling Letterkunde, Niewe Reeks, XV, XXI, XXX, XLIII), ll. 1925-28; cf. W. Goldin, *op. cit.,* p. 63, J. Frappier, *op. cit.,* p. 146, and Louise Vince, *The Narcissus Theme in Western European Literature up to the early Nineteenth Century* (Lund, 1967).

51. A. van Gennep, *Manuel du folklore francais contemporain* (Paris, 1946), I (ii), pp. 672.

52. *The Golden Bough,* part II: *Taboo and the Perils of the Soul,* (London, 1936), pp. 92 ff.

53. Bächthold-Stäubli, *op. cit.,* I p. 682.

54. *L'Art religieux à la fin du moyen âge en France* (Paris,1922), p. 365.

55. Cf. ms. B.N.fonds francais 1393, fol 112: a young man sees himself in a mirror divided into two halves, one of which is skeletal.

56. v. Otto Paecht, "René d'Anjou-Studien I", *Jahrbuch der Kunsthistorischen Sammlungen in Wien* LXIX (1973), 88-90.

57. G.F Hartlaub, *op. cit.,* p. 100.

58. Otto Paecht, *op. cit.,* p. 90 note.

59. Both are reproduced by Ernst Buchner, *Das deutsche Bildnis der Spätgotik und der frühen Dürerzeit* (Berlin, 1953).

60. O. Paecht, "Dévotion du roi René pour sainte Marie-Madeleine et le sanctuaire de Saint Maximin", *Chronique Méridionale, Arts du Moyen Age et de la Renaissance* I (1981),p.19. Lecoy de la Marche agrees that the portrait of the king proper is the work of René himself; v. *Le Roi René, sa vie, son administration, ses travaux artistiques et littéraires* (Paris, 1875), II pp. 72 ff.

61. Otto Paecht, *op. cit.* (Note 59), p. 18. Also reproduced in Joan Evans, *op. cit.* (note 35), plate 52.

62. Ed. A Langfors, *Romania* XLVII (1921), 511-531, and L (1924), 14-53.

63. v. G.A. Brunelli, "Jean Castel et le *Mirouer des Dames,*" *Le Moyen Age,* 4me série, XI (1956), 98 note.

64. Cited by C. Martineau-Génieys, *Le thème de la mort dans la poésie francaise de 1450 à 1550* (Paris, 1878) (Nouvelle Bibliothèque du Moyen Age VI), p. 194.

65. Cited by I. Siciliano, *Francois Villon et les thèmes poétiques du Moyen Age* (Paris, 1934), p. 233, note 5.

66. ms. B.N.fonds francais 15216, cited by I. Siciliano, *ibid.,* p. 233.

67. *Les Vers de la Mort,* ed. F. Wulff et E. Walberg (Paris, 1905)(Société des Anciens Textes Français), strophe XI, p. 10.

68. Ed. F. Ed. Schneegans, *Romania* XLVI (1920), pp. 537-570, ll. 299-300.

69. *op. cit., (v.* note 62), p. 110.

70. Ed. Stefan Glixelli, *Les Cinq poèmes des trois morts et des trois vifz* (Paris, 1914), pp. 55-56, ll. 36-46.

71. v. Alberto Tenenti, *La vie et la mort à travers l'art du quinzième siècle* (Paris, 1952) (Cahiers des Annales VIII), p. 67.

72. *De naturis rerum,* ed. Thomas Wright (London,1803) (Rerum britannicarum medii aevi scriptores), p. 239: "Vis igitur expressum conditionis tuae speculum intueri, intuere testam capitis hominis jam putrefacti et in pulverem reducti."

73. Reproduced by Paecht, *op. cit.* (note 55), p. 100.

RESUME

Prenant comme point de mire le sous-titre, *Miroer salutaire*, de la *Danse Macabré* (édité par Guyot Marchant, 1486), cette étude se propose de démêler les acceptions multiples du terme-clef. A l'époque déjà, *se mirer* ne voulait plus dire "se regarder dans un miroir" mais plutôt "se regarder intérieurement", "méditer sur soi-même". Par ailleurs l'image du miroir s'associe au thème de la mort. Le miroir reflète la réalité entière; il joue sur divers plans; il est à la fois instrument physique et métaphysique. Plus, il fournit un modèle à notre contemplation. Notons que pour chaque signification du terme il faudrait remonter à une source biblique ou patristique (cf. le *miroir de connaissance* chez saint Augustin, etc). Peu à peu, le *speculum* est donc devenu un art de vivre. Or, si le miroir peut nous renvoyer une image de la réalité idéale, il nous renvoie toujours celle de la réalité vecue: il s'agit alors d'un miroir *repoussant.*

A tout ceci s'ajoute chez la *Danse Macabré* la notion du mort: une espèce de sosie du vivant qui se contemple; le mort parodie le vivant (thème du soi-autre) et le met en garde, à travers le miroir.

Le miroir peut être magique, diabolique, divinatoire. Parfois il révèle plus à un tiers qu'à celui qui se mire. Il devient alors, sous la plume de certains, véhicule de l'ironie ("tout est vanité" devant la mort); il dévoile notre narcissisme et notre amour-propre.

La superstition populaire et certaines oeuvres littéraires démontrent que l'ancien symbole du miroir n'est pas complètement perdu pour nous.

THE ENGLISH CADAVER TOMB IN THE LATE FIFTEENTH CENTURY: SOME INDICATIONS OF A LANCASTRIAN CONNECTION

Pamela M. King

The fashion for presenting the deceased as a decaying corpse or skeleton on tombs never achieved more than limited popularity in Britain. From the earliest examples to the accession of Elizabeth I there survive records of around one hundred and seventy-five only, from the costly "double-decker" to the shroud brass. As the fashion did not arrive here until c. 1424, whereas early Continental examples can be confidently placed in the last quarter of the previous century, it is evidently derivative. It is my belief that it was imported from France and the Low Countries by people who travelled there for reasons of state in the early fifteenth century. Explanations for the phenomenon which go no further than to suggest that it was a product of the general aesthetic decline of late medieval, post-plague Europe do little to explain an individual instance; it should be possible to trace dissemination of the design within an identifiable milieu. This paper runs counter to the accustomed *Zeitgeist* approach to mortality themes: the choice of monument made by the present group of tomb-owners had more do to with whom they knew and where they had been, than with their reading, devotions, or contemplation of their final end. The group comprises four women and one man who died between 1465 and 1480, thirty-eight percent of surviving cadaver tombs from that period.

In indicating that the group may be designated as a "Lancastrian connection", it is not intended to suggest that the tombs in question belonged to those who joined battle in the "Wars of the Roses". Apart from anything else, the view that there was unbroken civil strife from 1399 until 1485 is fashionably dismissed as an historical myth, fuelled by Shakespeare and Tudor "golden age" propaganda.[1] "Lancastrian" in this context means rather those who, over a protracted period, owed special allegiance to the king in his distinct capacity as Duke of Lancaster. More specifically, the network of loyalties may be traced back to the Roet sisters (fig.1). Catherine Roet, before she became the wife of John of Gaunt, was married to Hugh Swynford, a Lincolnshire knight, by whom she had a son

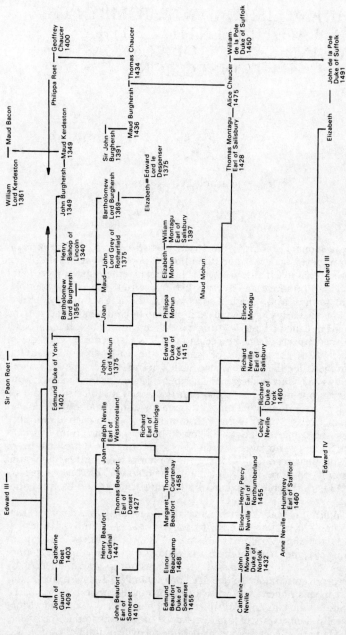

E.A. Greening Lambourne, 'The Arms on the Chaucer Tomb at Ewelme', *Oxoniensia* V (1940).
78-93.

Fig. I

Thomas. Thomas was keeper of Richard II at Pontefract Castle and was accused of his murder by Adam of Usk. As John of Gaunt's mistress, during the period of his marriage to Constanza of Castille, Catherine was guardian of Henry IV's sisters. She was mother to the Beauforts who were retrospectively legitimised when John of Gaunt eventually married her. Her sister, Philippa, was married to Geoffrey Chaucer, and was Constanza of Castille's lady-in-waiting. Geoffrey and Philippa's son, Thomas Chaucer, held Queen Isabella in his capacity as Constable of Wallingford.[2] The close allegiance between Chaucers, Swynfords, Beauforts and the Crown continued throughout the period of the Lancastrian dynasty.

The first tomb-owner under consideration, chronologically, appears as a comparative unknown. John Baret, burgess and draper of Bury St Edmunds[3], left a chantry chapel which appears to be more of a proclamation of faith in the Lancastrian cause than in the life to come. The tomb, in St Mary's church, is a stone mensa bearing a single corpse effigy, a *memento mori* verse[4], and a series of scrolls declaring the Lancastrian motto, "Grace me Gouerne". On the decorated ceiling above, the motto is repeated in a design of collars of Ss, the Lancastrian livery. When and why Baret was awarded the livery has never been clear; Tymms, who edited his long will, suggests that it was a result of services rendered to the king on his visit to Bury in 1433 or 1447.[5] Certainly Baret was awarded an annuity by the Crown in 1441, which he shared with another Bury man, the poet Lydgate.[6]

Baret's will names many friends and relations and also shows that he owned a manuscript of the *Siege of Thebes* and of the *Disce Mori*. Firstly, however, it is interesting because of the three men whom he names as habitual advisers in matters of property, William Jenney, John Heydon, and Thomas Heigham. Jenney, lawyer, J.P. and several times member of parliament for Suffolk, was a shrewd and lucky man "made by the law"[7], an extreme court partisan allied to Cardinal Beaufort. Heydon was an official of the Duchy of Lancaster, from 1444-45 Deputy Steward of the North Parts under William de la Pole, husband of Alice Chaucer.[8] Both were implicated in the events in Bury in 1447-48 which lead to the death of the Duke of Gloucester.[9] Heigham served on commissions with the other two and was another Lancastrian partisan.[10] Baret numbered among his friends, therefore, three of the party of de la Pole, Earl and later Duke of Suffolk, veteran of the French wars, appeaser, Duchy official and husband of Chaucer's grand-daughter. Baret also bequeaths a spoon to "my lady Poole dwellyng at Bermonddsseye"[11], undoubtedly the same lady.

The family bequests in Baret's will concern principally the Drurys of Rougham. His wife was sister to Sir William Drury, and his niece, Catherine Whitwell, was married to Sir William's son Thomas (fig.II). These apparently insular connections might be passed by, were it not for a passing reference in the seventeenth century *Chorography of Suffolk* to a shroud brass now missing:

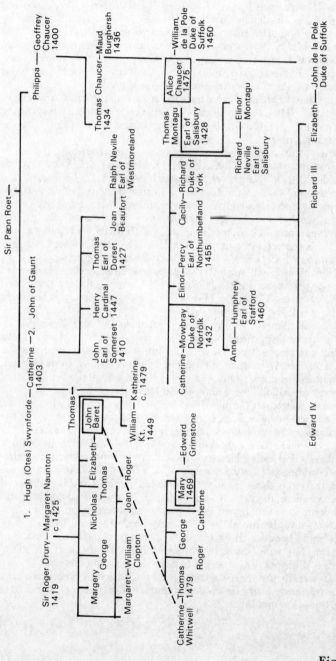

Derived from I and from genealogies of the Drurys in
J.J. Muskett, *Suffolk Manorial Families* (Exeter, 1900), i, 345-47

Fig. II

A portrait of a woman in her winding sheet about whose head are these armes p'pale France and England quarterly a labell of three points ermine and azur a chevron (ermine drawn) charged with 3 bores heades coupe. About the armes these wordes, 'These be the armes of Dame Catherine Swynford sometyme Duchesse of Lancaster that by S'r William (sic) Sewynford had sonne and heyre S'r Thomas Sewynford knight, father to Dame Catherine, wife to S'r Will'm Drury knight the w'h S'r Willia'and Dame Catherine among other had Marie the wife of Edward Grymstone esquier that god hath endued with great vertue and beautye and here is interred (who dyed on the 6th of March a'o Dni 1469).[12]

The deceased is John Baret's niece, therefore, and great-grand-daughter on her mother's side of Catherine Roet. This establishes for Baret more than a simple local affiliation, a clear family connection with the Lancastrian court circle, not hitherto acknowledged.

Mary Drury of the lost shroud brass was married to Edward Grimstone, another associate of de la Pole, involved in the negotiations in which the latter, as the king's proxy, arranged the marriage of Henry VI to Margaret of Anjou.[13] Storey describes him as "a well known partisan of the court" who sat on the jury in Bury dealing with Cade's rising.[14] He was also involved in negotiations with the Duke and Duchess of Burgundy in the 1440s, and it was probably on one of his frequent continental visits that he commissioned Petrus Christus to paint his portrait. In this, the first portrait of an Englishman in a domestic setting, he is shown proudly holding his collar of Ss. Not only does the portrait place him firmly within the "party" in question; it also shows how this group may be seen acquiring continental cultural tastes, a point to return to. Mary Drury was Grimstone's second wife, he her second husband. When she died she was only twenty-seven. He died in 1478 and is buried under an armoured effigy in the parish church at Rishangles.

Grimstone was one of the Keepers of the King's Jewels and Treasurer of the Chamber from 1448 "during good behaviour".[15] He had an associate and co-feoffee John Norris, Clerk of the Great Wardrobe until 1446, Keeper of the Queen's Jewels to Margaret of Anjou until 1450, and brother of Agnes Bulstrode, the next tomb owner.[16] Norris was, with Grimstone, involved in de la Pole's faction who were blamed for the failures in France in the 1440s. He was condemned by Cade and features in the popular song, "On the Popular Discontent at the Disasters in France".[17] His allegiances are nowhere better attested than in the fortunate survival of the original roundels of glass at Ockwells Manor. Among them are to be found the arms of Edmund Beaufort, Henry VI, Margaret of Anjou, John de la Pole and Richard Bulstrode of Upton.[18] The last was Norris's nephew, son of Agnes. Agnes's effigy in the church at Upton, Bucks, is all that remains of a brass to her, her husband and eleven children. It is the first known example of a kneeling shrouded effigy, anticipating the "resurrection brasses" of the early sixteenth century.[19] Richard Bulstrode was "master of the revels at the manor of Pleasance", an office of the Duchy of Lancaster. He was pardoned by the Yorkists, but later took part in the Duke of Buckingham's rising against Richard III in 1483.[20] As the Bulstrodes were a comparatively insignificant family of Buckinghamshire landowners with interests in London[21], it is probable that Richard gained preferment through his mother's family influence.

One name recurs in the emerging picture of this milieu, that of William de la Pole, third husband of Alice Chaucer whose double-decker tomb at Ewelme is one of the most splendid of the genre. Alice, grand-daughter of the poet, ended life as a considerable rural magnate in her own right. She first appears in records after the death of her second husband, Thomas Montacute, Earl of Salisbury, who was killed by a shot from the walls of Orléans in 1428, and was succeeded as commander there by de la Pole.[22] After the couple were married, it is evident that they commanded a vast fortune. For example, after the death of Alice's mother in 1437, she was given seisin of lands in Berkshire, Lincolnshire, Southampton, Suffolk, Essex, Cambridge and Oxfordshire. It was in this year that she and her husband founded the almshouses at Ewelme, and he became High Steward of the Duchy of Lancaster North of the Trent.[23] During the 1440s, William de la Pole's influence increased, principally owing to his continuing promotion by the all-powerful Cardinal Beaufort. The question of the royal marriage was in Beaufort's hands, and it was William de la Pole who was chosen as emissary in the suit with Margaret of Anjou. The marriage took place despite the fact many were in favour of prolonging hostilities with France. The ascendant party in the Lancastrian court under the influence of Beaufort may be broadly described as appeasers, opposed by Cade and Humphrey Duke of Gloucester who believed that the truce merely allowed the French king to strengthen his position. As a reward for services rendered, de la Pole became first Marquis, then, in 1448, Duke of Suffolk.[24] By that time, however, his position was threatened: as part of the price of the Angevin marriage England had relinquished her claim upon Maine, the gateway to Normandy, an extremely unpopular consequence. Then Suffolk was accused, albeit somewhat wildly, of the murder of Humphrey Duke of Gloucester. In fact Gloucester died, probably of a stroke, some days after their confrontation in Bury St Edmunds. The final straw was the eventual and overdue death of Beaufort himself. The king was forced, by an increasingly Yorkist Commons, to banish Suffolk, who escaped the angry London mob only to be killed at sea in 1450.[25] His death brings to an end the political ascendancy of the group in question. He was buried in the Charterhouse in Hull, a long-standing family benefaction; but his tomb, unfortunately, does not survive.

Alice Chaucer, however, survived her husband's discrediting and death comparatively unscathed. She remained, for the following twenty-five years of her life, active on her huge properties. She may have been safe because the Crown still relied on her for monetary assistance.[26] Her name is certainly linked, and not in the most complimentary manner, with Duchy partisans like Tuddenham, Hampden, Brews and Baret's friend Heydon in the *Paston Letters*.[27] Above all, she survived the change of dynasty because her only child, John de la Pole, was married to Elizabeth, sister of

Edward IV and Richard III.[28]

Not so fortunate was the last tomb-owner in the present group, Eleanor Moleyns, born in 1426 to Sir William Moleyns, a friend of Thomas Chaucer's. Eleanor's parents were married at Ewelme, originally the Burghersh family manor, since her mother's step-grandfather was Sir John Burghersh, Thomas Chaucer's father-in-law (fig. III). Connections with the Chaucer family were further reinforced by the marriage of Eleanor's aunt to John Hampden, a feoffee of Thomas Chaucer's. Eleanor's widowed mother later married Edmund Hampden.[29] After the death of her father at the Siege of Orléans, Eleanor became a ward of Thomas Chaucer.[30] When she was fourteen, he granted her marriage to Robert Hungerford, member of another well-established Lancastrian family, who then adopted the title Lord Moleyns. He spent most of his time in France and was imprisoned there during the struggle for Normandy in 1453. The ransom for his release cost his wife and mother almost all that they had, including most of Eleanor's dowry. Around the same time, Eleanor and Robert's son was married to one of the daughters of Henry Percy.[31]

With her fortune gone and her son married into a staunch Lancastrian family, Eleanor Moleyns was in the worst possible position when the Yorkists gained the throne. Her husband's extreme unpopularity with Richard Duke of York is attested in the *Paston Letters*.[32] After attempting to defend the Tower of London with Lord Scales in 1460, he escaped to on the Continent. His mother was arrested in 1461, and at the end of the year he was attainted, forfeiting all property. Thereafter he appears to have joined Margaret of Anjou in Scotland. In 1462, Eleanor was placed under surveillance.[33] Her husband was beheaded in Newcastle after the Battle of Hexham in 1464, after which much of their land was granted to Richard of Gloucester, later Richard III. Her son, Thomas, was charged with high treason, hanged, drawn and quartered near Salisbury in 1469, leaving no male heir, but only a baby daughter, Mary.[34] Eleanor Moleyns thus had none of the bargaining power of an Alice Chaucer and, bereft of all inheritance, she remarried an obscure gentleman called Oliver Man-yngham. She was commemorated by a modest shroud brass in the sanctuary of Stoke Poges church, near her parents' home. The inscription, according to Gough, was:

His hoc lapide sepelitur corpus venerabilis domine Eleanore Mullens baronisse, quam primitus desponsavit dominus Robertus Hungerforde miles et baro, et hanc postea nubita honorabilis dominus oliverus manyngham miles quorum animabus propicietur deus. Amen.[35]

The brass is now missing.

There are records of thirteen cadaver tombs or brasses whose owners died between 1465 and 1480. I believe that at least the five discussed here were personally known to one another. Of the other nine, the first is

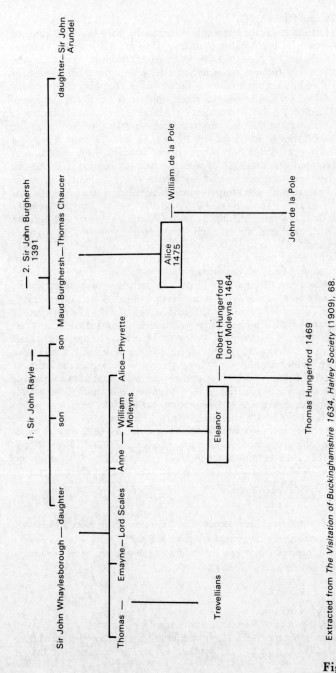

Extracted from *The Visitation of Buckinghamshire 1634, Harley Society* (1909), 68.

Fig. III

Thomas Bekynton, bishop of Bath and Wells, secretary and emissary abroad for Henry VI in 1432-39 and 1442. The tomb is said to have been erected by the bishop himself in 1451.[36] He may have taken the idea from what he saw on the Continent or from Henry Chichele, Archbishop of Canterbury and England's first cadaver tomb-owner, whose official and favourite he had been.[37] William Catesby (ob. 1471) was intimately connected with Henry VI's court[38] and Richard Willoughby (ob. 1472) was one of a Northern group of allies who held lands in the Duchy of Lancaster for whom similar patterns are traceable.[39] Joan Walrond (ob. 1477) was the daughter of a Berkshire J.P. who appears in records with John de la Pole and William Norris. Her daughter, Elizabeth Fetiplace, also chose the same type of monument.[40] One of the others was a Fellow of New College, Oxford, and the remaining four are very obscure minor landowners. In the case of these last, although no personal details can be found, there could be some connection with those studied since one belongs to Buckinghamshire and two of the others are buried in East Anglia.[41] In the 1480s another group of Lancastrian tomb owners is discernible in Hertfordshire.[42]

Making the case for the manner in which a devotional fashion travelled, however, does not explain why the cadaver effigy in particular should have been popular with these people. The solution to that question can be only suggested, rather than proven. Perhaps the most important factor to be taken into account is the support of the group for Margaret of Anjou, who, being the daughter of René, noted for his patronage of and participation in the arts, would have imported certain tastes with her. René's own tomb was surmounted by a painting of *le roi mort*, a putrefying corpse sitting on a throne in robes of state. It has been suggested that, owing to René's marked lack of success in matters of state, he devised the tomb in conscious parody of that of his ancestor, Robert the Wise of Anjou (ob. 1343) on which Robert is shown enthroned in majesty in a similar position. The same *memento mori* motif also appears with René's coat of arms in Egerton 1070, a book of hours in which this illuminaton at least could be in René's own hand.[43]

On the other hand, the idea could have been imported directly from observation of Continental examples, since the group was a well-travelled and well-cultivated one. Not only do we have Grimstone's portrait as a testimony to that; in 1444 William de la Pole had luxury household goods which he had imported delivered to him by the keepers of the port of Sandwich.[44] Alice Chaucer was the poet's grand-daughter, and even though Baret's *Disce Mori* is the only literature on a specifically mortality theme that seems to have been owned by the group, there is evidence of literary patronage. Alice we know commissioned the *Virtues of the Mass* from Lydgate[45], and her second husband, Thomas Montacute, has long been associated with Lydgate's translation of Deguilleville's *Pèlerinage de la Vie Humaine*, partly because of the frontispiece.[46] More important than that, however, must be the relationship between William de la Pole and Charles d'Orléans, each at one time prisoner in the custody of the other.[47] That the two men were personal friends is beyond doubt - de la Pole is said to have been awarded custody of Charles because his price was actually below

cost. The editor, Shirley, seems to have acquired the two poems of
Charles's, which appear with details from Chaucer's dream poems in
Harley 7333, from Lydgate, who in turn got them from Alice Chaucer.[48]
Charles d'Orléans also wrote an acrostic in praise of Anne Moleyns,
mother of Eleanor and family friend of the Chaucers.[49] The circle
was one familiar with Continental tastes.

All this does not exclude the possibility that these people took their lead
from their elders in their own country in choosing their tombs. One of the
earliest lay cadaver tomb-owners is Sir John Golafre (ob. 1442) who acted
on commissions with Thomas Chaucer, was knight of the shire for
Berkshire when Chaucer was Speaker in the last house of Commons
opened by Henry V, and was co-feoffee of William de la Pole.[50] He was
related to the Burghersh family and married two de la Pole ladies as his
first and third wives. Golafre was, with Chichele, a staunch supporter of
Beaufort and Henry V when the latter was still Prince of Wales.[51]

Probably a combination of the above factors led to the limited
popularity of cadaver tombs with these people. Certainly it seems that
there is a body of evidence to suggest that the fashion for cadavers was not
a general innovation, but a select trend passing amongst members of a
discernible group, to be picked up later by lesser persons living in the same
area or owing some debt of allegiance or admiration. Admittedly there are
unknown quantities - the tombs considered are chance survivals; people
are not always in a position to choose their tombs personally; not even a
majority of the followers of Margaret of Anjou favoured the design even
then, and she had neither the resources nor the privilege of determining
the design of her own tomb. On the other hand, none of the supporters of
Humphrey Duke of Gloucester seems to have a cadaver tomb; presumably
the design smacked too much of French influence for the hard-line
pugilists. Nor, for that matter, do any die-hard Yorkists favour the design.
The attribution to friends of the Queen and those who owed allegiance to
the Beauforts and the Crown in its specific capacity as Duke of Lancaster
appears to stand. There is, however, one exception: it seems from his will
that Edward IV had in mind for himself a tomb of the cadaver type.[52] But
he was unlucky.

NOTES

1. John Gillingham, *The Wars of the Roses* (London, 1981), 1-14.
2. Florence R. Scott, "A New Look at 'The Complaint of Chaucer to his Empty
   Purse'," *ELN* II (1964), 81-87. This discussion of the strength of the poet's case
   for requesting an annuity from Henry IV conveniently summarises the
   relationships in question.
3. M.D. Lobel, *The Borough of Bury St Edmunds* (Oxford 1935), 159.
4. Pamela M. King, "Eight English Memento Mori Verses from Cadaver Tombs,"
   N&Q XXVIII (1981), 495.
5. Samuel Tymms, ed., *Wills and Inventories from the Registers of the Commissary of Bury
   St Edmunds, The Archdeacon of Sudbury*, Camden Society XLIV (1850), 15-42.
6. *CPR, 1441-46*, 28, "The like grant of survivorship to John Lidgate, Monk of
   Bury St Edmunds, and John Baret, esquire, of 71, 13s, 4d yearly from Easter
   in the eighteenth year out of the issue of the counties of Norfolk and Suffolk

by the hand of the sheriffs thereof ..."

7. J.S. Wedgewood, *History of Parliament* (London, 1936), 500-01.
8. R. Somerville, *History of the Duchy of Lancaster, 1265-1603,* I (London, 1953), 425, 430, 453, 594.
9. R.L. Storey, *The End of the House of Lancaster* (London, 1966), 55-57, 46-47.
10. e.g. *CPR, 1467-77*, 248.
11. Tymms, *Wills and Inventories*, 36.
12. D.N.J. MacCulloch, *The Chorography of Suffolk*, Suffolk Records Society (London, 1976), 74-75. I am indebted to Dr. Charles Kightly of York for this reference and for guidance throughout.
13. C. Knight Watson, "Instructions given by King Henry VI to Edward Grimston and Notice of a Portrait of Edward Grimston", *Archaeologia*, XL (1866), 452-82. I follow throughout Watson's account of Grimstone.
14. R.L. Storey, *The End of the House of Lancaster*, 79n.
15. *CPR, 1446-52*, 130. The terms of the award may be connected with Grimstone's alleged involvement in the plot to put Margaret Beaufort and John de la Pole on the throne, alluded to in R.L. Storey, *The End of the House of Lancaster*, 74n.
16. J.S. Wedgewood, *History of Parliament*, 637-38.
17. Thomas Wright, ed., *Political Poems and Songs relating to English History, Composed during the Period from the Accession of Edward III to that of Richard III*, ii. (London, 1861), 222.
18. Margaret Wood, *The English Medieval House* (London, 1965), 358-59; and *VCH Berkshire*, iii. 103.
19. e.g. Spryng brass, Lavenham, Suffolk (1486).
20. J.S. Wedgewood, *History of Parliament*, 130-31.
21. *CCR, 1461-68*, 367; *1468-76*, 264, 372.
22. *CPR, 1422-29*, 474, 477, 478. *Complete Peerage*, xii. 444.
23. *CFR, 1431-37*, 346; *CPR, 1436-41*, 80; *Complete Peerage*, xii. 445.
24. *Complete Peerage*, xii. 446.
25. The role played by Suffolk in national affairs throughout the period in question may be found in E.F. Jacob, *The Fifteenth Century, 1399-1485* (Oxford, 1961), 473-95; and R.L. Storey, *The End of the House of Lancaster*, chapter ii.
26. *CPR, 1446-52*, 431 indicates that she proved indispensable in raising funds to send an army to Gascony in 1452.
27. Norman Davies, ed., *The Paston Letters and Papers of the Fifteenth Century* (Oxford, 1976), ii passim; and *PRO Lists and Indexes* xii, *List of Early Chancery Proceedings*, i. 235, no.77; 245, no.164.
28. Further details of Alice and William de la Pole are to be found in A.S. Harvey *The de la Pole Family of Kingston Upon Hull* (Yorkshire, 1957); and E.A. Greening Lambourn, "The Arms on the Chaucer Tomb at Ewelme, with a note on the early manorial history of the parish," *Oxoniensia* V (1940), 80ff.
29. *Complete Peerage*, ix. 42; and *The Visitation of Buckinghamshire 1634*, Harley Society (1909), 68.
30. Martin B. Ruud, *Thomas Chaucer* (Mineapolis, 1972), 12-13.
31. *Complete Peerage* ix, 618-21.
32. Norman Davies, ed., *Paston Letters*, ii. 233-34.
33. *CPR, 1461-67*, 181; and *Complete Peerage*, ix. 620.
34. *Complete Peerage*, ix. 621; and J.S. Wedgewood, *History of Parliament*, 485.
35. R. Gough, *Sepulchral Monuments in Great Britain*, ii. (1786), 207.
36. Kathleen Rogers Cohen, *Metamorphosis of a Death Symbol: The Transi Tomb in the Late Middle Ages and the Renaissance* (Berkeley, 1973), 68-69.
37. Ibid. and E.F. Jacob, *Archbishop Henry Chichele* (London, 1967), 90-96 for the date of Chichele's tomb which Cohen has misread, and 27-28 for the appointment of Bekynton.
38. R.M. Sergeantson, "The Restoration of the Long-Lost Brass of Sir William Catesby," *Associated Architectural Societies* XXXI (1911-12), 519-24, for an account of the brass at Ashby St Legers, Northants. J.S. Wedgewood, *History of Parliament*, 164, for an account of Catesby's political career.
39. Nikolaus Pevsner, ed., *The Buildings of England, Nottinghamshire* (Harmondsworth, 1951) 207, Wollaton Willoughby's will is preserved in *Testamenta Eboracensia* iii, Surtees Society 45 (1864), 170-72.

40. H.T. Morley, "Shroud Brasses of Berkshire," *Berkshire Archaeological Journal*, XXXIII (1929), 34-39, for the brasses in Childrey. *CPR, 1461-67*, 278, 363, 389, 559, 570, all support connections with the group in question.

41. Philip Astley (ob. 1467), Standon, Herts; Robert Brampton (ob. 1468), Brampton, Norfolk; Thomas Flemyng (ob. 1472), New College, Oxford; William Gurney (ob. 1472), Stone, Bucks; John Glemham (ob. 1480), Glemham Parva, Suffolk.

42. e.g. John Leventhorpe (ob. 1484), Sawbridgeworth, Herts, and William Robert (ob. 1484), Digswell, Herts.

43. Kathleen Rogers Cohen, *Metamorphosis of a Death Symbol*, 88-89 and figs 33,34.

44. *CCR, 1435-41*, 396, 399. The list includes two fardels with twelve "quysshones", six "valences", twelve "coverlytes", seven "celours", seven "testeris", one white "coverlyte" and "celour of tapserie", four "tapits" of green and fourteen of "tapserie" with figures (ymaginibus), all bought and purveyed in France.

45. Henry Noble MacCracken, *Minor Poems of John Lydgate*, EETS E.S. 107 (1911), 87. St John's College MS, Oxford, 56 has a title which reads, "Hyc incipit interpretacio misse in lingua materna secundum Iohannem litgate monachum de Buria ad rogatum domine Countesse de Suthefolcia."

46. BL Harley MS 4826, f.1 has a pasted on picture of the poet presenting his work to his patron who is shown as a soldier in armour with a shock of curly hair. For discussion see Derek Pearsall, *John Lydgate* (London, 1970), 172-77.

47. Enid McLeod, *Charles of Orléans, Prince and Poet* (London, 1969), passim.

48. Henry Noble MacCracken, "An English Friend of Charles of Orléans," *PMLA* XXVI (1911), 142-80.

49. Eleanor Prescott Hammond, "Charles of Orléans and Anne Molineux", *MP* XXII (1924), 215-16. In the acrostic, the surname is "Molins"; the conflation of the Moleyns family with the Molineux family is an error.

50. e.g. *CPR, 1416-22*, 140; *1436-41*, 148, 200, 250, 257, 505, 537.

51. *VCH Berkshire*, iii. 406; iv. 346. Martin B. Ruud, *Thomas Chaucer*, passim.

52. Charles Ross, *Edward IV* (London, 1974), 417: "upon the same stone to be laid and wrought with the figure of Death with a scutcheon of our armour …".

RESUME

Cet exposé traitera d'un petit groupe d'Anglais commemorés par des *transis*, c'est-à-dire des tombeaux ou des plaques de cuivre où le mort est représenté comme un cadavre en voie de putréfaction ou un squelette. L'origine première de ce type de tombeaux ne nous concerne pas, puisque les principaux tombeaux en Europe remontent à une époque antérieure à celle du groupe en question. Toutefois, ce qui n'a jamais été exploré, c'est le problème de la transmission de l'iconographie du cadavre du continent en Angleterre et à l'intérieur même du pays. Comme cette forme de tombeaux n'a connu qu'une popularité limitée en Angleterre, il est nécessaire d'expliquer son existence autrement qu'en offrant une simple définition de l'atmosphère esthétique qui a favorisé cette popularité. L'exposé examine les hypothèses qui permettent de présenter les preuves de la transmission d'une mode de dévotions dans un milieu bien défini.

L'échantillon présenté est limité à des personnes mortes entre 1465 et 1480 dans une région déterminée. J'ai choisi cette période parce que ceux qui sont morts alors ont vécu pendant les années de guerre civile entre York et Lancaster, époque où il est aisé d'identifier des modes suivies exclusivement par l'une ou l'autre faction. Bien sûr, un seul exemple ne peut servir de preuve concluante; mais il fournit les éléments d'une hypothèse fondée sur l'étude des liens familiaux et des allégeances politiques.

Nous examinons également la possibilité qu'avaient les gens de ce milieu de voyager à l'étranger, particulièrement en France, et l'intérêt général qu'ils portaient aux arts, afin d'établir qu'ils étaient particulièrement sensibles à toute nouvelle mode esthétique.

Les propriétaires de tombeaux examinés en détail sont: John Baret (ob.1467, Bury St Edmunds, Suffolk); Mary Grimestone (ob.1469, Thorndon, Suffolk); Agnes Bulstrode (ob. 1472, Upton, Bucks); Alice de la Pole/Chaucer (ob.1475, Ewelme, Oxfordshire); Eleanor Moleyns (ob.1476, Stoke Poges, Bucks).

D'autres personnes commémorées de la même façon à cette époque sont mentionnées comme d'autres figures clefs qui contribuent à la constitution de leur milieu.

DEATH IN THE RENAISSANCE, 1347-1656

Peter Burke

In the last few years, death has become a major professional concern of social and cultural historians, especially in France, thanks in particular to the work of Philippe Ariès and Michel Vovelle.[1] Now firmly on the historical map, the territory of death had in fact been reconnoitred earlier, notably by Emile Mâle, by Johan Huizinga, and in the somewhat neglected work of Alberto Tenenti.[2]

For some reason the bulk of this research, from Mâle onwards, has concentrated on France. However, to discover what was distinctively French about attitudes to death in the fourteenth and fifteenth centuries it is of course necessary to look at other countries. Similarly, we can only say what attitudes were distinctively medieval after looking at other periods, such as the Renaissance. In this essay I shall try to describe some Italian attitudes to death and to discuss how far these attitudes changed between the fourteenth and the seventeenth centuries, trying to make it as clear as the evidence allows whose attitudes are in question; clerical or lay, learned or popular, male or female.[3]

I should like to begin with a paradox. There is a conspicuous absence from Huizinga's chapter on 'the vision of death', and indeed from his whole book, and that is the Black Death, which killed about a third of the population of Europe in 1347-8, and recurred locally at irregular intervals for centuries thereafter.[4] The macabre sensibility which Huizinga describes so well but makes no serious attempt to explain looks extremely like a reaction to this massive disaster. In other words, 1347-8 offers us a striking example of the influence of *l'histoire événementielle* on *l'histoire des mentalités collectives*.[5] It is for these epidemic reasons, rather than an eccentrically precise definition of the Renaissance, that this paper bears the dates 1347-1656. Like 1347, 1656 was a terrible year for plague in Italy, Rome and Naples being struck with particular severity. In between these dates the worst years for plague were 1576, when Venice was particularly affected, and 1630-1, when northern Italy suffered more generally, from Milan to

Florence.[6]

Now comes the paradox. Italy suffered like France, and as much as France, from the catastrophe of 1347-8 and also from the later visitations of the plague. There can be little doubt of the psychological shock of the plague, at least in the short-term. Boccaccio may describe it calmly enough in the introduction to the *Decameron*, but the chronicles of the time suggest that people were quite stunned by the event, *stupefatti*, as the Sienese chronicler Agnolo di Tura put it: 'everyone expected to die ... everyone believed that the end of the world was come'.[7] And yet, in the long term, if we are to believe Burckhardt and his followers, Italian sensibility remained curiously resilient, immune from infection by the macabre.

The great question is therefore whether we are to believe Burckhardt or not. In attempting to give an answer I shall adopt the familiar scheme of thesis, antithesis, and synthesis, first summarising the Burckhardtian view, then passing to the criticisms which have been, or may be, levelled against it, and ending by trying to reformulate Burckhardt in suitably modified terms.

Burckhardt did not have very much to say explicitly about attitudes to death in Renaissance Italy, but the remarks on the subject scattered about his writings do suggest fairly definite conclusions. In his most famous book, *The Civilisation of the Renaissance in Italy*, the 'cult of graves' receives a brief mention. In the study of Renaissance art in Italy, this brief note is amplified into an eight-page discussion of the splendid tombs *(Prachtgraben)* of Renaissance princes, prelates, and even professors. The *Notes on Renaissance Sculpture* add a few more examples.[8] The conclusion which emerges is that Renaissance tombs express what Burckhardt called 'the modern sense of fame'.

Burckhardt's point can be amplified and it has been amplified in more recent studies of Italian Renaissance tombs and monuments, notably in the fine essay on tomb sculpture to which the late Erwin Panofsky devoted his last years, in what looks like a modern academic version of preparation for death.[9] From the comparative point of view, what is most striking in these Italian funerary monuments is what isn't there. In Italy we do not find the *transi*, the putrefying corpse, the worms, the toads. Even skeletons are relatively rare.[10] Instead we find the virtues; pyramids of fame; equestrian figures, as in the case of Can Grande and others in fourteenth-century Verona; standing figures, as in the tomb of doge Mocenigo at Venice, dating from 1476; seated figures, as in the case of Michelangelo's Medici tombs; or reclining figures, seeming to sleep or to meditate, images not so much of death as of petrified life. These figures have been interpreted as 'self-assertive', the expression of a glorification of man.[11] The impression is heightened when we learn that Renaissance tombs often follow classical models of apotheosis and incorporate triumphal arches, as in the case of Bernardo Rossellino's monument to the distinguished Tuscan humanist Leonardo Bruni, where the arch is combined with two winged victories: a monument which has been described as 'the quintessential memorial of Renaissance man'.[12] Again,

Michelangelo's Medici tombs are generally interpreted as statements – however cryptic – about fame, immortality, and apotheosis.[13] It may seem difficult to resist the conclusion, implied by Burckhardt and stated explicitly by Panofsky, that what we find here is 'a basic change of outlook: a rejection of christian concern for the future in favour of pagan glorification of the past'.[14] This view was in fact summarised more than three hundred years earlier by John Webster in his *Duchess of Malfi*, when he made Bosola complain that 'princes' images on their tombs ... are not carved with their eyes fixed on the stars, but as their minds were wholly bent upon the world, the selfsame way they seem to turn their faces.'[15]

So far the art historians; ordinary or 'total' historians like myself, the general practitioners of the profession, tend to be somewhat sceptical of arguments from changes in visual imagery to changes in mentality, unless there is supporting evidence from other sources, such as texts. The point is not that images are worth less, evidentially speaking, than texts, but simply that it is dangerous to rest general conclusions on one type of evidence alone. In addition, historians using images as evidence run two more specific dangers. One is assuming that changes in images over time reflect changes in attitudes to life, ignoring the fact that images have a certain degree of autonomy, that they change for internal as well as for external reasons. A second danger resides in the fact that images can only juxtapose; they cannot say anything about the possible relationship between the elements juxtaposed in this way; the pagan and christian elements in the Bruni tomb, for example. The pitfalls in the way of anyone trying to derive fifteenth – or sixteenth – century attitudes to death from an inspection of images alone have been pointed out in a recent study of the macabre in the German Renaissance.[16]

Is there any textual support for the Burckhardtian view of death in the Renaissance? To a limited extent there is. One might begin with the inscriptions on tombs, such as that of Filippo Decio, professor of law at Pisa in the sixteenth century, which boasts of his salary of 1500 ducats a year; a striking example of materialist and competitive attitudes carried to the grave.[17] I am not suggesting that Decio was typical of his age or even his profession in this respect, but it is a point of some significance that Renaissance culture permitted the public expression of attitudes such as his. Would this have been possible earlier? I doubt it.

A similar stress on immortality through fame can be found, less crudely expressed, in the writings of humanists and poets. Not long after the plague of 1347-8, Petrarch was writing of the triumph of fame over death and describing Laura as beautiful in death, like the figures on Renaissance tombs; the real Laura had simply escaped from the prison of the body. The fifteenth-century humanist Aurelio Brandolini was another writer who emphasised the triumph of fame over death. 'Do not Plato and Aristotle', he wrote, 'seem to be alive today ... whose doctrine and fame fill the whole world?'[18] Although it was a medieval Italian, pope Innocent III, who had emphasised the misery of the human condition, the horror of death and the corruption of the body in a treatise which was often reprinted in the later fifteenth century, it may be significant that no fifteenth-century Italian editions of this treatise have been discovered.[19] In the seventeenth century, when macabre themes invaded European poetry for a second time, Italian poets seem to have been less concerned than their contemporaries in other countries with the physical horrors of death.[20]

Literary evidence thus appears to confirm the impression of the distinctiveness of Italy derived from images. At the same time, however, this literary evidence raises doubts about the traditional interpretation of the classical imagery of Renaissance tombs. These doubts are most acute in the case of Michelangelo, whose poems on death are difficult to interpret as 'pagan', whatever we think of the Medici Chapel.[21] Texts raise the possibility that the imagery on Renaissance tombs may have been misunderstood by Burckhardt and his followers. There is nothing necessarily unchristian in declaring death to be a triumph; St.Ambrose did this, for example, in his funeral oration on the emperor Theodosius.[22] What has often been described as 'syncretism' might be better understood as the appropriation of a classical vocabulary to deliver a christian message; not the medieval message of the need to fear death (or the medieval 'joyous death' for that matter), but a christian message nonetheless.

If the primary qualification to the Burckhardtian thesis is a hermeneutic one, a second qualification is sociological. The evidence discussed so far comes from the world of the ruling class, humanists, and artists. It may not reflect the views of more than a minority within these groups. Nothing has been said till now about the attitudes of ordinary Italians. The 'new history of death', as it has been called, the history written by Ariès and Vovelle, Chaunu and Lebrun, has been concerned to reconstruct the attitudes of ordinary people. Is it possible to do this for Italy as it has been done for France?

Vovelle's main sources, in his well-known study of eighteenth-century Provence, were wills; some 30,000 of them. Italy, like France, was a notarial culture, and kilometres of wills survive in the notarial archives of Milan, Venice, Genoa and elsewhere. I have not tried to emulate Vovelle's virtuoso statistical study, nor has any other historian of Italy, so far as I know. However, it is sufficient to inspect a few hundred Italian wills, whether male or female, patrician or plebeian, to become aware of the persistence into the seventeenth century and even beyond of traditional attitudes, medieval attitudes. The wills reiterate the time-honoured formulae declaring that life and death are in the hand of God; that nothing is more certain than death, but nothing more uncertain than its hour; that it is better to live in the fear of death than to suffer death unexpectedly while hoping to live longer; and so on. The testators carefully bequeath their souls, in the majority of cases, to Almighty God, to the Blessed Virgin, and to the whole court of heaven. The detailed dispositions suggest an abiding concern for the exact place of burial – the family chapel for the rich, the altar of the confraternity for many townspeople – and also a concern for the precise manner of burial; in the habit of a Capuchin, perhaps, or followed to the grave by a precise number of priests or poor men, carrying torches the weight of which is usually specified. The interest of testators in the masses to be said for their souls, as many as possible and as quickly as possible, remains intense; indeed, I think I see evidence for an inflation of masses in the seventeenth century.[23]

Other kinds of document, where they can be found, confirm this general picture. Autobiographies or diaries of shopkeepers or craftsmen are not common but they do exist, and it may be instructive to compare the attitudes to deaths in the family expressed, at a distance of more than a century and a half, by Giovanni di Pagolo Morelli of Florence and by Gianbattista Casale of Milan. When Giovanni's son Alberto died in 1406, his father recorded that the boy 'commended himself repeatedly to God and to His mother the Virgin Mary'.[24] When Gianbattista's son Benedetto died in 1563, Casale wrote that he 'finished his life in the bosom of holy mother church after having made a good confession'.[25] In each case the grief-stricken father appears to have derived some consolation from the fact that his son made a good death in the traditional manner, even if Giovanni was tormented by visions of his son for a long time afterwards.[26]

The persistence of traditional attitudes is confirmed by the testimony of popular literature – literature for the people if not literature from the people – such as the sermons of Jacopo Passavanti in the fourteenth century and those of Girolamo Savonarola in the fifteenth; or the Italian translation of *The Art of Dying Well* attributed to Nikolaus von Dinkelsbühl, a translation which has been described as a 'best-seller' in late fifteenth-century Italy;[27] or the dialogue between the living and the dead which is illustrated with an impressive woodcut of a skeleton on horseback carrying a large scythe and begins, 'Io sono il gran capitano della morte/Che tengo le chiave de tutte le porte'.[28]

Contemporary accounts of Italian reactions to the plagues of 1576, 1630-1, and 1656 tell the same story. Despite the existence, emphasised by Carlo Cipolla in a series of fascinating local studies, of an educated minority with a secular-minded approach to matters of hygiene, the majority turned to the consolations of traditional religion.[29] The attitudes to death revealed at Naples in 1656, for example, do not seem to have changed much from the attitudes revealed at Siena in 1347-8. Although the archbishop, in tune with the new ideas about hygiene, prohibited 'every public demonstration of repentance' *(ogni publica dimostrazione di penitenza)*, his prohibition was unsuccessful. Ordinary people *(la plebe*, according to our source, a physician), made the stations of the cross at various churches in order to implore divine mercy. Girls walked barefoot, with crowns of thorns on their heads; men whipped themselves or carried heavy crosses on their backs, or walked with skulls in their hands or chains on their feet, with ashes smeared over their faces.[30]

It is obvious that what was described, from Burckhardt to Panofsky, as "the Renaissance attitude to death" was actually a minority view, and also that the view of even this minority may not have been as radically new (let alone "pagan"), as used to be thought. All the same, there are signs of change. The inscription on Filippo Decio's tomb, already cited, is one of the most spectacular, which does seem to express, in its crude way, the new 'sense of fame' to which Burckhardt refers. The classical tradition offered consolations complementary to or even alternative to the tradition of Christianity, consolations which were real enough to some individuals, as a final example may suggest. When Filippo Strozzi, the opponent of the Medici, killed himself in 1538, he left a suicide note recommending his soul to God in the hope of being given a place beside Cato of Utica and other virtuous men (*altri simili virtuosi uomini*), who had ended their lives in the same way.[31] The history of suicide in early modern Europe, and its relation to the stoic revival, remains to be written, but the example of Filippo Strozzi may be enough to suggest that some Italians of the Renaissance paid more than lip-service to classical values, and that the history of Italian attitudes to death between the fourteenth and the seventeenth centuries reveals shifts as well as continuities.

NOTES

1. Philippe Ariès, *Western Attitudes toward Death* (Baltimore, 1974); idem, *L'homme devant la mort* (Paris, 1977), trans. Helen Weaver (London, 1981); Michel Vovelle, *Piété baroque et déchristianisation* (Paris, 1973).
2. Emile Mâle, *L'art religieux à la fin du moyen âge en France* (Paris, 1908); Johan Huizinga, *The Waning of the Middle Ages*, trans. F. Hopman (London, 1924); Alberto Tenenti, *La vie et la mort à travers l'art du XV siècle* (Paris, 1952); idem, *Il senso della morte e l'amore della vita nel Rinascimento* (Turin, 1957).
3. On Italy, besides Tenenti, see Millard Meiss, *Painting in Florence and Siena after the Black Death* (Princeton, 1951), and the special number of *Quaderni Storici*, 1982, *I Vivi e i morti*, ed. Adriano Prosperi.
4. Elisabeth Carpentier, *Une ville devant la peste* (Paris, 1962) deals with Orvieto in 1347-8, but places the city in a wider context.
5. This is the theme of a conference at Aix organised by Michel Vovelle for September 1983.
6. On 1576, see Paolo Preto, *Peste e società a Venezia* (Vicenza, 1978); on 1630-1, Carlo Cipolla, *Cristofano and the Plague* (London, 1973).
7. Agnolo di Tura, "Cronaca senese," in *Rerum Italicarum Scriptores*, XV, part 6, ed. A. Lisini and F. Iacometti (2 vols, Bologna, 1932), II, p. 555.
8. Jacob Burckhardt, *Civilisation of the Renaissance in Italy* (1860), trans. S.G.C. Middlemore (new ed., New York and London, 1945), pp. 89-90; idem, *Die Kunst der Renaissance in Italien*, in his *Gesamtausgabe* (14 vols, Berlin-Leipzig, 1930-4), VI, 181-8; idem, "Randglossen zur Skulptur der Renaissance," *ibid.*, XIII, 302-10.
9. Henriette s'Jacob, *Idealism and Realism* (Leiden, 1954); John Pope-Hennessy, *Italian Renaissance Sculpture* (3 vols, London, 1958); Erwin Panofsky, *Tomb Sculpture* (London, 1964).
10. s'Jacob, pp. 177f.
11. *Ibid.*, p. 182.
12. Pope-Hennessy, ii, p. 37.
13. Charles de Tolnay, *The Medici Chapel* (Princeton, 1948), esp. pp. 63-7.

14. Panofsky, p.67.
15. John Webster, *The Duchess of Malfi*, act iv, scene 2, quoted in s'Jacob, p. 188.
16. Jean Wirth, *La jeune fille et la mort* (Geneva, 1979), pp. 8-13.
17. The inscription is printed in A. Terrasson, *Histoire de la jurisprudence romaine* (Paris, 1750), p. 418.
18. Charles Trinkaus, *In our Image and Likeness* (2 vols, London, 1970), i, p. 313.
19. Innocent III, *De miseria humanae conditionis*, ed. Michele Maccarrone (Lugano, 1955), pp. xx – xxii.
20. J.M. Cohen, *The Baroque Lyric* (London, 1963), pp. 45-46. To the examples he cites (Marino, Achillini, Ciro de Pers, and Pier Francessco Paoli), one might add the poems on death by Francesco Bracciolini, Giovanni Canale, and Tommaso Gaudiosi, in *I Marinisti*, ed. Giovanni Getto (Turin, 1954), pp. 260, 425, 453-4, 457.
21. See, for example, Michelangelo, *Rime*, ed. Enzo Girardi (Bari, 1967), numbers 86, 102, 118, 128, 285, 293, 295 (the same numbering in other modern editions). No. 86 plays with the idea of the *mors mortis* in a way not unlike St Bernard (see Leclercq, below, p. 197). For a brief discussion of Michelangelo's attitude to death, see Tenenti, *Il senso della morte*, pp. 317-8, 328, 341, 373-5, 405.
22. Sabine MacCormack, *Art and Ceremony in Late Antiquity* (Berkeley, Los Angeles, and London, 1981), p. 145.
23. These remarks are based on my sampling of wills in the Archivio di Stato in Milan and in Venice. I am grateful to the SSRC for funding this research. Compare the findings on Naples in Maria Antonietta Visceglia, "Corpo e sepoltura nei testamenti della nobiltà napoletana (xvi-xviii secolo)," *Quaderni Storici* L (1982), 583-614.
24. Giovanni Morelli, *Ricordi*, ed. Vittorio Branca (Florence, 1956), pp. 455-6. On this incident, see Richard Trexler, *Public Life in Renaissance Florence* (New York, 1980), pp. 172-5.
25. Giovanni Battista Casale, "Giornale", ms in Milan, Biblioteca Ambrosiana, fondo Trotti, no. 413, f. 3.
26. I should like to thank Kenneth Hyde for reminding me of this point during the conference.
27. Anne J. Schutte, "Printing, Piety and the People in Italy: the First Thirty Years," *Archiv für Reformationsgeschichte* LXXI (1980), 11.
28. *Il contrasto del vivo & del morto* (Venice, 1522). There is a copy of this edition in the British Library (pressmark C.57.1.7.(36)). The publisher, Bindoni, specialised in popular literature, especially booklets of four to eight pages.
29. Cipolla, *Cristofano,* and also his *Faith, Reason and the Plague,* trans. Muriel Kittel (Brighton, 1979).
30. Angelo Della Porta, "Della Peste di Napoli", ms in Paris, Bibliothèque Nationale, Ital. 299, ff. 139-58.
31. The note is printed in Jacopo Nardi, *Istorie della città di Firenze* (2 vols, Florence, 1858), II, p. 235. Compare the discussion of Borromini's suicide in 1667 in Rudolf Wittkower, "Francesco Borromini, his Character and Life," repr. in his *Studies in the Italian Baroque* (London, 1975), pp. 153-66.

RESUME

Après E.Mâle, J. Huizinga et Alberto Tenenti, Philippe Ariès et Michel Vovelle (pour ne citer qu'eux) approfondissent en historiens le thème de la mort en France. Pour l'attitude des Italiens, en vue d'une comparaison fructueuse, il nous faut remonter à Burckhardt d'une part et de l'autre tenir mieux compte de la peste que de certains ne l'ont fait. Historien de l'art, si l'on veut, Burckhardt ne nous fait pas entrevoir la stupéfaction, l'effroi de la population. Il se fonde avant tout sur la statuaire, la splendeur des tombes, sur la *gloire*, sur le *triomphe* classique qui expriment la sensibilité d'une élite. Il nous montre la vie pétrifiée plutôt que le *transi*. Selon Panofsky, il s'agit ici d'une glorification du passé et non d'une vision eschatologique et chrétienne.

Certains poètes et humanistes idéalisent, eux aussi, et à l'encontre de leurs rivaux européens, détournent les yeux des avanies de la mort.

En revanche, les sonnets de Michel-Ange n'ont rien de païen. Se pourrait-il que le monde chrétien se soit en somme servi d'un vocabulaire et de formes antiques pour formuler un message orthodoxe? L'étude de textes très directs (testaments, mémoires, etc) nous met sur la piste: l'homme du peuple n'a que faire de la gloire qui se survit. Son attitude devant la mort est toujours celle de ses ancêtres: c'est Dieu qui règne et le Panthéon n'a rien à y voir. Il est conservateur, il se fie à la tradition, aux prières de l'Eglise. Les *Arts de bien mourir* se vendent et se lisent; leurs illustrations restent macabres. Les actes de pénitence s'accomplissent envers et contre les règles de l'hygiène.

Il y a eu un certain syncrétisme de deux formes de consolation: le stoïcisme peut être celui de Caton comme il est celui du Christ. Il faut faire la part des choses.

DRAMA

HELL AND THE DEVIL IN THE MEDIEVAL FRENCH DRAMA: VISION OF DAMNATION OR HOPE FOR SALVATION?

Cynthia Foxton

The link between Hell and the devil on the medieval French religious stage and the subject of death is simple and direct. Part of the devil's traditional rôle in plays was to remove to Hell the bodies and/or the souls of wicked characters who died, or who were killed, in the course of the action. Critics have normally tended to assume that the aim of such scenes was to 'edify' the spectators by frightening them with a glimpse of the possibility of damnation. Petit de Julleville, for instance, said, 'Etait-ce ... pour faire rire les spectateurs qu'on montrait les démons, quand une bataille avait jonché la scène de cadavres, accourant avec des brouettes pour emporter les âmes?''; Raymond Lebègue, under the heading of 'Les diableries édifiantes', noted that they 'rappellent au public que les diables sont toujours prêts à induire les hommes au péché et à s'opposer à la miséricorde divine, et que les méchants vont immanquablement en enfer.'.[2]

The usual mental image of the medieval French stage Hell probably tends to be based on the kind of set which was built for the vast Passion performed over twenty-five days at Valenciennes in 1547. According to manuscript directions this Hell was fitted out with elaborate props and special effects:

item en Enfer souvrant le gouffre sortoit feu et fumee avecq diables doribles formes et lucifer seslevat hault sur un dragon iectat feu et fumee par le goeulle puis on voigt boulir la chaudiere plaine de damnez. daultres aussi en des roues tournantes.[3]

The Valenciennes manuscript was illustrated by Hubert Cailleau with a series of day-by-day miniatures set into the text, also a larger picture which purports to depict the whole stage as it was organised for the performance. This shows a series of sets strung apparently in a straight line between Heaven at one end and Hell at the other. Recently there has been considerable critical discussion and even controversy about the authenticity of this overall arrangement, and also about the details of some of the sets, for instance Heaven.[4] However this debate does not seem to affect Hell as portrayed by Cailleau, for it corresponds very closely with the manuscript directions quoted above.

Cailleau's Hell consists of a two-storey tower-like structure, the lower half of which is occupied by the traditional dragon's mouth entrance, the *gueule d'enfer*. Inside the monster's jaw, which is presumably hinged since it is gaping open, we can see a cauldron full of naked souls, while in the storey above, whose walls are cut away to reveal the interior, other souls are fixed to a wheel. Devils swarm out of the *gueule*, one leans from a little window beside it and another devil, probably Lucifer himself, is riding on a dragon high above the roof, pushed up on an apparently rigid chain; other dragons stand guard round the top of the tower. This Hell seems very much a concrete vision of fiery retribution.

Other records exist of Passion performances which appear to have made use of a fairly lavishly equipped Hell, at, for example, Ségur, near Montferrand (today Clermont-Ferrand) in 1477, and Mons in 1501. For Ségur the accounts list such items as 'une faysse de cercles pour fere la golle d'enfer', hoops over which the Hell-mouth must have been built up; 'une charretee de espine que fut achaptee pour mectre a l'entour du chaffault d'Enfer', thorns apparently being stuck around the whole structure; 'quatorze livres de pouldre de colabrunes et ... charbon', gunpowder for the cannons or 'colabrunes' which are also listed, and charcoal to be burned probably in the fires of Hell, plus 'neuf livres podre de seelpetre', an explosive.[5] At Mons are mentioned 'pentures ... servant au pendre la gueule du Crapault d'Enffer', supports for the *gueule*; 'pluiseurs sacquiés de mousset', sacks of moss presumably to adorn the structure; 'une caudiere'; 'deux petis soufflés'; 'deux serpens d'oziere' and 'le molle d'un draghon', wicker snakes and a mould for a dragon; 'une buze de fer et une fourquette servant à jecter feu', a primitive firearm and a sparking trident; 'deuz grandes keuwes (= cuves in dialect form) pour faire les tonnoires en Enffer' and 'carbon fauldre ... pour servir à l'Enfer'.[6]

The text of some of the surviving Passion plays also contains scenes where, having claimed a sinner's soul, the devils inflict practical tortures on it, or rather on a dummy substitute for a live actor. In the *Passion d'Auvergne*, which is thought to be part of the same play as was performed at Ségur, the devils roast the soul of the Bad Thief over the fire, then begin to eat it.[7] In the *Passion de Gréban*, which was one of the sources for the Passion at Mons, the soul of Judas is nibbled by Lucifer, then beaten with clubs by a team of devils and finally lowered on a pitch-fork into a 'pit', most likely a sunken area in the bottom of the set.[8] In the same scene in the *Passion de Michel*, which was performed at Angers in 1486 and also contributed to Mons, the gnawing by Lucifer is omitted, but to compensate the devils beat the soul at greater length, then put it into the pit.[9]

In theory, such elaborate sets of Hell and practical torture scenes as these could reasonably be interpreted as an attempt to produce a live vision of damnation to send shivers down the spines of onlookers. Yet it does seem pertinent to ask how typical they really were of the medieval French religious stage as a whole.

The fact is that, taking all surviving texts together, soul-claiming scenes with indications of prolonged practical torture are considerably outweighed by scenes in which, during or just after the journey back to Hell, the devils *talk* about torment, without any sign in the script that they actually carry out any of their threats in any but 'token' form, or at all. Nor is this confined to simple plays. For example, in a short *Jeu des Trois Rois* from a manuscript in the Bibliothèque Sainte-Geneviève in Paris, there is a scene after the Slaughter of the Innocents where two devils come to claim the soul of King Herod when, as is traditional at this juncture, he commits suicide. They describe Herod's past crimes and the tortures they plan to inflict in punishment – beating, boiling in the cauldron and exposure to snakes and scorpions. At this point, however, the script is cut off by the direction 'Cy l'emportent en enfer'.[10] The soul of Herod is also claimed, though, by the devils in the much longer and more complex *Passion d'Arras* and the *Passion de Gréban*, in which, as we have already seen, the devils torment Judas at length. Not so Herod. In *Arras*, his soul is offered by Satan to Lucifer, who orders it to be put '...ou plus parfont d'infer,/En plonc boullant et en metal'. The devils scurry about collecting '... gros crapaux et couleuvres,/Serpens, laisardes et dragons,/Araignes et escorpions' and stoke up the fire; but no sooner is the torture begun than the script ends.[11] In *Gréban* the pattern is at first similar, the soul being presented and Lucifer prescribing torture by molten lead: 'estrenez l'en plonc bien boulu/conffit en metal tout ardant', but the script is cut off even sooner with an immediate direction 'Icy font les deables tempeste' – literally, a din, a frequent way of ending *diableries*.[12] In *Arras* the whole scene is over in about twenty-eight lines, in *Gréban* a mere ten, which in performance would represent only a few minutes. It is possible that the devils could have gone on to mime a longer torture, but without directions specifically to this effect it is surely unwise to speculate, and better to admit that either torture was cut out altogether, or reduced to a brief token. Why, though, should full-blown torment scenes be so relatively rare, and apparently rationed even in plays which do sometimes indulge in them?

It seems relevant to note that we can deduce from some documentary sources, and from the text of some plays, that the entrance to Hell was probably opened only to let a devil pass in or out, and shut again at once. The directions for the *Mystère de l'Incarnation* at Rouen in 1474 mention 'une grande gueule se cloant et ouvrant quant besoing en est'.[13] In the *Passion de Semur*, when the devils approach Hell with the soul of John the Baptist, one of them calls to Lucifer, 'Maistre Sathanas, je t'aporte/Une ame, ovre nous la porte'.[14] In the *Passion d'Auvergne*, immediately after delivery of this same soul, the entrance is ordered to be closed: 'Sarre la gorge, sarre, sarre!/Accop, Enfer, garde la bien!'.[15] 'La gorge' is almost certainly the *gueule d'Enfer*, which we have seen existed when *Auvergne* was performed at Ségur. These two scenes suggest very strongly that souls were sometimes merely thrust quickly into the entrance to Hell, which was then closed, and the episode left at that, but they do not explain positively why.

For this I think we have to move off for a moment at something of a tangent, to consider not what happened to the souls inside Hell, but rather what was done with the devils themselves, and in particular with Lucifer.

Several independent sources suggest that Lucifer was usually housed in the upper storey of Hell, above the *gueule*. In the prologue to a Nativity play in the Sainte-Geneviève manuscript, which concerns the Fall of Man, there is a line where a devil speaks of putting Adam's soul 'Ou premier estage d'enfer,/Avec noz maistre Lucifer'.[16] In the *Passion d'Arras* and *Gréban* there are lines where Lucifer orders devils who are about to leave Hell, or being sent to be punished by their fellows after failing him, to go 'la dessoubz' or 'en bas', therefore implying that he himself is positioned above both exit and the place where torture took place.[17]

Now precisely such an arrangement seems to be in operation in the famous miniature in the Book of Hours of Estienne Chevalier painted by Jean Fouquet in 1461 which apparently depicts a performance of a play about the *Martyre de Sainte Apolline*. Among the sets is Hell, in the form of a tall, narrow-looking two-storey wooden box, with an open *gueule d'enfer* filling the lower half; a devil is peering out from just inside it. In the top, directly above the *gueule*, is the torso and head of a devil who seems to be giving orders to others on the ground and is therefore probably Lucifer. Judging by comparison with the figures, the whole structure of Fouquet's Hell cannot be much higher than two men, that is, about four and a half metres. Although the sideways-on angle makes this harder to assess, its width looks less. It seems reasonably safe to say, though, that the overall size does not appear bigger than a large walk-in cupboard.

Hell as depicted by Hubert Cailleau for Valenciennes in 1547 (see above) seems about the same size, or only a little larger. However in the upper storey of the tower Cailleau has painted not Lucifer, who is above the roof, but a wheel with souls round its rim. The relevant point about this wheel is that in this position it would have remained on display even when the *gueule d'enfer* was closed. In the kind of set shown by Fouquet, though, the presence of Lucifer in the upper storey of the cramped structure would surely mean that all torture props that might have existed – cauldrons, wheels, or the like – would have had to be confined to the lower storey, presumably inside the *gueule*. Indeed, even the manuscript directions for Valenciennes, if studied carefully, do not exclude the interpretation that the cauldron and the wheel were revealed only when the 'gouffre d'Enfer' – surely the *gueule* – was opened. Hubert Cailleau did not illustrate the manuscript, in fact, until 1577, all of thirty years after the event, and it is not proven beyond doubt that he actually attended the performance at all.[18] It can be argued therefore that in placing the wheel outside the *gueule* he may have been mistaken. At any rate, the balance of the evidence does seem to be that torture props in the stage Hell were probably kept inside the *gueule*. Now obviously, if the *gueule* were normally closed, save for devils' exits and entries and to receive souls, the result would be that for much of the time Hell would not appear at all as a vision of damnation. It would instead merely show the closed Hellmouth, with Lucifer, if included in the cast, up above. If there was no Lucifer, as was generally the case in shorter plays, Hell would probably have consisted only of the *gueule*.

If this suggestion is correct, it might perhaps account for the fact that some of the longer French religious plays contain verbal descriptions of the geography and nature of the infernal regions; these may have been meant to compensate for a lack of such details before the spectators' eyes. In the *Passion de Semur*, for example, the resurrected Lazarus describes the pains of Hell as follows:

```
... sont les dampnés
En feu ardant, sans nul sejour,
Quil ne leur fault ne nuyt ne jour,
Et cy sont en ce feu ardant
Grands bos et grans serpens lardans.
Les ungs sont a terre estendus,
Les autres sont en plonc fondu;
Selon ce qu'il ont plus mespris,
Sont de la chaleur plux espris,
Puans, poris, malheurés,
Ayreux, laix et deffigurés
Sont tousjours et plains de grevance;
Pour ce qu'il n'ont fait penitance,
En ce monde de leurs pechiers,
Seuffrent ses painnes, ces meschiefz,
Quil toujours leur durent sans fin.[19]
```

Accounts by Lazarus of Hell are also found in the *Passion de Gréban* l.15836 – 15856 and *Michel* l.14683 – 14731.

Briefer references to traditional torments, such as the cauldron, reptiles, molten lead, the pit and so on, are scattered throughout countless *diableries*, just as we have seen above in the *Jeu des Trois Rois de Sainte-Geneviève*, the *Passion d'Arras* and *Gréban* in the Herod-claiming scene. In the *Passion de Semur* the devils boast rather more freely of the tortures they plan for a very special soul, that of Jesus when He descends into Hell:

Baucibus

...

Je la tourneray en la roye,
Je la mectray ou puis d'enfert,
Je la vous lieray de fert,
En gresle, en froidure, en tempeste ...

Desroy

...

Je le pendray de cloux ardans,
Je ly aracheray les dans,
Je le vous randray conffondu.
Je le mectray en plonc fondu
En pugnaissie et en ordure ...[20]

Another quite common device was to reel off a list of the types of
sinner held in Hell, for instance in the *Passion du Palatinus*:

Li roy, li conte et li princier,
Li apostoile et li legat,
Li cardinal et li prelat,
Li moine noir, li jacobin,
Li cordelier, li faus devin,
Li avocat, li amparlier,
Li robeur, li usurier,
Clers et lais de par tout le mont ...[21]

Lists occur also in *Semur* l.5334 – 5346 and *Arras* l.18173 – 18218 and
l.20869 – 20874, while the *Passion de Sainte-Geneviève* l.828 – 892 links
particular types of sin with specific tortures, for example the covetous
are punished by fire, the malicious by alternating fire and ice, and
so on.

In the *Passion de Gréban* the very language of the devils is crammed
with terms which suggest fire and monsters, for example:

que l'horrible maignie
des dampnés vous guident et mainent
et a tels tourmens vous ramainent
qu'au parfont du gouffre infernal
ardez tous en souffre eternal.[22]

To this extent, then, some plays did create a vision of damnation,
but it was a mental, imaginative one rather than a concrete one before
the eye. In some ways this was an advantage, for it overcame the limita-
tions that sheer feasibility imposed on those tortures that were actually
performed, allowing *diableries* to fill out what would otherwise have

been a simplified or perhaps even altered version of current popular ideas of Hell. (It is a noticeable difference between stage Hells and those evoked in other forms, such as the *Vision of St. Paul, St. Patrick's Purgatory* and similar narratives, that the cauldron seems much more important on the stage than elsewhere, presumably because it was easier to provide and handle than many of the other traditional torments.) Verbal description, where it occurs, is certainly an attempt to create a *kind* of vision of Hell; however, this happens only in wordier texts, which are in a minority. A great many plays were simply too brisk to spend time developing the subject, and in these Hell would seem both visually *and* imaginatively reticent about the details of damnation.

Moreover even word-pictures of damnation have to be set against the fact that in terms not just of visibility to the audience, but also of time, the stage devil's main serious function was not the torment of the dead, but rather the temptation of the living. This is true whether we survey the whole field of medieval French religious drama, or look inside individual plays. Because nobody wicked dies during the action, there are many texts, especially of the saint and miracle type, in which temptation is the devil's only rôle, for example the *Mystère de Saint Martin, Mystère de Saint Sébastien*, several of the Cangé *Miracles de Nostre Dame*, the *Job* play in the *Viel Testament* series, and many others. Even in plays where the devil's rôle is mixed, soul-claiming scenes are more often than not outnumbered by temptations. In the *Jour du Jugement*, indeed, there are no less than five *diableries* before the final judgement scene, in which the devils interfere with the living by siring, aiding and abetting the Antichrist. In the Passion plays, because of more time tending to be devoted to developing the public life of Jesus as well as Holy Week, temptation became more important in the devil's rôle in the fifteenth century, especially in the *Passion de Michel* which contributed to the text of several important performances. In the fourteenth century Passion plays *Palatinus, Autun* and the *Passion de Sainte-Geneviève* the devil does not tempt at all, in *Semur, Arras* and *Gréban* from the first half of the fifteenth century tempting is fairly balanced against soul-claiming – about four scenes each – but in *Michel* there are six temptations to only two soul-claimings.

The message of temptation scenes was by and large a hopeful one, because the devil was often seen to be defeated, sometimes by quite ordinary people as well as by Jesus and the saints. In one of the Cangé *Miracles de Nostre Dame*, for instance, a wife refuses to be unfaithful to her absent husband, and the devil is reduced to framing her through her more pliant uncle.[23] Even where temptation at first succeeds, the devil may lose the soul later through a sudden repentance and/or the intercession of the Virgin or a saint. The obvious example is the *Miracle de Théophile*, but there are others, for example a *Miracle de Saint Nicolas et d'un Juif* where, after the intervention of the saint, a soul is literally snatched from the devil's claws at the last moment.

The subject of repentance brings us back to the question of why certain plays make the devils hurry some souls so abruptly off to Hell, yet have them torture others at length. If we look carefully at the context of these 'full-blown' soul-claimings, we see that the aim is probably not so much to dwell on the damnation for its own sake as to contrast it with the possibility of salvation, which the victim has wilfully rejected. The elaborate torture of Judas's soul in *Gréban* and *Michel*, mentioned earlier, follows a long scene in which he has conspicuously refused the opportunity to repent, and the grisly fate of the recalcitrant Bad Thief's soul in *Auvergne* is followed by a scene in which the Good Thief's soul is conducted by the Angels to Limbo to await salvation. Not only did the French medieval religious drama remain on the whole reticent about the devil in relation to the dead, as opposed to the living, but even when it did expand on damnation it was often in the spirit that such was the fate only of those who refused all their *life* to repent of their sins. The drama did not undertake to treat of the afterlife for its own sake, but left this to other literary forms; its own focus was very much on life *before* death.

NOTES

1. *Les Mystères* (Paris, 1880), vol. 2, p. 273.
2. *Le Mystère des Actes des Apôtres* (Paris, 1929), p.159.
3. E. Königson, *La représentation d'un mystère de la Passion à Valenciennes en 1547* (Paris, 1969), p.39.
4. See Henri Rey-Flaud, *Le cercle magique* (Paris, 1973), pp.122-136.
5. Archives reproduced by A. Bossuat, "Une représentation du Mystère de la Passion à Montferrand en 1477," *Bibliothèque d'Humanisme et de Renaissance* V (1944), 334-345.
6. *Le livre de conduite du régisseur pour le mystère de la Passion jouée à Mons en 1501*, ed. G. Cohen (Paris, 1925), pp.497-563.
7. Ed. G.A. Runnalls (Genève, 1982), ll. 3804-3817.
8. Ed. G. Paris and G. Raynaud (Paris, 1878), ll. 22078-22176.
9. Ed. O. Jodogne (Gembloux, 1959), ll. 24025-24070.
10. Ed. A. Jubinal, in *Mystères inédits du quinzième siècle*, (Paris, 1837; reprinted Genève, 1977), pp.135-136.
11. Ed. J.-M. Richard (Arras, 1891), ll. 5506-5534.
12. *Ed. cit.*, ll. 7985-7995.
13. G. Cohen, *La mise en scène dans le théâtre religieux français du moyen âge* (Paris, 1926), p. 97.
14. Ed. E. Roy in *Le mystère de la Passion en France du XIVe au XVIe siècle* (Dijon, 1903/4, reprinted Genève, 1974), pp.3-189.
15. *Ed. cit.*, ll.663-664.
16. Ed. A. Jubinal, *op. cit.*, p.20.
17. *Arras, ed. cit.*, ll. 13115, *Gréban, ed. cit.*, l. 33488.
18. See Rey-Flaud, *loc. cit.*
19. *Ed. cit.*, ll. 5266-5281.
20. *Ed. cit.*, ll. 8449-8452 and ll. 8462-8466.
21. Ed. G. Frank (Paris, 1922), ll. 1314-1321.
22. *Ed. cit.*, ll. 17458-17462.
23. *Miracle de la Marquise de la Gaudine.*

RESUME

Le rôle du Malin dans le théâtre du Moyen Age ne s'élucide pas aisément: la diablerie a-t-elle pour but de faire rire, d'édifier ou de terrifier les spectateurs? La *gueule d'enfer* (que l'on connaît par des descriptions de la scène et par des miniatures du 15e siècle, notamment celles d'Hubert Cailleau et du *Livre d'Heures d'Etienne Chevalier*), le feu, les tourments sous toutes leurs formes sont-ils typiques? Le répertoire connu de ce théâtre montre qu'en gros la punition physique est presque toujours de courte durée (ou même absente, laissée à l'imagination); c'est-à-dire qu'elle est le plus souvent décrite, le plus souvent verbale. La *gorge d'enfer* s'ouvre et se referme, alors que Lucifer seul reste visible au-dessus de la porte fatale. La représentation physique est évidemment limitée par les maigres ressources de la scène, mais (ce qui est plus important) le théâtre en question a pour thème principal la tentation, surtout à partir du 15ᵉ siècle.

Le diable est souvent battu. Il y a miracle, refus du péché. L'ultime péché n'est pas tel ou tel crime mais bien le refus du pardon. La réticence d'approfondir le thème de la punition ne tient donc pas uniquement à la difficulté de la mise en scène, mais tout au contraire au désir de montrer l'ultime drame de la vie vécue, de la tentation à laquelle d'aucuns succombent alors que tant d'autres s'y refusent.

THE DEATH OF CHRIST IN FRENCH PASSION PLAYS OF THE LATE MIDDLE AGES: ITS ASPECTS AND SOCIOLOGICAL IMPLICATIONS

Edelgard E. DuBruck

That there was a preoccupation with death in French lyric poetry and didactic writings during the last centuries of the Middle Ages is by now an established fact. The reasons for this emphasis have been researched since the first quarter of this century (actually since Huizinga's work), and some of the scholars present here have contributed significantly to the results of this activity.[1] Later, it was found that this preoccupation should neither be characterized as macabre- and horror-orientated, nor as "morbid" as many researchers had done, and that more emphasis should be placed on the implications of religious teachings for the late-medieval attitude toward death.[2] Definite aspects of the literary treatment of death remain: the suddenness of death (possibly without religious preparation), the *ars moriendi* tradition, the elegiac contemplation of transitoriness (especially in poetry of lamentation), the pre-Renaissance treatment of death as enemy on one hand, as gate to paradise (immortality) on the other, macabre realism (with religious – *contemptus mundi* – or non-religious overtones), and death as leveller (with sociological implications). Generally it could be said that this preoccupation was more physical than metaphysical; Helinant's *Vers de la mort* have not created a tradition and can still at most be compared to Ronsard's *Hymne de la mort*.

What remains to be done is a sociological study – to complement the literary aspects – as to how people died in the late Middle Ages (by *milieu*), how death, dying and mortality were expressed linguistically by the dying, the survivors, and by the narrator; furthermore, how late medieval accounts of Saints' Lives and of the life of Christ reflect what happens to spiritual subject-matter when it is aimed at a certain social *milieu*, specifically, how the death of a saint, or of Christ, were depicted, and why this manner was chosen. Some attention will of course be given to the interrelationship of iconography and literature.

81

It is true that the death of Christ, of all episodes in the Passion sequence, would be depicted in close adherence to the Gospel accounts, and that the *fatiste* would hesitate to touch that particular moment of the myth. As Maurice Accarie emphasised, "on peut interpréter la vie de Jésus; on ne peut pas interpréter sa mort".[3] However, for our purposes, namely, to investigate how fifteenth-century people felt and thought about death, and how religious teachings influenced their attitude toward life and death[4], it is imperative that we consider not only the moment of Christ's death in these plays, but rather the circumstances, actions and reactions of bystanders, their lamentations, and the reasons for them. In that sense we shall indeed interpret Christ's death in its various aspects.

The events of the crucifixion comprise the first thirty verses of Chapter 19 of the Gospel according to St. John. It is the most explicit, compared to the synoptic gospels. The episodes are:

1) Pilate scourges Jesus.
2) He is given a crown of thorns and the purple robe of a king (of the Jews).
3) He is smitten.
4) The priests wish to crucify Him – Pilate renders Him to the Jews.
5) Jesus bears His cross to Golgotha, where He is crucified between two thieves.
6) Pilate writes a sign to be affixed to the cross, saying that Christ is the king of the Jews.
7) The soldiers take His garments, tear them into four parts except for the coat for which they cast dice (to fulfil Scripture).
8) Scene of the women by the cross. Jesus entrusts His mother to his favourite disciple.
9) To fulfil Scripture, Jesus says, "I thirst". He is given vinegar.
10) Jesus dies.

Scenes not mentioned here are: the Barrabas episode (Matt. 27, 15-21; Mark 15, 7-15; Luke 23, 18-20), the dream of Pilate's wife (Matt. 27,19), Pilate's washing his hands (Matt.27,24), the Jews spit on Christ (Matt. 27,30), revile and mock him (Matt.27, 39-43; Mark 15, 18-20; Luke 23, 35-37). Among the seven last words are omitted, "My God, my God, why hast Thou forsaken me?" (Matt. 27, 46; Mark 15, 34) and "Father, into Thy hands I commend my spirit" (Luke 23, 46); furthermore, the apocalyptic words to the women (Luke 23, 28-31), and when Jesus talks to the good thief (Luke 23, 42-43).

A *Passion* of 129 stanzas of four lines each (octosyllabic) of the tenth century found at Clermont-Ferrand depicts the following events in "archaic" narrative style, interrupted at times by direct speech:

1) Pilate renders Christ to the Jews.
2) He is clad in purple and given the crown of thorns.
3) He is mocked.

4) He carries His cross.
5) He addresses the women.
6) Mercenaries take His clothes and cast dice for them.
7) He is given vinegar to drink.
8) The two thieves are crucified on each side.
9) Christ speaks to the good thief.
10) Two stanzas feature a prayer by the unknown author, hoping that we (mankind) will be pardoned, too, like the thief.
11) After ominous signs in nature, Christ dies within the next two stanzas. ("God, why hast Thou forsaken me?")

In these forty verses, the author has followed mostly St. John and St. Matthew, and he pays special attention to the suffering of the Mother of God. The language is a mixture of Provencal and Old French.

The *Passion du Palatinus* and the *Passion d'Autun* (both c. 1300) derive from the same source, which, in turn, goes back to the so-called *Passion des Jongleurs* (early 13th century, narrative). *Palatinus* (c. 2000 verses) was intended to be staged, has certain scenic effects, and on occasion, atrocious realism. There is a diversity of tone, metres, gestures, and actions, there are lyric parts and prayers, and short scenic indications at the beginning of each of the thirty-seven scenes. The text is dialogue, the stanzaic form has been abandoned. There is the following sequence:

1) Caiaphas determines that Jesus will be crucified.
2) Herod sends Marquez to the smith, to forge three nails.
3) The smith claims his hands are swollen, and does not wish to make the nails.
4) His wife volunteers for the job; she would do it even without payment. She is convinced that Jesus committed the crime of which He is accused.
5) At Golgotha, Caiaphas accuses Jesus in obscene language.
6) One of the soldiers hammers in the nails, regretting that Christ was allowed to live that long.
7) Christ receives the crown of thorns: "Ce soit par sa pute destinee!" (p. 244).
8) A Jew mocks Him.
9) Pilate is to affix the sign. He refuses to alter it to say: "He said He was the king of the Jews".
10) Our Lady speaks to her Son (twenty lines).
11) Christ entrusts her to St. John.
12) Christ says: "I am thirsty" and is given vinegar.
13) "My God, why hast Thou forsaken me?"
14) Caiaphas decides to hang the thieves at His sides.
15) Longinus cuts Jesus's side with his lance and begs Christ's forgiveness, which he receives.
16) Jesus dies: "It is finished".
17) Long lament by Our Lady (changing metres).

The whole text comprises 282 lines, octosyllabic.

83

The corresponding scenes in the *Passion d'Autun* (Biard) look similar, but seem more archaic and sober. Here, Jesus is sometimes designated as "doux agneau" . The Jews have recourse to a formula, which reminds us of the *chansons de geste*: "Nous avons droit, et il a tort,"[5] where death seems a consequence of an ontological argument (which then turns into an ethical judgment based on ideology, as in the case of the Franks vs. the Saracens). *Autun* also has the scene of the smith and his wife, and the Veronica scene after Christ's death. Among the seven last words we find: "Into Thy hands I commend my spirit". Without going into further detail, we should mention that in this *Passion* we occasionally have dialogue interrupted by narrative passages.

Thus far, we have followed the development of the Crucifixion plot in the various passion plays preceding Gréban's and Michel's: its gradual enlargement by elaboration and by the addition of apocryphal elements is clearly noticeable. Our examples were taken somewhat at random, of course; our choice does not exclude the possibility that other elaborations may be observable in passion plays or fragments not mentioned here. But our aim is the fifteenth-century plays and, in particular, the phenomenology of Christ's death in them. Gréban's *Mystère de la Passion* (1452) and Jean Michel's 1486 adaptation enlarge the crucifixion scene by some 2450 verses. While they retain the sequence of scenes from earlier passions, certain aspects of the death of Christ are emphasised, such as the mocking and tortures (active element) and the lamentations of women and disciples (passive element, especially in Jean Michel). In the main section of our study we shall therefore analyse these aspects and then come to some conclusions concerning the sociological implications of the late-medieval crucifixion scene. We are using the Michel text in Jodogne's edition[6], not only because it is convenient, but also because Michel has more scenic effects and indications than Gréban. It is interesting, in this context, that Michel's play ends with the crucifixion and omits resurrection and descent to Hell.

Starting with v. 26102, Michel has Caiaphas order a special cross for Jesus, "ce maulvais garson":

Nous la voulons plus grande,
plus lourde et aussi plus espesse;
car nous voulons par autre espece
luy acroistre plus son tourment;
et vecy la forme comment.
Par piéz et mains sera cloué
et bien fermement encloué
a la croix de grande haultesse,
pour endurer plus grande engoisse
et mourir a confusion. (26106-26115)

As Grifon explains this order to the carpenter, he reinforces the awesome features of the crucifix (26146-53). He goes into detail about the holes, which are to receive the nails, "qui sont gros et mal esguisés" (26159). He also encourages the carpenter to make the holes rather too far apart from one another than too close (26232-33). Once more the carpenter insists that he has never made such a heavy and strong cross. Grifon and the carpenter together can hardly move it.

Pilate then sends to the smith for "de gros clous et longs et moussus." Hedroit, the smith's wife, is willing to forge the nails. Once more, Brayart specifies: "qu'ilz soyent gros et pesans, moussus, mal uniz, mal perçans, a grosse teste rabatue" (26211-13):

Hedroit: Si la pointe est si mal aguë,
Comment perceront ilz la peau?
Brayart: A coups et force de marteau
nous le ficherons jusques au bout
et luy froisserons nerfs et tout
pour luy faire plus de doleur. (26214-19)

Later, Hedroit proudly shows her nails, "forts et pesants/Pour durer jusques a mille ans/Sans jamais pourrir de roulleure" (26281-83). Later, when Christ's clothes are taken away, they stick to His back, and when they are torn off, parts of the skin tear: "Se semble ung mouton qu'on escorche;/la peau s'en vient avec l'abit" (26360-61). The Jews then mock Him. Pilate, trying to stop them, only reinforces the feeling of compassion the audience experiences at this point. Roullart, soldier, indicates that he would kick Jesus in the shin if He does not walk fast enough with the cross. Others, like Dragon, note Christ's feebleness and the trouble He has in dragging Himself along. Symon Cyreneus is finally recruited to carry Jesus's cross, and the dialogue between Symon and the soldiers takes the form of a grim *rondeau*, casting an ironical light upon the entire scene. Here is a good man, opposed to carrying the cross of shame (instinctively opposed to hastening Christ's death), and upset because this common (but free) man is, once again, forced by someone of superior social status. The scene reminds us of the *vilain* incidents in Chrétien's romances.

The interlude with the devils (27054-27103) serves to suggest to them a "temptation" of Pilate's wife, who is to prevent Christ's death.[7] At first sight, this seems a paradox, yet it must be understood from the viewpoint of the devils, who are afraid of losing the redeemed from Hell.

On Calvary, Christ is denuded "tout aussi nud qu'ung ver de terre" (27157) "au point/qu'il sortit du ventre sa mere" (27162-63). Meant as a humiliation, this action closes the cycle of Christ's incarnation, and, in medieval religious thought, a "ver de terre" is nothing but a cocoon of the beautiful soul about to be resurrected. Concerning the exact method of crucifixion, we hear in vv. 27234-37:

Il est bon que vous l'estandez
sur terre et l'atachez d'ung bout
premier qu'on le dresse sur bout;
vous en ferez myeulx a vostre aise.

Grifon then proceeds to nail one arm, realistically describing how the nail is indeed not sharp enough to pierce both the hand and the wood; the other arm has to be stretched "bien troys doiz de distance" (27266), which is done with the help of a rope, "tant que vous pourrés / ensemble jusque aux nerfs desjoindre" (27282-83). The pulling by the various soldiers becomes, again, a *rondeau grinçant*,[8] and indeed the episode has been compared to stringing and tuning an instrument.[9]

Since there is only one nail left, and to hasten things, the feet of the Saviour are to be nailed one upon the other. Again, we are witness to atrocious pulling. After the job is finished, Brayart still wants to make sure that the nails hold firm. Pilate then affixes the sign in several languages. Lifting up the crucifix is again done linguistically in the form of a *rondeau*, which reflects the great effort necessary to erect and to steady the cross. Mocking continues:

Es tu la Jesus? Tu te esbas;
tu as bon temps. Es tu bien aise?
Presche nous cy, mais qu'il te plaise,
de tes beaux faiz du temps ancien. (27416-19)

Then it is the turn of the two thieves. Jesus starts speaking the seven last words, given here in Latin with, each time, the French periphrase following. The mocking of Christ continues in *rondeaux* and in simple dialogue. After a long lamentation by the Holy Virgin, Jesus entrusts her to St. John.

Mocking continues. The soldiers draw straws for Christ's clothes, but for the coat use a new game, dice, invented by Satan, who explains to Grifon the infernal symbolism of numbers one to six. Already, the process of dying is taking too long for the soldiers, and Grifon brings his hatchet to hasten death, "pour coupper cuisses et cuissos" (28217). There is a darkness, and the bystanders are seized with horror. Jesus speaks His fifth word ("I thirst"), is given vinegar and gall, while some advise to shorten these torments. His words, "Consummatum est" are followed by another lament of Mary, then He yields up His ghost with "O Pater, in manus tuas", to the great despair of Satan, for whom Christ's fateful descent into Hell is now imminent.

In this record of Christ's agony accentuated by mocking and tortures, special attention was obviously given by Gréban and Michel to 1) the instruments of torture (blunt nails, hammers, heavy and coarse unfinished wood, a hatchet), and 2) the actions of torture (forging, hammering, stretching, humiliation by mocking, spitting – as a competition in the *Passion d'Arras* – denuding, cutting with a lance by Longinus, in a later scene). Christine Martineau-Génieys has called our attention to the cult that developed around Christ's blood (beginning with the Longinus incident) and His wounds, to the point that some late *mystères* speak of a "pressoir mystique", in which Christ's body is used like grapes in a wine press (Eucharist).[10] The way in which Michel's *mystère* presents the torture scenes is by slow exposition and linguistic reinforcement, either as statements of grim pleasure by the torturers (repeated with crescendo and innuendo) or remarks of compassionate awe by various bystanders.

The "passive" reflection of the torture scenes and Christ's death is of course provided by the lamentations of the women and St. John, and the commentary by God. Of these let us examine the passage given to Veronica and two monologues by the Mother of God.

Veronica, the well-known apocryphal figure, applies her cloth to Jesus's face and carries off His image (p. 392).[11] She addresses Christ (octosyllabic lines), then His perspiring face (lines of six syllables), and finally *la véronique*, the holy features immortalized in colour on the cloth (lines of seven syllables), ending in an exhortation to all Christians (decasyllabic lines in alternation with lines of six syllables).

Veronica's monologue, in which feminine rhymes prevail, offered the audience a chance to contemplate what had happened; it provided relief after the long torture scenes; it invited compassion, a form of loving atonement for all humanity. The miracle of the face's imprint became a visible sign for beauty restored, a kind of "private" resurrection, indeed, prefiguration of the Resurrection to come, one last moment of relief before the dramatic scenes of Christ's final struggle.

Michel furthermore added to the crucifixion scene two lamentations by the Mother of God, one before her fainting, the other afterwards. In the first, she sings a *chanson* of twenty lines with a very artistic rhyme scheme:

> Doleur vient de moy repeller
> ce que amour veult interpeller
> et suis entre deux si estraincte
> que je ne sçay qui appeller
> ne comme triste expeller
> de moy qui me tient si contraincte.
> Je suis mere astraincte
> de doleur actainte

en ceste passion tant saincte
et ne puis obvier mon deul.
O mon filz, ou est ton doulx oeul
dont en cy gracîeux acueul
maintes foys m'avoyes regardee?
Helas, ou est le humble recueil
par qui surmonste tout orgueil?
Et present ... (p. 417).

The dominating rhyme elements are here -*ainte* and -*ueil,* and the sadness and suffering are indeed in the sound rather than in the meaning of the verses. The lyric art of the author is (here as elsewhere) in the choice of rhyme sounds and in the metric structures, comparable to Symbolist poetry.

The Virgin's address in the *pietà* scene (p. 433) is by far the most expressive *plainte.* It is colloquial, in simple language, a true complaint of a mother for her dead child. Our Lady is "believable" on the level of simple humanity in the audience, played most likely by a beautiful young woman, as we see her still today in fifteenth-century paintings, statuary and carvings. Her phrases come in short periods, interrupted by sobbing. Octosyllabic lines alternate with groups of three-syllable verse. She describes Jesus in appositions as "mon cher enfant" , "mon amour" , "de mon bien le plus", "ma fin", "ma parfaicte lumière", "ma joye", "ma lÿesse première et derrenière", pondering all He meant to her. Then she remembers His childhood, the pleasure she derived from holding Him, kissing His hands; but now all pleasure has turned into pain.

The overwhelming effect of this monologue is in the phrasing and in the simple, poignant language. There are no concrete images, no complicated rhetorical apparatus, no allegories, and, as in the entire *Mystère*, no allusions to classical antiquity or mythology. The colloquial immediacy of Mary's lamentation makes it comparable to spiritual poetry of the sixteenth century (cf. Marguerite de Navarre, *Chansons spirituelles).*

As mentioned above, the lamentations did provide rest for the audience, interspersed as they were among the torture episodes; but they also reinforced the pathos, the aspect of suffering endured during Christ's agony. They voiced, in fact, the audience's compassion. They *are* commentary, as Maurice Accarie suggested in his 1979 work on Jean Michel.[12]

This thought leads us to pondering, in general, the almost melodramatic manner in which Christ's death was portrayed in this late-medieval play. A later generation has condemned the passion plays precisely because of their gory, flamboyant aspects, and their irreverent manner of mixing grotesque elements with theological thought and doctrine. Christine Martineau-Génieys has mentioned the heightened sensibility of fifteenth-century people and has pointed to Franciscan influence.[13] However, at this point, I wish to advance arguments, some of which are not new, but most of which are in direct relationship to late-medieval religious teaching (partly Franciscan):

1. The manner of Christ's death was determined, in part, by Old Testament prophecies. Such details as the mocking and casting dice are all inserted with specific reference to this source. At a time when there was more and more emphasis on the gospels in pre-Reformation religious teaching, it was in the interest of the church to maintain the linkage between the Old and the New Testament. Therefore, many passion plays started, like Gréban's, with *Genesis* and reconstrued the entire cycle of Fall and Redemption.

2. The theory has been advanced (again supported by Biblical evidence) that Christ's death was meant to outwit the devil.[14] This is especially true for Gréban's *Passion*, which is much more dualistic than Michel's and opposes the realm of devils and Hell and its hierarchies to that of God and the angels. The concept of outwitting goes back to the age of crusades and the medieval epics, and ultimately to pagan societies and their own conflicts and battles. The theory has been translated, in religious terms, into a system of satisfaction: Christ had to die to redeem mankind and thereby to cancel the blemish cast on God's universe by the Fall. The manner of Christ's death in agony and ignominy was therefore not influenced by the agents of Hell, in whose interest it was to cause a delay or to avert this event. The more Christ was tortured, the closer would be the moment of outwitting, of satisfaction. It goes without saying that only the more sophisticated people among the audience would be able to grasp this significance and therefore "accept" torture and mocking.

3. The suffering of Christ emphasises man's own sinful mortality and the decrepitude of the body. The more He is tortured in the eyes of the audience, the more meaningful and imminent will Redemption become. Like Mathias Grünewald's *Altarpiece*, the spectacle of the crucifixion teaches the onlookers to despise the body *(contemptus mundi)* and to look forward to the hereafter.

4. To view torture, and to hear mocking and lamentations, help the audience to achieve catharsis by compassion *(imitatio Christi)*. Christ's death becomes the death of man, everyone's preoccupation, as we have stated already. In this context, the flagellation of Christ is like self-flagellation, a phenomenon mentioned already by Huizinga and explained, insufficiently, by the modern appositive, "collective neurosis".

5. The circumstances of Christ's death are to emphasize the brutality of the Jews in an age when Jews were persecuted as heretics.[15] Nathan asks Jesus on p. 406:

Mais cuydoye tu tousjours mener
guerre contre la sinagogue?
Cuydoye tu estre si tres rogue
que nous ne te peussons grever?

Many other passages could be cited in support.

6. Christ's death, especially the wounds inflicted and the blood shed and used (by Longinus), becomes – as it were – a celebration of Holy Mass, at the same time a re-enactment of the Sacrifice of Abraham (itself derivable from pagan rituals), a topic tremendously popular in late-medieval sculpture and iconography. The tortures and bloodshed, which hasten the death and bring about new life, are therefore seen as necessary and acceptable by the audience. It should be remembered, however, that there are explicit records of the misuse of Holy Mass and the Eucharist in the fifteenth century.

7. Finally, the agony of Christ, visible to all, suffered by all, is an incarnation of abstract concepts. To sacrifice Christ is to take Redemption into one's own hands, as it were, to the point of profanation. To a crowd, which was still so frightened of dying unprepared[16], such a sacrifice meant reassurance. In this context, it is significant to note, once more, that Michel's play ends with the crucifixion as the logical finale and culmination of the passion events. It is a hard decision for a *fatiste* not to take advantage of the scenic effects of descent to Hell and Resurrection; his reason for this decision was no doubt to preserve Christ's death as climax of His public life (which Michel had emphasized much more than Gréban), and thus to spiritualise the passion play.

No matter which interpretation we prefer among these seven proposals, Christ emerges in fact as a kind of scapegoat, or in German "Sündenbock" (someone punished for someone else's sins), according to a theory advanced by R. Warning.[17] Rather than choose one of these interpretations, however, the author of this study wishes to consider all of them taken together in syncretism. Together they show, in extraordinary clarity, that late-medieval people viewed the crucifixion and the death of Christ to remedy their own fears, which were real in a society where death was a daily companion. According to the findings of the 1975 Strasbourg Colloquium of medieval historians, *La Mort au moyen âge*[18], famine and pestilence remained formidable factors in sensitising people to the presence of death, and constant anxiety speaks through the wording of Last Wills, sermons, baptismal ceremonies, and funeral rites which multiplied at that time. More than in any other period, death – like the death of Christ – was a social event; more than at any other time, reflections about man's sinful state led inevitably to the thought of death.[19]

In viewing the crucifixion, the audience of the passion plays therefore contemplated their own death 1) by *imitatio/compassio (ars moriendi)*; 2) by suppression, fixing their attention upon the dying Christ instead; 3) by hoping for eternal life and Redemption practically brought about by themselves, by the work of their hands, in building props and acting on stage, in choreographing, as it were, their own final moments. In writing and staging the death of Christ in the particular manner we have discussed, fifteenth-century French playwrights showed that they had understood the needs of their audience.

NOTES

1. Selected sources: E. Döring-Hirsch, *Tod und Jenseits im Spätmittelalter* (Berlin, 1929); W. Rehm, *Der Todesgedanke in der deutschen Dichtung vom Mittelalter bis zur Romantik* (Halle, 1928); A. Tenenti, *La vie et la mort à travers l'art du XVe siècle* (Paris, 1952); E. DuBruck, *The Theme of Death in French Poetry of the Middle Ages and the Renaissance* (The Hague, 1964); K. Jankofsky, *Darstellung von Tod und Sterben in mittelenglischer Zeit* (Duluth, 1970); T.S.R. Boase, *Death in the Middle Ages* (London, 1972); Ph. Ariès, *L'Homme devant la mort* (Paris, 1977); C. Martineau-Génieys, *Le Thème de la mort dans la poésie française de 1450 à 1550* (Paris, 1978).
2. Jankofsky (see above), *passim*.
3. M. Accarie, *Etude sur le sens moral de la Passion de Jean Michel* (Genève, 1979), p. 114.
4. See also E. DuBruck, "Death and the Peasant: A Testimony on Fifteenth-Century Life and Thought by Johannes v. Saaz", *Fifteenth-Century Studies* III (1980), 55-70.
5. *La Passion d'Autun*, ed. Grace Frank (Paris, 1934), p.96, v. 774.
6. Jean Michel, *Le Mystère de la Passion* (Gembloux, 1959).
7. In Biblical accounts, Pilate's wife tells her husband about her dreams and entreats him: "Have Thou nothing to do with that just man!" (Matt. 27, 19). In the late-medieval *mystère*, this incident translates into a "temptation" by devils, insinuating, possibly, unfaithfulness to Pilate. This shows, in turn, a tendency toward explicitness in demonstrating psychological motivation which, apparently, fifteenth-century people began to require. I have had occasion to investigate this aspect in my recent article, "The Perception of Evil in the *Mystère de la Passion* by Jean Michel (1486)", to appear in *Michigan Academician* XV (1983).
8. On the use of the *rondeau* in late-medieval drama, see L. Müller, *Das Rondel in den französischen Mirakelspielen und Mysterien des 15. und 16. Jahrhunderts* (Marburg, 1884) and H.Chatelain, *Recherches sur le vers français au 15e siècle* (Paris, 1907), ch. xiii.
9. R. Warning, *Funktion und Struktur. Die Ambivalenzen des geistlichen Spiels* (Munchen, 1974), pp. 206 ff.
10. Martineau-Génieys (*supra, n.* 3), p. 108.
11. On Veronica, see *New Catholic Encyclopedia* XIV (New York, 1967), p. 625.
12. Accarie (*supra, n.* 3), p. 108.
13. Martineau-Génieys, p. 101; see however E. DuBruck, *The Theme of Death*, p. 41, on St. Bernard de Clairvaux.
14. R. Warning (*supra, n.* 9), p. 169 and *passim*.
15. See F. Heer, *The Medieval World* (New York, 1963), ch. 13; H. R Trevor-Roper, *The European Witch-Craze of the Sixteenth and Seventeenth Centuries* (New York, 1969), p. 109, and E. DuBruck, "Thomas Aquinas and Medieval Demonology", *Michigan Academician* VII (1974), 173.
16. On the emphasis upon oral confession in the late Middle Ages, see *New Catholic Encyclopedia* IV (New York, 1967), 132. Also: T.N. Tentler, *Sin and Confession on the Eve of the Reformation* (Princeton, 1977).
17. Warning, pp. 184 ff.
18. Collection "Recherches et documents", 25.
19. There is no doubt that in Michel's play as a whole emphasis is on life rather than death. Instead of long passages of fire-and-brimstone moralising, we discover picturesque scenes in streets and markets, we overhear fishermen talking about the day's catch and merchants about sales opportunities. There is even some indication that life's successes may be taken as an early assurance by God that with His help evil has been defeated, and that suffering and the crucifixion were but calvary stations on a pilgrimage (cf. E. DuBruck, "Changes of Taste and Audience Expectation in Fifteenth-Century Religious Drama", *Fifteenth-Century Studies* VI (1983), 86).

RESUME

Quand on compare les Mystères du XVe siècle aux textes bibliques dont ils s'inspirent ou à des Passions plus anciennes, on constate qu'ils présentent les épisodes de la Crucifixion sous une forme très réaliste, voire mélodramatique. Tous les témoignages contemporains relatifs à ces scènes nous permettent de supposer que les spectateurs voyaient dans la mort du Christ: 1) l'accomplissement des paroles de l'Ecriture; 2) la défaite de Satan; 3) la promesse de la Rédemption; 4) une forme de catharsis s'opérant par la compassion; 5) un meurtre perpétré par les Juifs; 6) un équivalent de la Messe; 7) une matérialisation d'idées abstraites assez proche d'un sacrifice tribal. Les actions et les réactions des figurants, les tortures et les lamentations sont destinées à toucher la sensibilité d'un public qui cherche à remédier à sa peur de mourir en état de péché par la *contemplatio, l'imitatio/la compassio*, et par la représentation de la *Redemptio*. Dans une société où la mort était une présence familière, où la famine et les épidémies ne cessaient de rappeler à l'homme combien précaire est sa vie, cette peur était certes très réelle. Une inquiétude constante se fait jour dans la langue des testaments, sermons, cérémonies baptismales, rites funéraires qui prolifèrent alors. Plus qu'à toute autre époque la mort, comme celle du Christ, avait un caractère public. La manière dont les dramaturges du XVe siècle ont écrit et fait représenter les scènes de la Crucifixion montre qu'ils comprenaient les besoins profonds de leur public.

LITERATURE

DANTE'S IDEA OF PURGATORY, WITH SPECIAL REFERENCE TO *PURGATORIO* XXI, 58-66

★

Kenelm Foster

The Catholic doctrine of Purgatory was first defined by the Second Council of Lyons in 1274, when Dante was nine years old and Aquinas only a few months dead. With a slight difference in the wording this definition was repeated by the Council of Florence in 1439, and reaffirmed in the next century by the Council of Trent as a sufficient statement, against Protestant denials, of the Catholic belief in a place or state of temporary and purificatory suffering after death. The definition runs as follows (with a few words added to bring out the logical sequence): "The Holy Roman Church ... teaches that those who after baptism fall into sin are not to be rebaptised; instead, they will obtain forgiveness of such sins by doing penance for them. If, however, thus truly repentant and in the love of God, they should die before making satisfaction for these their sins ... by bringing forth fruits befitting penance, then their souls are purified after death by purgatorial or cleansing punishment *(poenis purgatoriis seu catharteriis)*; which punishment can be lightened by the prayers of the living ..." (Denzinger, *Enchiridion Symbolorum* , ed. 20, 464).

Such, for the past seven centuries, is all that Catholics have been taught as "de fide" about Purgatory. Note that nothing is said about either the place of Purgatory or the manner of the suffering it entails – except, by implication, that this is only for a time. There is no mention of fire. This double silence, so to call it, obviously left great liberty to the imagination of a poet like Dante. But it was, I think, at a deeper level that the dogma left our poet the liberty that his genius, especially his genius as a moralist, was most happy to take advantage of. I will explain what I mean by a brief analysis of the terms of the 1274 definition, followed by an outline of the structure of the *Purgatorio*.

The definition took for granted three basic points in New Testament Christianity: (1) that sinful man needs to be reconciled with God; (2) that such a reconciliation has in fact been effected, and perfectly, by the self-immolation and the resurrection to new life of the God-Man

Jesus Christ; (3) that the medium through which individuals come to share in this life of the risen Christ, and so are reconciled to God, is faith expressed sacramentally in baptism, as St. Paul explains in Romans ch. 6: in baptism we both "die with" Christ – which is our death to sin – and rise with him to "walk in newness of life". And it was from this scriptural starting-point that the Church proceeded to her doctrine of Purgatory, the whole point of Purgatory being to remedy relapses into sin on the part of those who had once been brought into perfect harmony with God. No baptism, no Purgatory. Note however that Purgatory is not the *first* remedy envisaged by the Church for post-baptismal sin. The first remedy is to do penance for such sin. Purgatory only comes in because of the brute fact of death – of death, that is, as either forestalling or interrupting the needful work of penance. In essence indeed Purgatory *is* that same work, but carried out in the special conditions of *post-mortem* existence; where if the work has been begun on earth, it is completed; and if not even begun, it is carried out *in toto*, from start to finish. The only thing absolutely required of the sinner in this life, if he is to be admitted to Purgatory, is that he die, as the Lyons formula puts it, repentant and "in the love of God", i.e. desiring reconciliation with Him – as did Dante's penitent Sienese lady Sapìa: "Pace volli con Dio in su lo stremo/de la mia vita" – "I wanted peace with God when I came to the end of my life" (XIII, 124-5).

My present concern is with this teaching only in relation to Dante, and not to test his orthodoxy but simply as a clue to his meaning. For where that meaning is obscure it is not unreasonable to look to the accepted teaching to shed some light on it; and where the meaning is clear it is historically pertinent to ask how far, if at all, it represents an original development or application of the dogma as commonly received. My working hypothesis is that Dante's thirty-three cantos about "that second kingdom/where the human spirit is purified/and becomes worthy to rise to heaven" (I, 4-6) are, in intention at least, Catholic; a point which none of his early commentators dreamed of calling in question. This is not of course to say that Dante had been at pains to look up the Lyons definition for himself; he would have got all the instruction he needed from the doctrinal sermons of the Friars, at S. Maria Novella, for example, or S. Croce.

Allusions to the belief of ordinary Catholics in Purgatory – in terms especially of its practical consequence of prayers for the dead – emerge most often and most distinctly in the earlier cantos of *Purgatorio*; less so in the long middle section from Canto IX to XXVII; still less in the last six cantos, XXVIII – XXXIII, describing the poet-protagonist's return to the Garden of Eden, his meeting with Beatrice, his visions concerning the Tree, symbolic of Divine Justice. In this last section the properly purgatorial theme, as Catholic dogma defines Purgatory, is virtually left behind. The encounter with Beatrice, painfully penitential though it is, presents nothing purgatorial in that quasi-technical sense, for Beatrice is not in Purgatory, nor, save in a highly specialised sense, is Dante. Consequently I leave these concluding cantos out of account. My business is with the two main preceding sections: the so-called 'Ante-Purgatorio', Cantos I-VIII inclusively, and then the long middle section, Cantos IX-XXVII, which may be called 'Purgatory proper', on the strength of Virgil's remark to Dante when the poets, at the start of their second day on the Mountain, are approaching the Gateway to this middle region: "Tu se' omai al purgatorio giunto", "You are now arrived at Purgatory" (IX, 49). Artistically this separation of the lower from the middle regions of the Mountain, of the Ante-Purgatorio from the circles of purification proper, was exceedingly felicitous, but it involves theological questions, as we shall see.

As regards the Ante-Purgatorio, I pass quickly over Cantos I and II, in part because as narrative they are only prolegomena to what follows, but chiefly because the dominant figure here, the unbaptised pagan Cato, raises theological issues too complex to be dealt with in the time at our disposal. Enough to say here (a) that Cato is in no sense undergoing the pains of the Dantean Purgatory, (b) that he functions, here at the foot of the Mountain, as a symbol of those natural virtues which it is the purpose of the middle, properly purificatory section – 'Purgatory proper' – to restore, though only as a preparation for the higher life of direct union with God, whose focal symbol, in this part of the *Commedia*, will in fact be Beatrice (cf. XXXI, 133-145); and (c) that Dante's Purgatory, no less than that envisaged in Catholic dogma, is exclusively for the baptized; which was not the case with Dante's Hell. So much, at present, for Cato. What should not, however, be overlooked in Canto I is the series of thematic pointers, so to call them, which here at the very start of the *cantica* serve to alert the reader to certain concepts which will in fact govern the whole subsequent process of chastisement and purification, namely Love, Virtue, Liberty and Humility; these four ideas being indicated, respectively, by Venus (as the morning star), the planet of love (lines 19-21), by the four stars near the Southern Pole, symbolising the Cardinal Virtues (lines 22-27, 37), by Virgil's praise of Cato for his love of liberty (lines 71- 75), by the reed, symbol of humility, with which Virgil, in obedience to Cato, girds Dante (lines 94-95, 133-36). The whole movement of Dante's Purgatory is governed by Divine *Love*; requires profound *humility* on the side of man; and has for its effect the restoration of lost *virtue* and spiritual *liberty*.

The first souls we meet undergoing any penalty are those in Canto III who died excommunicate, their penance being to remain at the foot of the Mountain thirty times as long as they had spent under the ban of the Church, unless this delay is shortened by prayers offered for them on earth (lines 136-41). Then come the various Late-Repentant (Cantos IV-V) and finally, before Purgatory proper begins, that cross-section of the late 13th century European upper class in the lovely Valley of the Princes (VII- VIII). In a variety of ways the same *negative* penalty is imposed on all these souls. Desiring intensely the sight of God, and conscious that there is that in them which gets in the way of that vision, they are in fact being held back from the process of inward purification which alone can remove the obstacle (V, 55-57, cf. XIII, 85-90). Their suffering is all in this delay, this forced inactivity; aware as they are that meanwhile their characters remain unchanged, unreformed, those characters which, like Eliot's *Animula*, have issued "misshapen" from the "hand of time". In sharpest contrast are the souls on the seven Terraces of Purgatory proper, whose sufferings, recounted in Cantos X – XXVII, are strictly reformatory, cathartic, in that they are here shown being cleansed from one or other of the seven traditional Capital Vices, pride, envy, anger, sloth, avarice, gluttony, lechery, in that order; which plainly is that essential purification which the souls in Ante-Purgatorio are for the time being prevented from even beginning. Hence it may be presumed, I think, though this is left unstated, that all the souls destined after death to climb the Mountain of "probing Justice" (III, 3) will in the event suffer on one or other of the seven Terraces. Young Manfred, for example, down among the loitering excommunicates cheerfully confesses that his sins were "horrible", well knowing that their needed purification will certainly come in God's good time. Similarly the witty Belacqua must be destined for the circle of Sloth (IV, 109-35). Conversely, Sapìa and Dante's friend Forese Donati, on the Terraces respectively of Envy and Gluttony, remember that their sojourn among the Late-Repentant had been shortened, for the one by the prayers of a saintly fellow-citizen, for the other by those of his devout widow (XIII, 124-29, XXIII, 85-90).

The fact is that Dante has separated, yet kept in living connection, the two aspects of Christian penance which the Lyons definition had left indistinct. According to that definition, you will recall, souls go to Purgatory to complete by purgative suffering, *poenis purgatoriis*, the "penance" due from them for post-baptismal sins; it being assumed that, while each such sin has been forgiven, the sinner is not thereby quit of all punishment for it; in technical language the removal of his guilt, *culpa*, does not as such mean he is no longer *reus poenae*, that is, required in justice to accept a punishment for having incurred it. Now implicit in all this is a certain view (a) of the necessary inward effects of sin, and (b) of how, granted these effects, sins do in fact get remitted or forgiven. Here we are talking, of course, not of the so-called 'original sin' attaching to 'fallen' human nature as such – for that *ex hypothesi* had been removed from the souls in Purgatory by baptism – but of particular 'actual' sins committed since baptism. Of the essential effects of such sin, and of what is involved in its forgiveness, the clearest account I know is that of St. Thomas (*Summa theologiae* 1a2ae. 85-87; 109, 7), which reduced to essentials is as follows: (a) The effects of all 'actual' sin are, first a resulting *macula* or 'stain' in the soul, and then that incurred liability to punishment, the *reatus poenae* mentioned a moment ago. The metaphor of stain itself connotes that of God as the Source of spiritual 'radiance' from which the sinner as such has in fact culpably distanced himself, thus incurring, so long as he remains unrepentant, a certain spiritual darkening and deformity. (b) As to the forgiveness of the sin, this consists precisely in the removal of that 'stain', that is of that self-distancing from God which was the sin's proper and primary effect. By God's forgiveness therefore is meant that He reunites the soul with Himself. Now the soul unites with God principally in the will. It follows – granted, as we have seen, that, besides the 'stain', the sin involved a liability in justice to punishment – it follows that the 'stain' of a man's sin cannot be removed "unless the man's will accept the order of divine justice; that is to say, unless he either spontaneously takes it on himself to punish his past sin, or else bear patiently whatever punishment God may send him" *(Summa theol.* 1a2ae. 87, 6). In other words, the being forgiven one's sins involves a readiness to do penance for them; which, as St. Thomas goes on to explain, alters the nature of the punishment. This is a point of some importance for an understanding of the torments suffered by the penitents of Dante's terraces:

> Either way (of the two just mentioned, in which the punishment may be willingly borne) the punishment has the character of a 'satisfaction' (i.e. of expiation). Now expiatory punishment loses somewhat of the nature of punishment. For it is of the nature of punishment that it goes against the will; and though expiatory punishment absolutely considered is against the will, nevertheless in the here and now it is voluntary. Indeed, speaking quite simply, *simpliciter*, it is voluntary; only indirectly, *secundum quid*, is it involuntary ... In conclusion, therefore, once the stain of sin has been removed, that is, once the sin is forgiven, if any punishment remains, it will not be punishment in the strict sense but rather expiation. *(ibid.)*

The distinction drawn here between the voluntary *simpliciter* and the voluntary *secundum quid* is directly relevant to the passage referred to in the title of this talk, but before we come to that a query remains concerning the relevance of the Lyons definition of 1274 to Dante's middle section, Cantos X-XXVII. Certainly, the torments described in these cantos seem to tally with the *poenae purgatoriae* of the definition. On the other hand the definition only speaks of those *poenae* as the means whereby sinners do *post mortem* penance for their sins; so that *prima facie* it might be maintained that, as envisaged in the Lyons dogma, the *poenae* are only "satisfactory", in the sense of paying off a debt; that what they are thought of as delivering sinners from is only the *reatus poenae*, not the *macula*, of sin; so that the souls in Purgatory, as the definition conceives of Purgatory, would correspond only to those souls in Dante's poem whom he places in the Ante-Purgatorio, and whose punishment *there* leaves them, as we have seen, inwardly quite unchanged. But such a narrowly reductive reading of the 1274 definition would certainly be unhistorical – a point I obviously cannot set out to prove here; let it suffice to refer you to the exhaustive article 'Purgatoire' in vol. 13, part 1 of the *Dictionnaire de théologie catholique*, cols. 1191-1250. And it would be unhistorical even granted, what is true, that the Fathers assembled at Lyons in 1274 were not concerned to incorporate into the definition of Purgatory the most recent theological reflections on the working of divine grace in the soul of penitent sinners; for example, St. Thomas's analysis in the *Summa* 1a2ae. 86 of how the 'stain' of sin may be removed, and the soul thereby restored to that *nitor*, as Thomas calls it, that 'radiance' which sin had obscured; an analysis to which the reader of Dante has every right to appeal in corroboration of what the poet shows us on his seven terraces of purification. "The human soul", says Thomas, "has a twofold radiance: from the refulgence of the natural light of reason, by which its actions are guided, and from the refulgence of the divine light of wisdom and grace, which bring those actions to perfection" (86, 1). And then on the recovery of the *nitor*, once it had been lost: "The stain of sin continues in the soul after the sinful act. The reason is that the stain ... denotes a certain loss of radiance owing to the soul's withdrawing from the light of reason or of divine law. So long therefore as a man stays withdrawn from that light, the stain remains in him; upon his return, however, to the light of reason and of God ... the stain is removed ... not, however, in such wise that he at once returns to his former state. There must be an act of will in the direction contrary to that which brought him into the state of sin ..." (86, 2) These few words anticipate the whole process of moral catharsis exhibited on Dante's seven terraces.

You will have noticed St. Thomas' stress on the role of the human will in the recovery from sin, and how moreover he saw the *nitor*, the 'brightness' thereby recovered as including a 'refulgence' from the light of natural reason. This 'humanistic' strain, so to call it, this confidence in free will and rationality in the religion of Aquinas and Dante is as recognisably Catholic as the opposed Lutheran stress was to prove, in the event, characteristically Protestant. That it involved, however, in the *Purgatorio* no inattention to the properly Christian factor comes out clearly in the lines spoken by Forese Donati assimilating his and the other penitents' willingness to suffer to that displayed by Christ on his way to Calvary "... and not once only, as we circle this road, is our pain renewed – I say pain and should say joy, for that desire leads us ... which led glad Christ to say 'Eloi', when he delivered us with his blood" (XXIII, 70-75; cf. Matt. 27. 46).

And that same stress, thus associated with Christ, on pain willingly borne brings us at last to the great lines of Statius in Canto XXI, explaining how the penitent souls on the Mountain become aware, individually, that their moment of release has come – that this one or that one is now free to go on to Paradise. Let me recall the circumstances. Towards the end of Canto XX Dante and Virgil are surprised by a sudden trembling of the Mountain, followed by a great cry. The trembling at once calls up for Dante a classical precedent, but the cry recalls the song of the angels at the birth of Christ (Luke

2. 13-14); while together they touch off in him a keen desire to know their cause; a desire – so we are told at the start of the next canto – arising from the thirst for knowledge which is natural to man (cf. Aristotle, *Metaphysics* I, i, 980a 21; *Convivio* I, i, 1) and which, nevertheless, only the waters of divine Grace can finally slake (XXI, 1-3; cf. John 4. 13-15). It is at this point, against this closely woven backcloth of humanist and Christian motifs, that our two poets are joined by a third figure; and it was, we are told, as when the two disciples on the road to Emmaus were joined by the newly-risen Christ (Luke 24. 13ff). Virgil's question to the stranger about the earthquake at once follows, and the latter's answer, after which the pagan-turned-Christian first-century poet reveals his identity. But our concern is only with what Statius says about the earthquake.

It has, he says, no natural explanation, being the outward effect and sign of an inward spiritual event: a soul's – in this case his own – discovery that its purification is now complete: the Mountain, he says, "trembles when some soul feels itself to be pure ... and that cry follows. Of the purity the will alone gives proof (*sol voler fa prova*); which, wholly free now to change place and company, seizes on the soul unawares and empowers it to will (*di voler le giova*). It wills indeed before, but is held back by desire (*non lascia il talento*) which Divine Justice, going counter to the will, turns to the torment, as it was once turned towards sin" (XXI, 58-66). The process of purification, here epigrammatically described, is what we have already heard stated very simply by St. Thomas, when he said that on the sinner's part "there must be an act of the will in the direction contrary to that which brought him into the state of sin" (*Summa theol.* 1a2ae. 86, 2; 87, 6); he must, that is to say, choose or accept a displeasure contrary to his former illicit satisfactions. To denote this purgative choice, or willing acceptance, Dante here uses the current Provençalism *talento* (line 64), but stiffening, as it were, its normal meaning of wish, inclination, desire (cf. *Inferno* V, 39; X, 55) to give it the sense of a concrete option, of an actual willing of *this* and not *that*, in the here and now. With this meaning of *talento* in mind the other key-terms in the passage are easily understood. *Anima (alma)* is the soul or psyche as the subject of any experience or activity. It is represented here as in two stages: in and prior to the moment of deliverance described in lines 61-63, from "Of the purity" down to "empowers it to will". This moment consists essentially in the soul's suddenly finding itself willing, and *wholly* willing, its own deliverance. What leads it to that discovery is its own appetitive capacity; which, as the capacity of a nature endowed with intelligence, is called 'will' (and not, for example, 'instinct'). Now this will is shown here, first as a power or faculty ((*il) voler*, line 61), then as an actual willing (*voler, il talento*, lines 63 and 64), and then once more under its aspect of power or faculty (the *voglia* of line 65); this ringing the changes between will as faculty and will as actual volition being the poet's way of rendering a certain division in the will of the suffering souls, prior to their moment of final release and peace. Prior to this moment, that is to say, their will is divided in the sense that while its natural bent, the *voglia* of line 65, is towards joy, Divine Justice – to which it is entirely yielded up – holds it to the acceptance of temporary pain as the price of eventual joy, this acceptance of pain being, as we have seen, what Dante here calls *il talento*, line 64. But at a certain point in time – which only God, not the soul, can determine and foresee – that grip of God's justice on the will is relaxed, so that it is suddenly free to issue into an actual volition *entirely in line with its natural bent* – into the decision, that is to say, to leave Purgatory. At this point the will is re-unified, and this to the point of perfect oneness with itself, of perfect spontaneity; unified, that is, no longer as heretofore in Purgatory, in total submission to God's punishing justice, but as totally identified with its own intrinsic desire for joy.

In all this two points of theological psychology are particularly noteworthy: (1) the hidden presence of God as *directing* the whole process: (2) the manner in which the soul at a certain moment becomes aware that its purification is complete. A word on each point: (1) Any actual willing presupposes an end apprehended as desirable; which apprehension, however, may be, and often is, in a mind other than that of the subject willing, as when the latter is merely obeying orders or following advice. And normally, of course, that other mind is itself human. But at least twice in the *Commedia* Dante points to situations where the psyche in its willing is directly subject to the directing mind of God: that of the new-born child envisaged in *Purgatorio* XVI, 85-90, and that of the souls undergoing their catharsis, as described here in Canto XXI. The new-born child spontaneously and immediately desires joy, as being still enclosed, as it were, in the creative joy of its Maker; only through an inborn flaw in its nature ('original sin') will its desire in fact go astray: "Issues from the hands of Him who loves it/before it exists ... the little simple soul, which knows nothing,/save that, proceeding from a glad Maker,/it turns eagerly to whatever delights it ..." This spontaneous turning towards joy, at once natural and God-caused, is the 'voglia' – the will's natural bent, as I have called it – mentioned by Statius in Canto XXI, 65. By contrast,the force enclosing and directing the souls undergoing catharsis, and precisely *as* undergoing it, is not God's joy but His justice. But they too, like the new-born child, "know nothing", in the sense that for as long as the purgatorial process continues all the *knowledge* that this entails is in God's mind, not in theirs; all they know is that they love Him and must obey Him – obey, that is, by suffering for as long as He pleases. In His will is their peace – though it is peace in pain. Here, it seems to me, Dante's thought on Purgatory anticipates that of the great St. Catherine of Genoa, 1447-1510 (see her *Treatise on Purgatory* , translated by C. Balfour and H.D. Irvine, London, Sheed and Ward, 1946). (2) The term of the purgatorial process is a moment of self-knowledge, when the soul finds itself not only, as hitherto, desiring the end of the process, but as no longer actually willing its continuance; so that there is nothing now left for it to will but the joy that awaits it in Paradise; to which it therefore now directs itself. In this way, at this moment, it both rises to the height of its dignity as a self-governing rational nature, and at the same time entirely surrenders itself to its Divine Lover, that "infinite and ineffable Good" who "speeds to love as a ray of light to a bright body" (XV, 67-69).

RESUME

1)   Exposé et brève analyse du dogme du purgatoire, formulé pour la première fois officiellement par le second concile de Lyons en 1274: "L'Eglise Catholique Romaine déclare et enseigne que tous ceux qui, après le baptême, commettent un péché peuvent obtenir le pardon par la pénitence. Or, l'âme de ceux qui meurent, repentants et dans l'amour de Dieu, avant d'avoir fait réparation par les fruits du repentir, sera purifiée (*poenis purgatoriis seu catharteriis*) et nettoyée punitivement. Cette punition peut être allégée par la prière des vivants."

L'on remarquera que ni dans cette formulation du dogme ni dans celle promulguée par les conciles de Florence (1439) et de Trente (1547), on n'a tâché de localiser le purgatoire ou de décrire les peines qu'il entraîne (sauf pour dire qu'elles sont transitoires). Cet état de chose laisse toute liberté à l'imagination du poète.

2)   Or, le génie de Dante se déploie librement d'une autre manière encore. La formulation ci-dessus ne distingue pas entre les éléments purement pénaux et expiatoires des souffrances infligées et leur valeur morale et cathartique: elles sont *suffisantes*, quant à la Justice divine et réparatrice, c'est-à-dire qu'elles remédient à un état de chose; elles amènent un renouveau, une métanoia exemplaire. Dante s'est servi de la liberté qu'on lui laisse d'appuyer plus ou moins fortement sur un des deux aspects de la question: punition ou régénération. Sans laisser de côté l'aspect expiatoire, il a mis l'accent sur la réforme de l'âme. Si la punition figure largement dans l'Ante-Purgatorio (III-VIII), la catharsis domine les chants X à XXVII. Tel est l'esprit qui informe l'humanisme chrétien de cette seconde tranche de l'oeuvre.

3)   Tout ceci est mis en évidence tout particulièrement dans les tercets 58 à 66 du canto XXI. Statius, sur le point de quitter le purgatoire, y décrit pour Dante et Virgile comment il avait su que son heure était venue. Sa connaissance, tout intérieure, tirait sa source de sa propre volonté à lui. Quand il se voulut libre du tourment, il le fut. L'activité de la créature, toute subjective et volontaire, ne pourrait s'exprimer plus clairement. En d'autres mots, c'est l'assentiment de l'individu à la grâce divine qui aboutit à la perfection de l'âme.

THE CHANGING VISION OF ARTHUR'S DEATH

Fanni Bogdanow

When I was asked if I would contribute a paper to this Colloquium, I agreed to do so with both joy and sadness: joy at the privilege of being able to pay public hommage to Professor Eugène Vinaver whose example and encouragement have been my lifelong inspiration; and sadness at the thought that he, to whom we all owe so much and in whose memory this Colloquium is being held, is no longer with us.

It is perhaps not inappropriate that the theme of this Colloquium is "Death in the Middle Ages". Eugène Vinaver himself not only edited the *Works* of Sir Thomas Malory to which Caxton gave the collective title *Morte Darthur*, but in a series of memorable studies he revealed Malory's conception of the Death of Arthur.[1] For Malory, Mordred's rebellion and the subsequent battle on Salisbury Plain where Arthur was mortally wounded only succeeded because the country had been previously weakened by dissension which had been, in the words of Vinaver, the outcome of a 'conflict between two forms of human love and fidelity[2] : the passionate feudal loyalty of man to man and the self-denying devotion of the knight-lover to his lady.'[3] For when after the discovery of Lancelot and Guenevere's love, Guenevere is condemned to death, 'it is Lancelot's loyalty to Guenevere that causes him, in his anxiety to protect her, to act with such rashness as to kill unwittingly the man he loves most – Gareth, Gawain's brother; and it is genuine grief that turns Lancelot's most faithful friend, Gawain, into a mortal enemy'.[4] The theme of 'divided allegiances' was, of course, already implicit in the story and characters of Malory's 'French Book', the thirteenth century Vulgate *Mort Artu*[5], but in making this theme the *leitmotiv* Malory was able to endow the narrative with a more poignant meaning.

In reshaping the story of Arthur's death, Malory is continuing in the tradition of earlier writers, each of whom had modified and reinterpreted the version of his predecessors in order to convey his own particular vision of the rise and fall of the Arthurian kingdom. The first comprehensive account of the passing of Arthur forms part of Geoffrey of Monmonth's larger *History of the Kings of Britain*[6] written in 1136. Since the Church Fathers medieval writers had seen in history the workings of the hand of God and great calamities were explained as God punishing the evil conduct of nations.[7] It was in this way that a sixth-century monk, Gildas, to whom Geoffrey of Monmouth is greatly indebted, had interpreted the recent history of his country in a work that bears the title *Concerning the Destruction and Conquest of Britain (De Excidio et Conquestu Britanniae).*[8] Gildas, of course, does not mention Arthur by name, though the timespan he covers includes the period when Arthur, if he were a historical reality, would have lived. Now Geoffrey of Monmouth saw the desolation of Britain in the same light as Gildas. But in his conception the Arthurian period was the high point of British history. For this reason it is only in the post-Arthurian period that Geoffrey introduces the theme of the British people falling away from righteousness and their consequent decline. The height of Britain's plight, in fact, comes when Cadwallader, the son of Cadwallo, one of Arthur's successors, falls ill. 'The Britons', so Geoffrey says, 'started to quarrel among themselves and to destroy the economy of their homeland by an appalling civil war.'[9] This was followed by a grievous famine and a deadly plague. 'The few wretches left alive ... emigrated to countries across the sea...'[10] and 'for eleven years Britain remained deserted by all its inhabitants.'[11] Cadwallader himself set sail for Brittany and his parting words underline the significance of the whole catastrophe:

> Woe unto us sinners, he cried, for our monstrous crimes, with which we never stopped offending God, as long as we had the time for repentance. The vengeance of His might lies heavily upon us ... When He, the true Judge, saw that we had no intention of putting an end to our crimes, ... He made up His mind to punish us for our folly. He has visited His wrath upon us ...[12]

In contrast to all this and clearly in order to avoid tarnishing the image of Arthur and Arthurian Britain, Geoffrey of Monmouth, without actually bringing in the symbol of the Wheel of Fortune, accounts for the disaster that ends Arthur's reign in terms of the medieval concept of Fortune. According to this notion, taken over from Boethius, the fickle Goddess Fortuna casts men down from prosperity to adversity without their having merited it. Arthur, seen throughout as a just, God-fearing and valiant king, had in the early years of his reign fought against the infidels, the Saxons, and had brought all Europe under his dominion, with the exception of Rome. Now the war at the end of Arthur's career which was again to take him overseas with such tragic consequences – Mordred's rebellion culminating in Arthur's death – is likewise presented as both a justifiable and an honourable expedition. Faced with the two equally intolerable alternatives of either paying tribute to Rome or of facing the certainty of another invasion of Britain, Arthur had no choice except to take up the Roman challenge and thereby, at the same time, fulfil the Sybilline prophecies of long ago that 'for the third time someone born of British blood shall seize the Empire for Rome.'[13] To underline the sudden and unjust reversal of Fortune the news of Mordred's treason will reach Arthur just as he touches the height of his glory and is about to march on Rome itself.

While later writers will largely respect Geoffrey's sequence of events, they will not always follow his interpretation. The anonymous author of the thirteenth-century Prose *Perceval*[14], a work intended to complete Robert de Borron's unfinished Arthur-Grail Arthuriad[15], is one of those writers who, like Robert de Borron himself, continued Geoffrey's idealisation of Arthur and the Arthurian world. To heighten Arthur's prestige and to emphasise that the misfortune that will shortly overtake him is undeserved, he systematically blackens the Emperor of Rome and raises the whole conflict from the level of a war of self-defence to the status of a Holy War. For the Emperor of Rome, in this version, not only allies himself to Sarrasins, namely the King of Spain and the Sultan, but forgets his position to the extent of marrying a pagan girl, the Sultan's daughter: *si meserra molt li emperere vers Dieu et vers sainte yglise, car il prist a feme le fille le Soudan, qui paiene estoit* ...[16] Arthur and his knights, on the other hand, are presented as the upholders of the True Faith who take up the Roman challenge not only for political reasons but to defend the interests of Christendom that the Emperor had wanted to enslave – *mestre en servitude.*[17] For the same reason, the conflict with Mordred is raised to similar dimensions. While in Geoffrey of Monmouth Mordred's army included both pagans (namely Saxons) and Christians: *Erant autem omnes numero quasi octoginta millia, tam paganorum quam christianorum*[18], in the Prose *Perceval* Mordred's sole allies are the heathen Saxons, the very same who under Hengist had treacherously made war on Arthur's father, Utherpendragon. And as if to stress this, the Prose *Perceval* has transferred the place of the final battle in which Mordred will be killed and Arthur mortally wounded from the banks of the river Camlan in Cornwall where it takes place in Geoffrey to an island belonging to a pagan king, Hengist's son, who had given asylum to Mordred.

With the Vulgate Cycle of Arthurian romances where the story of Arthur's death *(La Mort Artu)* is inextricably bound up with that of Lancelot and is preceded by that of the *Queste del Saint Graal* and of the flourishing of Lancelot's love for Guenevere (the so-called *Lancelot* proper), each the work of a separate author, Arthur's fortunes change and with them the conception of the causes underlying the Arthurian tragedy.[19] In the Prose *Perceval* the accomplishment of the Grail Quest had served to heighten Arthur's glory. Not so in the Vulgate Cycle. While the author of the *Lancelot* proper delights in juxtaposing two irreconcilable ideals, that of courtly love and divine love, the author of the *Queste del Saint Graal*, steeped in the theological teachings of St.

Bernard, condemned outright the former and underlined the failure of earthly chivalry on the spiritual plane. Moreover, like Gildas and Geoffrey of Monmouth, he sought to warn his contemporaries of the dire consequences that would befall them if they did not abandon their evil ways. And so he transferred the theme of the British people falling away from righteousness from post-Arthurian times to the days of Arthur, interpreting their future misfortunes as a consequence of their refusal to change their sinful life. Galaad, like Christ, had been sent to show them the way, but apart from the few elect and Lancelot who in the course of the *Queste* had repented of his unlawful love, the majority of Arthur's knights *se sont torné a peor vie et a seculer.*[20] Hence at the end of the Quest, the Grail, the symbol of God and His grace, abandons Arthur and his kingdom[21], making inevitable the civil strife that had been prophesied earlier in a warning vision.[22]

Now in the Vulgate *Mort Artu,* Mordred's rebellion will, as in the earlier versions, be the immediate cause of Arthur's downfall, but the events leading up to it will no longer redound to Arthur's glory. The Roman war is presented as only a secondary cause of Arthur's absence from his kingdom. The real reason is the internal conflict between Arthur's and Lancelot's lineage triggered off by the discovery of Lancelot's adultery, for shortly after his return from the Quest of the Grail he had relapsed into his former sinful existence. The Roman challenge only came while Arthur was already overseas waging war on Lancelot. Nor are Arthur and those of his lineage without responsibility for the strife that tears apart their fellowship and thus enables Mordred's rebellion to succeed. Unlike the author of the Vulgate *Queste,* the writer of the *Mort Artu* did not seek to condemn earthly chivalry on spiritual grounds. The real hero for him is Lancelot and, in order to keep the reader's sympathy for him, he skilfully shifts some of the blame for the dissension, and hence for the final disaster, away from Lancelot onto Arthur.[23] In order to convey the impression that Arthur himself had largely contributed to the situation that forced Lancelot to rescue Guenevere, with its tragic consequence – the death of Gauvain's beloved brother Gaheriet killed unintentionally by Lancelot – , the author of the *Mort Artu* relies in part on a parallel incident in the *Lancelot* proper. There, in the episode of the False Guenevere, Arthur had the genuine Guenevere wrongly condemned to the most severe punishment until Lancelot proved her innocence.[21] By analogy, the author of the *Mort Artu* implies that Arthur in condemning Guenevere to be burnt[25] had again acted wrongly, a fact confirmed when later the Pope, as in the False Guenevere incident, threatens to place Britain under an interdict unless Arthur agrees to take his wife back.[26] Similarly, each time subsequently that there is an opportunity to end the war with Lancelot, Arthur, encouraged by Gauvain, stubbornly prolongs it.[27] And to increase still further the reader's sympathy for Lancelot, the author presents him as torn between his love for Guenevere and his sense of loyalty to Arthur.[28] Malory, as Vinaver has shown, will use this theme of Lancelot's divided allegiance to explain Arthur's downfall; for the Vulgate author, however, it was above all a means of heightening the tension and tarnishing Arthur's role.

News of Mordred's treason will reach Arthur, in the Vulgate as in the earlier versions, after his successful campaign against the Romans.[29] But if the Vulgate underlines the theme of the sudden reversal of Fortune by introducing the symbolism of the Wheel of Fortune, this is not primarily to exculpate Arthur. Rather it is another device to lessen Lancelot's responsibility for the final catastrophe. The latter's indiscretion is now seen only as the ultimate material cause needed for Fortune to turn her wheel and cast Arthur down, for in Lady Fortune's own words; *tel sont li orgueil terrien qu'il n'i a nul si haut assiz qu'il ne le coviegne cheoir de la poesté del monde.*[30]

The doctrine of the Grail and that of the Wheel of Fortune are, of course, mutually exclusive. The Post-Vulgate *Roman du Graal,* which is a *remaniement* of the Vulgate Cycle enriched by material derived from the First Version of the Prose *Tristan,* is a more homogeneous whole than the Vulgate.[31] It centres on Arthur and the fortunes of his kingdom rather than on Lancelot, and here, for the first time, the narrative is endowed with a sense of tragic irony. For in this version Arthur's death is seen as the consequence of his own sin of incest. The Vulgate Cycle had, of course, already introduced the theme of Mordred being both Arthur's nephew and his son. On hearing of Mordred's treason, Arthur had exclaimed in the Vulgate that never did father do unto son what he will do, for he will kill him with his own hands:

Ha! Mordret, or me fez tu connoistre que tu ies li serpenz que ge vi jadis eissir de mon ventre, qui ma terre ardoit et se prenoit a moi. Mes onques peres ne fist autretant de fill comme ge ferai de toi, car je t'ocirrai a mes deus meins, ce sache touz li siecles, ne ja Dex ne vueille que tu muires d'autrui meins que des moies.[32]

In the Vulgate the theme of Mordred's incestuous birth seems, however, mainly to heighten the horror of the final tragedy and to shift the blame yet further away from Lancelot. If there is a vague suggestion that Arthur dies by the hand of Mordred because of his sin of incest, this notion is never developed in the Vulgate. In the last part of the *Lancelot* proper where we learn that Mordred is the son of Arthur and his sister, King Lot's wife, the hermit who tells Mordred of his future role is reprimanding Mordred, not Arthur: the latter's sin is not even mentioned:

Mordret, fet il, dont ne sez tu pour coi je te di que tu es li plus maleureus chevaliers del monde? Je le te dirai. Pour chou que tu feras encore plus de mal que tous lez hommes du monde; quar par toi sera mis a destruction la grant hautesce de la Table Roonde, et par toi morra li

111

plus preudoms que on sache, qui tes peres es. Et tu morras par sa main. Ensi sera mors li peres par le fil et li fils par le pere. Et lors tournera tout a noient tes parentés qui ore est li plus soverains du monde, si te pues moult hair quant tant de prodomme morront par tes mains.[33]

The Post-Vulgate *Roman du Graal,* on the other hand, elaborates the theme and establishes a direct link between Arthur's end and his sin of incest. We are told, in the portion of the narrative dealing with the beginning of Arthur's reign[34], how shortly after Arthur's coronation, Lot's wife, the Queen of Orkney, comes to Arthur's court with her four sons and how Arthur, not knowing that she is his sister, falls in love with her and begets the boy Mordred who is destined to destroy him and his kingdom:

Adont [conut] li freres carneument sa serour et porta la dame chelui qui puissedi le traist a mort et mist a destruction et a martyre la terre, dont vous porrés oïr viers la fin dou livre.[35]

When Lot's wife has returned to her country, Arthur has a terrifying dream foreshadowing his end. This dream is similar to the vision he is said to have had in the Vulgate *Lancelot.*[36] But while the purpose of the reference in the latter is to stigmatise Mordred as the serpent who will devastate Logres, in the Post-Vulgate its function is to underline Arthur's guilt. Merlin, who tells Arthur of the significance of his dream, informs him at the same time of his *grant desloiauté* without sparing his feelings. He calls him *dyables et anemis Jhesucrist*[37] and henceforth the knowledge of his sin pursues Arthur.

Not that Arthur's sin was a deliberate outrage. For tragedy does not exist where, to quote Aristotle, 'worthless men are seen falling from prosperity into misery'. Such a story 'would not arouse either pity or fear: pity is awakened by undeserved misfortune ...', when the 'fall into misery is not due to vice and depravity, but rather to some error'[38], and when, as Vinaver would add, there is a 'sense of human helplessness'.[39] Aware of this, the Post-Vulgate links with the motif of Arthur's tragic error a theme which plays but little part in the Vulgate, that of *aventure et mescheance.*[40] From the outset Arthur and his knights are destined to mischance: they are not just the victims of a universal law – Fortune – as they are in the Vulgate. An atmosphere of gloom hangs over Arthur's realm: the first adventure to take place after his accession to the throne is interpreted by Merlin as a sign of worse to come.[41] Pure accidents unleash catastrophes: Balain's Dolorous Stroke which inaugurated the fearsome adventures of the Grail and destroyed three kingdoms, though described as a 'sin which renews that of Eve our first mother'[42] was not a deliberate outrage, but an unintentional fault, the culmination of a series of mischances which befell the unhappy knight. Arthur's incest likewise was an accident, another example of the *mescheance* that overshadows the land.[43] And Arthur, who in contrast to the King of the Vulgate *Lancelot* never neglects his royal duties[44], could, like Balain, have said: 'Ceste male aventure est plus avenue par male meskeance que par autre chose'.[45]

But although Arthur, like Balain, transgressed unwittingly a divine command, his action is all the same a sin that will have to be expiated. In thus affirming that a sin committed *per ignorantiam* is a sin, our author is following the thought of St. Bernard who, contesting Abelard's assertion that one cannot sin in ignorance[46], reaffirmed the Old Testament teaching that: 'If anyone sins, doing any of the things which the Lord has commanded not to be done, though he does not know it, yet he is guilty and shall bear his iniquity'.[47]

Nothing, henceforth, can prevent the Lord's will from being done. At the beginning all that Arthur himself knows is that a child already conceived but not yet born will cause his death and the destruction of his realm. He attempts to find the child, but his efforts are all in vain, for God Himself has decreed that it shall be so. As Arthur is about to destroy the children born on the day that the 'evil child' is born, he is told in a divine vision that his action will be useless:

> Tu cuides par ceste chose destorner la destruction del roiaume de Logres; mais non feras, car elle averra tout ensi comme li fieus a l'anemi le t'a devisé.[48]

The series of events that will finally culminate in Arthur's fatal battle with Mordred are essentially the same as in the Vulgate.[49] But, anxious to endow Arthur with the stature of a tragic hero and to ensure that he and the fate of his kingdom should arouse 'pity and fear', the Post-Vulgate reverses the process of the Vulgate and shifts the sympathy from Lancelot to Arthur. The latter's own unwitting sin can only catch up with him because he himself is the helpless victim of an internal strife for which he was in no way responsible. The whole emotive theme of the 'conflict between two loyalties' is played down[50] and there is dissension between the knights of Arthur's lineage and those of King Ban, Lancelot's father, long before the death of Gauvain's beloved brothers. It was because Hector on his return from the Quest of the Grail had accused Gauvain of treason for having killed Erec and Palamedes that Arthur's relatives had wanted to make Arthur aware of Lancelot's disloyalty *pour meitre mortel haine entre le roy Artus et le parenté le roy Ban.*[51] In its account of Arthur's siege of Joieuse Garde and then Gaunes, the Post-Vulgate omits many of the details that had served in the Vulgate to exalt Lancelot at the expense of Arthur. Instead of relating the moving scene where Lancelot, attacked by Arthur, had refused to strike back, but rehorsed him and saved his life,[52] the Post-Vulgate author stresses Lancelot's less noble qualities. He underlines, for instance, that Lancelot would never have handed Guenevere back to Arthur had it not been for his fear that people would then have known that what they had heard about him was true.[53]

The sense of tragedy and pity for Arthur is heightened by the fact that just before the news of Mordred's treason Arthur, in conquering the Romans, had succeeded, as in Geoffrey of Monmouth, in forestalling an invasion of his homeland.[54] But above all it is the reappearance of the theme of *mescheance* that justifies the Arthurian tragedy and makes it emotionally convincing.[55] As Arthur journeys from Dover to Salisbury Plain there is no vision of the Wheel of Fortune either to warn him or to comfort him.[56] In the last battle as he fights bravely, he blames neither Fortune nor God for the calamity that has overtaken him. On seeing Mordred strike down Sagremor, Arthur utters in the Vulgate a cry of self-pity.[57] But in the Post-Vulgate his remark stresses the pathos of the death of so many good knights caused by the machinations of one bad man: 'Ah! God, what mischance that a traitor should kill so many good and loyal knights'.[58] And far from watching Mordred's approach with fear as he does in the Vulgate[59], Arthur bravely seeks him out, gives him the first blow[60] and warns him that his treachery has done him no good.[61] Similarly, when the last few survivors of the battle, Arthur, the Bishop of Canterbury, Blioberis, Lucan and Giflet see that none are left to fight and that Salisbury Plain is covered with their dead, they do not as in the Vulgate indulge in a long discourse on their misfortune[62]; they utter but a few words which reveal their deep realisation of the tragedy.[63] But it is Arthur himself who more than anyone is aware of the full extent of the mischance that has befallen them. He leaves the *champ douloureux* in great sorrow, and when the Archbishop attempts to comfort him, telling him that he has had good fortune in that he has remained alive and won this mortal battle, he can but say: 'Ah! if I am alive, what good does it do? ... I can see that I am wounded unto death. Ah! God, what mischance has befallen a great country through the treason of one bad man.'[64]

Aristotle underlines that there can be no tragic error without recognition of one's fault.[65] It is this that heightens the pathos. The Post-Vulgate does not deny Arthur such recognition. When in battle in the Noire Chapelle Arthur accidentally falls backward onto Lucan and crushes him to death[66], he blames Fortune alone in the Vulgate.[67] But in the Post-Vulgate, in a moment of insight, he realises that the misfortune that has overtaken him is a just retribution for the sin he has committed:

Giflet, (he says), I am no longer the King Arthur that they used to call the *rois aventureux* on account of the good fortune he had. He who would now call me by my right name should call me unfortunate and wretched.

Fortune did this to me; she has turned into my stepmother and enemy. And Our Lord whom it pleases that I should spend in grief and sadness what little of my life is left makes me realise that just as He once had the power to raise me through many beautiful adventures without my meriting it, so He now has the power to lower me again through ill adventures that I deserve on account of my sin.[68]

Nor is Arthur's death and the destruction of his once glorious fellowship the last in the series of mischances to befall his realm. Already in Geoffrey of Monmouth Mordred's two sons had, after their father's death, risen against the new ruler of Britain.[69] The Vulgate, anxious to exalt Lancelot to the end, presented him as the saviour of Britain, returning from Gaunes to vanquish in a battle at Winchester Mordred's two sons, who in this version had actually seized the country.[70] The Post-Vulgate keeps this incident[71], but overshadows Lancelot's success by a final tragedy. Echoing the chain of disasters that in Geoffrey of Monmouth's *Historia* overcame post-Arthurian Britain, the Post-Vulgate announced early in Arthur's reign that after his death there will rule such evil kings that the realm of Great Britain which God had so exalted will weep and lament over the good men of the past:

> Et aprés cellui temps regneront les mauvaiz hoirs de pis en pis si que le royaume de la Grant Bretaigne, que Dieu a orendroit si essaulcee, plorera et regretera les preudomes qui a cestui temps regneront. Car alors seront en ceste terre toutes les proesces tournees a neant.[72]

The names of the evil kings are passed over in silence, with the exception of one, King Mark of Cornwall, who had once been Arthur's faithful vassal.[73] But as irony and mischance would have it, Mark's loyalty to Arthur had turned to enmity when Arthur had given refuge to Mark's wife Yseut who together with Tristan had fled to Arthur's domain. During the life-time of Arthur and his knights, Mark had been unable to take revenge: his invasion of the kingdom during the time of the Grail Quest had ended in shame.[74] And so, after Lancelot's death, Mark invaded the country once more, destroying not only Camalot, but also the symbol of Arthur's former glory, the Round Table.[75]

This pessimistic vision is, however, not the last word of the French medieval writers on the Arthurian tragedy. The anonymous writer of the *Perlesvaus*[76], a thirteenth-century prose romance written after the Vulgate though probably before the Post-Vulgate[77], rehabilitates the Arthurian world. Arthur, like the majority of his knights, is *bien creanz en Dieu*[78] and the end of the Grail Quest, far from being a

115

prelude to his downfall, heralds a turn in fortune for the better. This is symbolised by the *reprise* in reverse of the theme of the Wheel of Fortune: the Demoiselle du Char who here signifies Fortune, bald since the day of Perlesvaus' silence, recovers her hair after the reconquest of the Grail Castle[79], signifying that Arthur's kingdom has been redeemed. Not that this means that there will be no wars in the post-Quest Britain of the *Perlesvaus,* but our author, whose aim is not so much to warn his contemporaries against the fatal consequences of personal sin[80] as to encourage them to fight against the external enemies of Christendom[81], deliberately takes an opposing stance to the Vulgate and suggests overtly how a catastrophe could be avoided. Although Lancelot does not repent of his love for Guenevere, he is discreet[82] and so does not cause the dissension which in the Vulgate and Post-Vulgate tears apart Arthur's kingdom. The traitor here is Keu, not Mordred (who is not mentioned), and when the former joins Brien des Isles in an attempt to take over Arthur's kingdom while the latter is away on pilgrimage to the Grail Castle, Lancelot will restore peace and secure Arthur's crown for him.[83] Nor is this all. In the Vulgate, Lancelot, despite his indiscretion, could still have saved Arthur's fellowship if only Arthur had followed Gauvain's advice when he appeared to him in a vision after his death and implored Arthur to ask Lancelot for help before facing Mordred in battle; but Arthur had refused to do so as he felt he had wronged Lancelot too much.[84] In the *Perlesvaus,* in contrast, where for quite different reasons Arthur and Lancelot had at one time become embroiled with each other, Arthur is more conciliatory. When faced with an attack from his old enemy King Claudas, he takes the advice of Lucan and becomes reconciled with Lancelot to the advantage of all.[85] The message of the *Perlesvaus* is no less clear than that of the other versions, but it is one of hope, as befits a work written by a man who, like St. Bernard, evidently deplored strife among Christian barons and sought to divert their energies by encouraging them to fight instead against the Infidels.

The references to Arthur's ultimate fate in some ways reflect the changing conception of his downfall. Geoffrey of Monmouth, eager to glorify Arthur even after the final tragedy, has the wounded monarch transported to the Isle of Avalon *ad sananda vulnera.*[87] The Prose *Perceval* accepts this version, but underlines the British hope of Arthur's eventual return.[88] The Vulgate *Mort Artu,* in contrast, which could not allow Arthur's destiny to detract in any way from that of Lancelot, rejects all possibility of a second coming. Arthur is taken to Avalon, but to no avail: the following day he is brought back and buried by the Noire Chapelle.[89] The Post-Vulgate, on the other hand, seeking to keep Arthur as the central character, stresses that he is the *roi aventureux* about whose end no one shall know the truth. When Giflet has Arthur's tomb opened, he finds nothing there except the helmet Arthur wore in the dolorous battle and he exclaims: 'Ha! dist Girflet, pour nient me travailleray je de enquerir le trespassement de monseigneur le roy Artus. Vraiement, c'est le *Roi Aventureux* dont nul home mortel ne savra la fin. Et tout ainsi qu'il vint au royaume de

Logres par aventure, par aventure s'en est il alé.'[90] The author of the *Perlesvaus,* for his part, wishing perhaps to stress the harmony of Arthur's fellowship, echoes Giraldus Cambrensis's reference to the discovery of the bodies of Arthur and Guenevere in 1191 in Glastonbury[91] and has Arthur buried by the side of his wife and their son Loholt.[92] Finally, Malory, coming at the end of the line, evaluates the possible veracity of all these conflicting references without opting for any of them, preferring to say: *here in thys worlde he chaunged hys lyff.*[93]

NOTES

1. See in particular, E. Vinaver, *Malory* (Oxford: Clarendon Press, 1929), pp. 95-99; *The Tale of the Death of King Arthur by Sir Thomas Malory,* ed. E. Vinaver (Oxford: Clarendon Press, 1955), pp. vii-xxv; *The Works of Sir Thomas Malory,* ed. E. Vinaver, 2nd edition (Oxford: Clarendon Press, 1967), I, pp. xciii-xcix, II, pp. 1615-1663; E. Vinaver, *The Rise of Romance* (Oxford: Clarendon Press, 1971), pp. 123-138; E. Vinaver, "The Shaping Spirit in medieval verse and prose", in *Sewanee Mediaeval Colloquium Occasional Papers* I (1982), pp. 9-18.

2. E. Vinaver, *The Tale of the Death of King Arthur,* p. xiii.

3. E. Vinaver, *The Works of Sir Thomas Malory,* III, 1622. For somewhat modified views of Malory's conception of the Arthurian tragedy, see among others: Winifred L. Guerin, "The Tale of the Death of Arthur: Catastrophe and resolution", in *Malory's Originality. A Critical Study of Le Morte Darthur,* ed. by R.M. Lumiansky (Baltimore: John Hopkins University Press, 1964), pp. 233-274; *The Morte Darthur, Parts Seven and Eight,* edited by D.S. Brewer (London: Edward Arnold, 1968), pp. 23-35; E.T. Pochoda, *Arthurian Propaganda. Le Morte Darthur as an Historical Ideal of Life* (Chapel Hill: The University of North Carolina Press, 1971), pp. 130-140; Mark Lambert, *Malory. Style and Vision in Le Morte Darthur* (New Haven and London: Yale University Press, 1975), pp. 124-221.

4. *Ibid.* p. 1621.

5. *La Mort le Roi Artu,* ed. J. Frappier (Geneva: Droz,1936).

6. Geoffrey of Monmouth, *Historia Regum Britanniae,* ed. Actom Griscom, (London, New York, Toronto: Longmans, Green and Co., 1929); E. Faral, *La Légende Arthurienne,* 3 vols. (Paris: Champion, 1929), III, pp. 64-303.

7. See E. Gilson, *La Philosophie au Moyen Age,* 2 vols. (Paris: Petite Bibliothèque Payot, 1976), pp. 168-172; André Vauchez, *La Spiritualité du Moyen Age* (Paris: Presses Universitaires de France, 1975), pp. 62-65; Robert W. Hanning, *The Vision of History in Early Britain from Gildas to Geoffrey of Monmouth* (New York and London: Columbia University Press, 1966), pp. 1-43. This conception of history goes of course back to the Old Testament (cf. A.M. Dubarle, *Le péché originel dans l'Ecriture* (Paris: Les Editions du Cerf, 1976), pp. 25-31).

8. Gildas, *The Ruin of Britain and other works,* edited and translated by Michael Winterbottom (London and Chichester: Phillimore and Co. Ltd., 1978).

9. *The History of the Kings of Britain,* translated by Lewis Thorpe (London: Penguin Books,1966), p. 280; 'Quo igitur, ut dicere coeperam, languente, discordio afficiuntur Britones et opulentam patriam detestabili discidio destruunt' (*Historia,* ed. Faral in *La Légende arthurienne,* III, p. 299-230 para. 203, lines 1-3).

10. *The History of the Kings of Britain,* trans. L. Thorpe, p. 281; 'Unde miserae reliquiae patriam, factis agminibus, diffugientes transmarinas petebant regiones' (*Historia,* ed. Faral, p. 300, lines 9-10).

11. *The History of the Kings of Britain,* trans. L. Thorpe, p. 282; 'Britannia ergo cunctis civibus, exceptis paucis, ... desolata per .XI. annos' (ed. Faral, III, p. 301, para. 204, lines 4-6).

12. *The History of the Kings of Britain,* trans. Thorpe, p. 281; 'Vae nobis peccatoribus

ob immania scelera nostra, quibus Deum offendere nullatenus diffugimus, dum paenitentiae spatium habebamus. Incumbit ergo illius potestatis ultio ... Ipse verus judex, cum vidisset nos nullatenus a sceleribus nostris cessare velle ... volens corripere stultos, indignationem suam direxit, qua propriam nationem catervatim deserimus.' (*Historia*, ed. Faral, III, p. 300, para. 203, lines 14- 25). In his *Vita Merlini (Life of Merlin: Geoffrey of Monmouth, Vita Merlini,* edited with introduction, facing translation, textual commentary, notes, index and translations of the Lailoken tales by Basil Clarke (Cardiff: University of Wales Press,1973), Geoffrey takes up again this theme. In referring to the disasters that befell post-Arthurian Britain, Merlin comments: 'Indeed, God suffers this disaster to come upon us because of our crimes, as a punishment for our folly.' (Lines 951-2: Nempe Deus nobis ut corrigat insipientes has patitur clades ob crimina nostra venire). Wace, on the other hand, who adapted Geoffrey's *Historia* into French (*Le Roman de Brut de Wace,* ed. Ivor Arnold, Société des Anciens Textes Français: Paris, 2 vols, 1938-1940) interprets Britain's misfortune as *mesaventure* (14673) and deliberately omits Cadwallader's parting words (14700).

13. *The History of the Kings of Britain,* trans. Thorpe, p. 234. 'En vaticinia Sibillae, quae veris testantur, ex britannico genere tertio nasciturum qui romanum obtinebit imperium' (*Historia,* ed. Faral, III, p. 251, para. 160 lines 18-20).

14. Referred to also as the *Didot Perceval* and published under this title by Roach (*The Didot Perceval according to the Manuscripts of Modena and Paris,* ed. William Roach (Philadelphia: University of Pennsylvania Press, 1941).

15. Robert de Borron is the first writer to have combined the Grail-Arthur themes. Of his work only the first part, the *Joseph* or *Le Roman de l'Estoire dou Graal,* and 502 lines of the second part, the *Merlin,* have been preserved in their original verse form in a unique late 13th century ms., B.N. fr. 20047. But both the *Joseph* and the *Merlin* were subsequently translated into prose. Robert's *Merlin* breaks off with Arthur's coronation, but in two of the manuscripts containing the prose *Joseph-Merlin* the work is completed by a prose *Perceval* which ends with an account of Arthur's death. On this Arthuriad see my chapter on "La trilogie de Robert de Boron: le *Perceval en prose*" in *Grundriss der Romanischen Literaturen des Mittelalters,* edited by Hans Robert Jauss and Erich Köhler (Heidelberg: Carl Winter, 1978), IV, pp. 513-535.

16. *Didot-Perceval,* ed. Roach, ms. *E,* 2386-2388; ms. *D,* 1779-1780.

17. *Didot-Perceval,* ed. Roach, ms. *D,* 1879.

18. *Historia Regum Britanniae,* ed. Faral, III, p. 275, para. 177, lines 22-24.

19. The whole of the Vulgate Cycle was edited by H.O. Sommer under the title *The Vulgate Version of the Arthurian Romances* (Washington: Carnegie Institute of Washington, 1908-1916); I, *L'Estoire del Saint Graal;* II, *L'Estoire de Merlin;* III, IV, V, *Le Livre de Lancelot del Lac;* VI, *Les Aventures ou la Queste del Saint Graal and La Mort le Roi Artu;* VII, Supplement: *Le Livre d'Artus;* VIII, *Index of Names and Places.* The *Lancelot* proper, the *Queste* and the *Mort Artu* have also been edited separately: *Lancelot, roman en prose du XIIIe siècle,* ed. Alexandre Micha, (T.L.F.: Paris, Genève, 1978-1982), 8 vols.; *Lancelot do Lac. The Non-Cyclic Old French prose* Lancelot, ed. Elspeth Kennedy (Oxford: Clarendon Press, 1980), 2 vols.; *La Queste del Saint Graal,* ed. A. Pauphilet (C.F.M.A.: Paris, 1923, 1949); *La Mort le Roi Artu,* ed. J. Frappier (Paris: Droz, 1936; revised edition, T.L.F., Genève: Droz, 1954). On the Vulgate Cycle, see J. Frappier, "Le Cycle de la Vulgate", in *Grundriss* IV, 536-589. F. Lot's view in *Etude sur le Lancelot en prose* (Paris: Champion, 1918), that the whole cycle, with the possible exception of the *Estoire de Merlin,* is the work of a single author, is no longer acceptable. It is now recognized that the cycle grew up in stages (the last three branches being written first) and that each of the branches is the work of an individual writer.

20. *Queste.* ed. Pauphilet, p. 271.8-9.

21. *Op. cit.,* p. 271.10-11 and pp. 274.28-275.4: 'Et en la maniere que je vos ai devisee perdirent cil del roiaume de Logres *par lor pechié* le Saint Graal ... Et tot autresi come Nostre Sires l'avoit envoié a Galaad et a Joseph et aus autres oirs qui d'ax estoient descenduz, par lor bonté, tot autresi en devesti il les malvés oirs par la malvestié et par la noienté qu'il trova en ax ...'

22. In a warning vision vouchsafed to Gauvain the reader learns of the *estrif* that will arise among Arthur's knights after their return from the quest of the Grail

(see *Queste,* ed. Pauphilet, p. 149.28-29).

23. Already in the *Lancelot* proper, the author, anxious to avoid presenting Lancelot's adultery as odious, had tarnished Arthur's role.

24. *Vulgate Version,* ed. Sommer, IV, 56-66; *Lancelot,* ed. Kennedy, I, 601-606.

25. *Mort Artu,* ed. Frappier, para. 93.

26. *Op. cit.,* para. 117. In the prose *Lancelot,* the Pope actually laid an interdict on Britain (*Vulgate Version* IV, 73). There is no reference to the Pope's intervention in the Non-Cyclic *Lancelot* which denigrates Arthur somewhat less than the Cyclic Version. In the former, as soon as Lancelot has proven the genuine Guenevere's innocence, the False Guenevere is condemned to death and Arthur takes his wife back (ed. Kennedy, I, 606-608). In the Cyclic Version, however, Arthur not only remains with the False Guenevere after his wife's innocence had been established, but accedes to the False Guenevere's request that the other Guenevere be exiled. And despite the Pope's interdict Arthur persists in his folly until the False Guenevere and her accomplice, both struck by a fatal paralysis, confess their deceit (IV, 73-83).

27. Thus, during the siege of Joieuse Garde, Gauvain urges Arthur to refuse Lancelot's generous terms for peace (ed. Frappier, 1936, paras. 109-110; especially para. 110, p. 117, lines 6-12). Similarly, after Guenevere has been restored to Arthur, Gauvain is determined to continue the war (see para. 119, p. 134.12-17; para. 127, p. 140.19- 141.1), a sentiment with which Arthur readily concurs ('mes il dist que, se la roine revenoit, que ja por ce la guerre ne remeindra entre li et Lancelot, puis qu'il l'avoit emprise' para. 117, p. 129.15-16).

28. For instance, when Arthur besieges Joieuse Garde, Lancelot is grieved not because he is afraid for himself, but because he loves Arthur: 'Quant Lancelos voit que li chastiax estoit assis en tel maniere del roi Artu et de *l'ome del monde qu'il avoit plus amé* et or le connoist a son ennemi mortel, si est tant dolenz qu'il ne set que fere, non mie por ce qu'il ait poor de soi, *mes por ce qu'il amoit le roi.*' (para. 109, p. 115.26-30).

29. Ed. Frappier, 1936, para. 163. In Geoffrey, Wace and the Prose *Perceval,* Guenevere had been Mordred's willing accomplice, but in the Vulgate she refuses Mordred's love and it is she who here sends to Arthur the messenger with the news of Mordred's treason.

30. Ed. Frappier, 1936, para. 176, p. 201.2-3.

31. The Post-Vulgate *Roman du Graal,* which has not come down to us in its complete form in any single manuscript, but has to be reconstructed from various fragments, consisted of: (1) an *Estoire del Saint Graal* similar to that of the Vulgate; (2) the prose rendering of Robert de Borron's *Merlin* followed by a series of incidents dealing with the early years of Arthur's reign known as the Post-Vulgate *Suite du Merlin;* (3) a *Queste del Saint Graal* and a *Mort Artu* both based on the Vulgate but remodelled.

The greater part of the *Suite du Merlin* has been preserved in ms. Brit. Mus. Add. 38117 (edited by G. Paris under the title of *Merlin, roman en prose du XIIIe siècle,* S.A.T.F., 2 vols., 1886) and Cambridge University Library ms. 7071 first identified by Professor Vinaver in 1945. A smaller fragment of the *Suite,* part of which overlaps with the end of the London and Cambridge mss., was found by E. Wechssler in ms. B.N. fr. 112 (ed. by H.O. Sommer under the title of *Die Abenteuer Gawains, Ywains und Le Morholts mit den drei Jungfrauen ..., Beihefte zur Zeitschrift für Romanische Literatur* XLVII, 1913). Finally, another portion of the *Suite* which largely fills the gap between the end of the fragment published by Sommer and the beginning of the *Queste* was identified by myself in mss. B.N. fr. 112 and 12599 (*La Folie Lancelot, a hitherto unidentified portion of the Suite du Merlin,* ed. F. Bogdanow, *Beihefte zur Zeitschrift für Romanische Philologie* CIX, 1965).

As for the Post-Vulgate *Queste* and *Mort Artu,* portions of these are found in mss. B.N. fr. 112, 343, 340, Bodmer 105 and a large number of manuscripts of the prose *Tristan.* I am at present completing a critical edition of the Post-Vulgate *Queste-Mort Artu* for the S.A.T.F.

In addition to these French mss., there also exists a Spanish translation of the *Suite du Merlin,* as well as Spanish and Portuguese translations of the Post-Vulgate *Queste-Mort Artu.* For more details, see F. Bogdanow, *The Romance of the Grail* (Manchester: Manchester University Press, 1966). (*Cf.* also note 49.)

32. Ed. Frappier, 1936, para. 164, p. 185.12-17.

33. *Vulgate Version,* V, 284.11-18.

34. Namely, the Post-Vulgate *Suite du Merlin* (ed. G. Paris). (cf. note 31.)

35. *Merlin, roman en prose du XIII siècle,* ed. G. Paris (S.A.T.F.: Paris, 1886), I, 147-8.

36. This vision, referred to by Arthur when he heard the news of Mordred's treason (ed. Frappier, 1936, para. 164, p. 185.12-17), is first mentioned in the *Lancelot* proper (V, 284.25-30) at the point where the hermit blames Mordred for the ill he will do.

37. *Merlin,* ed. G. Paris, I, 154. In the *Lancelot,* significantly, the hermit tells Mordred, *not* Arthur, the significance of the dream. He explains that Mordred, a man without pity, is the serpent: 'Et ses tu qui li serpens est? Ce es tu. Tu es vraiement serpens, quar tu es homs sans pitié et sans deboinaireté. Et tout ensi [com li serpens est douz el commmencement de son voler tout aussi] est il de toi, quar tu n'as mie esté el commencement de ta chevalerie trop fel ne trop crueuls, ains as esté deboinaires et piteus. Mais dez ore mais en avant seras tu drois serpens, et ne feras se mal non, et ocirras hommes a ton pooir. Et que diroie jou? Tu feras plus de mal en .i. jor que tous tes parentés ne face de bien en sa vie ...' (V, 284.33-40).

38. Aristotle, *On the Art of Poetry,* translated with an Introduction by T.S. Dorsch (London: Penguin Books, 1965), chapter 13.

39. *Le Roman de Balain,* edited by M. Dominica Legge with an Introduction by Eugène Vinaver (Manchester: Manchester University Press, 1942), p.XXIX.

40. There are, of course, references to *mescheance* in the Vulgate *Mort Artu,* but their significance is not the same as in the Post-Vulgate.

41. 'Che est la premiere aventure qui est a ta court avenue, si me poise moult que li commenchemens en est teuls, car li signes en est malvais et anieus.' (*Merlin,* ed. G Paris, I, 175).

42. 'Si m'est avis que nous avons recouvré en toi Evain notre mere' (*Merlin,* ed. G. Paris, I, 231).

43. The author stresses that Arthur could in no way have known of the Queen of Orkney's true identity, for he was totally ignorant of his sister's existence. Replying to Merlin's accusation, Arthur says: 'Anemis drois, de chou dont tu m'acuses ne pues tu estre certains, se tu ne ses vraiement que j'aie serour; mais che ne pues tu savoir ne tu ni autres, *quant jou meismes ne le sai.* Ne nus, che me samble, ne puet estre certains de ceste chose plus comme moi; *mais je n'en sai riens.*' (*Merlin,* ed. G. Paris, I, 154).

44. In the Vulgate *Lancelot* a friar reprimands Arthur as *li plus viex pechieres de tous autres pecheors* for having failed in his feudal duties, especially towards Lancelot's father, King Ban (see *Vulgate Version,* III, 215.37, 216.13-14).

45. *Merlin,* ed. G. Paris, II, 42.

46. In his *Traité du Baptême* (chapter IV), St. Bernard says: 'Il est probable que cet homme, qui soutient qu'il n'y a point de péché d'ignorance, ne prie jamais Dieu de lui pardonner ces sortes de péchés, et se rit du Prophète, quand il lui entend dire: ''Ne vous souvenez pas, Seigneur, des fautes de ma jeunesse ni de mes péchés d'ignorance (Psal. XXIV, 7)!'' ... 'Tous ces passages ne montrent-ils pas dans quelle ignorance grossière se trouve celui qui ne sait pas qu'on peut pécher par ignorance?' (*Oeuvres complètes de Saint Bernard* trad. par Charpentier, (Paris: Librairie de Louis Vivès, 1866, vol. 2, p. 546-547); *Patrologia Latina,* 182, 1041-42: 'Is forsitan qui asserit non posse peccari per ignorantiam, nunquam pro suis ignorantiis deprecatur, sed potius prophetam irrideat deprecantem et dicentem: *Delicta juventutis meae, et ignorantias meas ne memineris* (Psal. XXIV, 7) .... Numquid no ex his satis apparet, in quantis jacet ignorantiae tenebris, qui ignorat peccari posse interdum per ignorantiam'?

47. *Leviticus,* 5. 17. I am indebted to my colleague Dr. A.R.W.James for drawing my attention to the Old Testament references. On the conception of sin in the Bible, see David Daube, *Sin, Ignorance and Forgiveness in the Bible* (Claude Montefiore Lecture, 1960, The Liberal Jewish Synagogue, London); Stanislas Lyonnet and Léopold Sabourin, *Sin, Redemption and Sacrifice, a Biblical and Patristic Study* (Rome: Biblical Institute Press,1970).

48. *Merlin.* ed. G. Paris, I, 208.

49. The greater part of the Post-Vulgate *Mort Artu* has only survived in Spanish and

Portuguese translations; only two fragments of the French redaction have so far come to light, one in ms. B.N.fr. 340 and the other in Bodmer 105 (of which I am preparing a study). Except for one short fragment contained in ms. 1877 of Salamanca University Library, the Spanish rendering is known only from two early printed editions, Toledo 1515 and Sevilla 1535. The latter has been reprinted by Bonilla y San Martin: *La Demanda del Sancto Grial* (Nueva Biblioteca de Autores Espanoles, 6, Madrid, 1907). The Salamanca fragment was published by Karl Pietsch (*Spanish Grail Fragments*, The Modern Philology Monographs: The University of Chicago Press, 1924-25, 2 vols.). The Portuguese *Demanda*, preserved in a unique 15th century manuscript (no. 2594 of the Vienna National Library) has been published by A. Magne (*A Demanda do Santo Graal*, Rio de Janeiro, 1944, 3 vols.; 2nd revised edition, I, 1955, II, 1970). My paragraph references will be those of Magne's edition, but all my quotations from the Portuguese are based directly on the Vienna manuscript. For the relationship of the Hispanic texts, see F. Bogdanow, "An attempt to classify the extant texts of the Spanish *Demanda del Sancto Grial*": *Studies in Honour of Tatania Fotich* (Washington: The Catholic University Press of America, 1972), pp. 213-226 and F. Bogdanow, "The relationship of the Portuguese and Spanish *Demandas* to the extant French manuscripts of the Post-Vulgate *Queste del Saint Graal*", *Bulletin of Hispanic Studies* LII (1975), pp. 13-32.

50. But *not* altogether omitted.
51. Ms.B.N. fr. 772, f. 418a-b. Cf. Portuguese *Demanda,* para. 625.
52. *Mort le Roi Artu,* ed. Frappier, 1936, para. 115, p. 127.12 para. 116, p. 128.13. For the shortened Post-Vulgate account, see *Demanda,* para. 656.
53. 'E sabede verdadeyramente que Lancaloc nom lha dera, se nom fosse que entendiriam as gentes que era verdade o que diziam.' (Ms. 2594, f. 192c; Magne, para. 656.)
54. 'Ca lhi diserom que o enperador de Roma era en Bretanha com muy gram gente e queria filhar Gaula, e pois passar ao reyno de Logres e conquero-lo.' (Ms. 2594, f. 192d; Magne, para. 660.)
55. During the *Queste* section the gloom hanging over Britain had been lifted for a brief period.
56. *Mort le Roi Artu,* ed. Frappier (1936), para. 176, p. 200.20-201.8; *cf.* Portuguese *Demanda,* para. 663.
57. *Mort le Roi Artu,* ed. Frappier (1936), para. 190, p. 219.22-23: 'Ha! Dex, por quoi me lessiez vos tant abessier de proesce terriene...?'
58. 'Ay, Deus, camanha ma andança do traedor, matar os boos cavaleyros e os leaes!' (f. 193c; Magne, para. 666).
59. 'Ceste parole dist li rois Artus moult esmaiez' (*Mort le Roi Artu,* ed. Frappier (1936), para. 187, p. 215.7).
60. *Demanda,* para. 665. In the Vulgate, Mordret strikes Arthur first (*Mort le Roi Artu,* ed. Frappier (1936), para. 188,p. 216.6-7).
61. *Demanda,* para. 665.
62. *Mort le Roi Artu,* ed. Frappier (1936), para. 191, p. 220.17-221.7.
63. 'Diserom antre sy chorando: "Ay, Deus! Como aqui a gram dano e gram perda! Ay, Deus! que nos poderiades chus mal fazer? Ca nos veemos aqui todo [o] mundo jazer morto a marteyro e a door!"' (f. 193d; Magne, para. 667).
64. '"Ay! dise el rey, se eu escapey vivo, que prol me vem? Ca mia vida nom e nada, ca eu bem vejo que soo chagado aa morte. Ay, Deus! que foy fatal viir tam maa andança a hua gram terra, per traycom d'uu mao homem."' (f. 193d; Magne, para. 668.) The first part of this remark may have its origin in the Vulgate (*Mort le Roi Artu,* para. 191, p. 221.10-11), but the second belongs to the Post-Vulgate.
65. Aristotle, *On the Art of Poetry,* chapters 11 and 16.
66. *Demanda,* para. 671. According to most of the manuscripts of the Vulgate *Mort Artu* Lucan dies because Arthur embraces him too tightly (see ed. Frappier, para. 192, p. 222.9-13), but two of the manuscripts give the same version of Lucan's death as the Post-Vulgate.
67. See *Mort le Roi Artu,* ed. Frappier (1936), para. 192, pp. 222.20-221.1.
68. 'Giflet, eu nom soo rey Artur, o que soyam chamar rey aventuroso polas boas andanças que avia. Mas quem m'agora chamar per meu direyto nome, chamar-m'a mal aventurado e mizquinho. Esto me ffez ventura, que xi me tornou

121

madrasta e enmiga. E Nosso Senhor, que praz que vi[v]a en doo e en tristeza este pouco que ey de viver, e bem mo mostra: que asi como el quis e foy poderoso de me erguer per muy fremossas aventuras e sen meu merecimento, bem assi e poderoso de me dirribar per aventuras feas e mas, per meu mericimento e per meu pecado.' (f. 194b; Magne, para. 672).

69. Geoffrey of Monmouth, *The History of the Kings of Britain,* trans. L. Thorpe, p. 262.
70. *Mort le Roi Artu,* ed. Frappier (1936), para. 197-198. In Geoffrey, it is Arthur's successor, Constantine, who kills Mordred's two sons.
71. *Demanda,* para. 690-692.
72. *Die Abenteuer Gawains, Ywains und Le Morholts* ..., Ed. H.O. Sommer, *Beihefte zur Zeitschrift für Romanische Philologie,* 47 (Halle, 1913), p. 63.
73. See *Merlin,* ed. G. Paris, I, 230.
74. This incident is related in the Post-Vulgate *Queste* (ms. B.N. fr. 343, ff. 61a-72c; *Demanda,* para. 445-484).
75. F. Bogdanow, *Romance of the Grail,* pp. 264-270.
76. *Perlesvaus,* ed. William A. Nitze and T. Atkinson Jenkins (1932; reprinted New York: Phaeton Press, 1972), 2 vols.
77. On the date of the *Perlesvaus,* see my chapter in the *Grundriss der Romanischen Literaturen des Mittelalters,* ed. Reinhold R. Grimm (Heidelberg: Carl Winter, 1983), vol. IV/2.
78. *Perlesvaus,* ed. Nitze, line 63. Cf. lines 6628-6630, where the author, speaking of Arthur's knights, says: 'li plusor estoient bon chevalier. Ce n'estoit mie solement ferir; ainz estoient bien loial e verai, e croioient fermement en Deu e en sa doce mere ...'
79. *Perlesvaus,* ed. Nitze, lines 9946-7.
80. Not that the *Perlesvaus* in any way condones sin. He firmly condemns *luxure* and Lancelot, because of this sin, will not see the Grail (see lines 3749-3753).
81. The *Perlesvaus* is influenced no less than the Vulgate *Queste* by the teachings of St. Bernard, but while the Vulgate concretises above all the tenets of St. Bernard's contemplative theology, the *Perlesvaus* largely reflects St. Bernard's crusading ideology (for details, see my chapter on the *Perlesvaus* in the *Grundriss,* IV, 2).
82. Cf. *Perlesvaus,* ed. Nitze, lines 7602-7605.
83. *Perlesvaus,* ed. Nitze, lines 7107-7174, 7634-7749.
84. *Mort le Roi Artu,* ed. Frappier (1936), para. 176, p. 199.26-p. 200.6.
85. *Perlesvaus,* ed. Nitze, lines 8554-8660, 9429-9536.
86. Geoffrey, *Historia,* ed. E. Faral (in the latter's *Légende Arthurienne,* Champion, Paris, 1929, III, 278.57). Geoffrey develops the theme of Arthur's eventual return to health in his *Vita Merlini.* We are told that 'Morgan put the king in her chamber on a golden bed, uncovered his wound with her noble hand and looked long at it. At length she said he could be cured if only he stayed with her a long while and accepted her treatment.' (Ed. and trans. Basil Clarke, University of Wales Press, 1973, lines 934-938).
87. *Historia,* ed. Faral in *La Légende arthurienne,* III, p. 278, line 57.
88. *Didot-Perceval,* ed. Roach, ms. E, lines 2644-2652. Cf. F. Bogdanow, "La trilogie de Robert de Boron: le *Perceval* en prose" in *Grundriss,* IV/1, p. 531 including note IIIa.
89. *Mort le Roi Artu,* ed. Frappier (1936), para. 193, p. 225.20 para. 194, p. 227-14.
90. Bodmer ms. 105, f. 325a. Cf. *Demanda,* ed. Magne para. 683. The first writer to refer to Arthur's death as being *dutuse* is Wace (see *Brut,* ed. I. Arnold, S.A.T.F., 1938-40, lines 13285-90).
91. On Giraldus Cambrensis's reference, see E.K. Chambers, *Arthur of Britain* (London: Sidgwick and Jackson, 1927; reprinted 1966), pp. 112-114.
92. *Perlesvaus,* ed. Nitze, lines 7596-7600; 10189-10191. The *Perlesvaus* places the tombs in the *Isle d'Avalon* which, to judge from the description, was identical in the author's mind with Glastonbury (see *Perlesvaus,* ed. Nitze, II, 45-72).
93. *The Works,* ed. Vinaver, 1242. For the particular account of Arthur's ultimate fate in Grays Inn MS7 and its relationship to the other version, see Richard Barber, "The *Vera Historia de Morte Arthuri* and its place in Arthurian tradition", *Arthurian Literature* I (Brewer, Rowman and Littlefield: 1981), pp. 62-78, and Michael Lapidge, "An edition of the *Vera Historia de Morte Arthuri*", *Arthurian Literature* I, 79-93.

RESUME

Si Geoffroi de Monmouth le premier, au douzième siècle, a établi dans ses grandes lignes l'histoire de la mort du roi Arthur – l'absence, malencontreuse mais inéluctable, du roi, parti en guerre contre les Romains; la trahison de Mordret; l'ultime catastrophe, toutes choses dont la Fortune a été pour lui responsable – ce sont d'autres auteurs qui, au cours des siècles, ont su remanier et réinterpréter ce peu de faits, pour en faire surtout dans la post-Vulgate et chez Malory une véritable tragédie. Pour l'auteur du *Perceval* en prose (treizième siècle), la responsabilité de la mort du roi et de la disparition de son royaume chevaleresque incombe à la méchanceté de deux hommes: d'une part Mordret, dont le caractère est systématiquement noirci par l'auteur anonyme, et d'autre part l'empereur de Rome, ici allié aux païens et partant devenu ennemi de Dieu. Dans la *Vulgate* apparaît pour la première fois le récit de la conception incestueuse de Mordred, mais ce n'est pas ce péché qui, dans le grand cycle du *Lancelot-Graal,* fournit le moteur de la tragédie; la catastrophe finale naît de l'échec chevaleresque et moral de la Table Ronde. La glorieuse aventure du Saint-Graal achevée, la Table Ronde se reconstitue et retombe fatalement dans un monde séculier où le conflit tragique entre le roi et Lancelot amènera la mort d'un monarque lequel, par son désir de vengeance, aura été pour une large part lui-même responsable de sa mort et de celles des chevaliers de sa cour.

L'auteur de la post-Vulgate, et après lui Malory, ont choisi plutôt de souligner un péché que la Vulgate a peu exploité: le fait que Mordret est le fils incestueux du roi Arthur lui-même. Pour eux, en effet, le royaume d'Arthur est, presque dès ses débuts, soumis aux coups de la *mescheance;* par une ironie tragique, ce sera une faute commise dans sa jeunesse et en toute innocence par le roi lui-même qui entraînera plus tard la punition divine: la destruction de la Grande-Bretagne, la disparition du monde chevaleresque, la mort du malheureux père.

Une seule exception à cette manière de voir le rôle d'Arthur: le *Roman de Perlesvaus.* Là, en effet, il n'est jamais question de Mordret: le traître est Keu, dont les machinations seront déjouées précisément par Lancelot dont l'amour pour Guenièvre n'aura pas ici soulevé de conflit avec Arthur. Le royaume chevaleresque évitera ainsi la catastrophe, et saura réserver ses énergies pour un devoir supérieur et suprême: la lutte contre le monde païen.

DU BERCEAU A LA BIERE : LOUIS DE MALE DANS LE DEUXIEME LIVRE DES *CHRONIQUES* DE FROISSART

★

Peter Ainsworth

Qu'on accorde aux *Chroniques* de Froissart le titre de littérature ou non, les critiques sont généralement d'accord pour reconnaître au chroniqueur de Valenciennes le droit au nom d'écrivain. Or, Froissart n'a bénéficié jusqu'à présent d'aucune étude en profondeur de la valeur proprement littéraire de son oeuvre en prose.[1] On parle de ses dons de romancier, de journaliste; on explore tel ou tel aspect de son style mais, malgré la parution récente de plusieurs articles de fort bonne qualité[2], aucune tentative moderne n'a été faite pour tirer au clair la spécificité littéraire de l'ensemble des *Chroniques*. La dernière grande étude d'ensemble date des années trente[3], mais les pages consacrées par F.S. Shears au mérite littéraire de l'oeuvre en prose sont relative-ment peu détaillées, quoique suggestives. Sans prétendre qu'il soit possible de combler cette lacune, nous voudrions offrir au lecteur, dans les pages qui vont suivre, un examen assez poussé de quelques aspects proprement littéraires de cette riche *textualité* en évolution que sont les *Chroniques* : "dédoublement" des discours du texte (concurrence, à ce niveau, entre le récit et sa glose); motivation romanesque de cer-tains "effets de réel"; émergence, enfin, d'un texte *de connotation*[4], plus "spatial" que linéaire.

Les épisodes que nous nous proposons d'examiner ont été quelque peu négligés par les critiques littéraires des *Chroniques*: il s'agit d'événements survenus avant et après la bataille du Beverhoutsveld (3 mai 1382). Dans un article récent, J. van Herwaarden[5] nous présente une vue d'ensemble fort bien documentée de l'histoire des guerres entre les Gantois et leur seigneur, Louis de Mâle, comte de Flandre (1346-1384) qui succéda à son père Louis de Nevers, tué à Crécy. Le savant néerlandais nous signale fort à propos la très grande valeur historique des parties du Deuxième livre des *Chroniques* con-sacrées aux affaires de Flandre[6]: oeuvre de maturité qui offre au lecteur des aperçus intelligents et perspicaces sur les causes et consé-quences de ces différends.[7]

Froissart semble avoir très bien compris le danger représenté par les querelles privées entre familles (affaire de Jan Hyoens et Gijsbrecht Mayhuus, par exemple) dans une société urbaine dominée par des intérêts de clan et par l'influence des divers métiers. Il a vu aussi que cette société, surtout à Gand, n'était pas homogène, qu'elle était composée de plusieurs couches imbriquées, dont la plus importante, à ses yeux, était la *poorterie* (l'ensemble des bourgeois les plus riches).[8] Celle-ci, estime Froissart, aurait dû se déclarer solidaire de la politique comitale, au lieu de s'éclipser lâchement devant une série de démagogues présomptueux.[9] S'il exagère un peu la défaillance morale de la *poorterie* (la révolte de Gand fut dirigée par une coalition changeante réunissant *poorterie*, tisserands, et représentants des *menus mestiers*), Froissart a raison, selon van Herwaarden, de relever l'importance du Franc de Bruges, dont les représentants (d'une société plus agraire qu'urbaine) soutenaient le plus souvent les intérêts du comte contre ceux des villes.[10]

Les affaires de Flandre devaient toucher de près le chroniqueur de Valenciennes: clerc issu de la bourgeoisie hennuyère, Froissart contemple les événements de 1379-1382 avec un mélange d'horreur et de fascination.[11] Avant de nous raconter la journée de Roosebeke, il nous rappelle que les Maillotins de Paris, mais aussi tous les *villain* de France et de Normandie, n'attendaient que la défaite de la chevalerie française pour déferler comme une vague sur les *gentils* de leurs pays.[12] Froissart craint donc de voir sombrer l'ordre du monde, et J. van Herwaarden observe avec justesse que pour le chroniqueur, la bonne société, c'est un pays gouverné par un prince sage et juste qui veille sur la paix interne de son domaine (mais qui combattra toujours pour défendre ses intérêts légitimes) et qui bénéficie de l'appui de ses sujets, barons, prélats et hommes des bonnes villes. Contrat social basé sur l'aide *réciproque* des Ordres établis par Dieu, cette conception toute féodale de la société présuppose le respect du seigneur naturel, et exclut – chez celui-ci, mais aussi chez ses sujets – l'orgueil et la présomption.[13]

Or, si d'une part Froissart enregistre fort clairement sa désapprobation de l'orgueil des Gantois et de la présomption de leur capitaine, Philippe d'Artevelde[14], il est tout aussi clair d'autre part qu'il reconnaît le courage des rebelles.[15] Le chroniqueur mettra dans la bouche de Louis de Flandre lui-même les propos suivants, prononcés juste avant la bataille du Beverhoutsveld:

> 'Nous irons combatre ces mesceans gens; encore sont il vaillant, disoit li contes: il ont plus chier à morir par espée que par famine.'[16]

Nous avons vu déjà que Froissart ne craint pas de reprocher à la *poorterie* leur manque de probité morale et politique. Le comte, au contraire, paraît échapper à tout reproche de sa part, et van Herwaarden

126

estime que, pour Froissart, le blâme (en ce qui concerne l'insurrection) revient entièrement aux habitants de Gand, à leurs capitaines et alliés. Pour notre part, nous croyons qu'il faut être plus prudent à l'égard des sentiments du chroniqueur concernant la responsabilité morale de Louis de Flandre.

C'est dans le récit des journées précédant la bataille du Beverhoutsveld, et dans la suite de celui-ci, que nous croyons déceler les traces d'une attitude plus complexe, plus critique aussi peut-être, envers le rôle tenu par le comte Louis dans la genèse du conflit. L'attitude dont nous parlons ne s'exprime pas catégoriquement, pourtant. Bien au contraire, nous verrons que le texte de ces pages s'accompagne d'une *glose*, dont les éléments constitutifs, pour être disséminés, éparpillés dans la narration (et cela, à deux niveaux bien distincts – mais coordonnés – du texte), n'en sont pas moins cohérents. Bref, la narration de ces événements paraît *dire plus qu'elle ne dit*; elle sécrète un surplus de sens, et de ce point de vue-là elle se comporte comme un récit plus romanesque qu'historique. L'essence même de ce surplus de sens n'est pas tout simplement d'ordre didactique et moralisateur, cependant.

Il s'agit, au départ, d'une juxtaposition de discours concurrents ou même complémentaires. Nous allons voir qu'une glose biblique (débitée "franchement", c'est-à-dire en guise d'*exemplum* déclaré, par d'Artevelde, ou rapportée : prédication des Frères dans la ville de Gand avant le recours aux armes par les Gantois) vient commenter, en un premier temps, l'énonciation de la situation politique. Celle-ci, à son tour, se trouve consignée dans les propos de d'Artevelde et des Frères, donnés – respectivement – en style direct et indirect. Jusqu'ici, la glose fournit donc une *interprétation* des événements prise en charge par les dirigeants des Gantois. Froissart, en revanche, s'abstient de tout commentaire: il se contente de reproduire la glose didactique et moralisatrice à l'intérieur d'un récit assez neutre.

Le "surplus de sens" dont nous avons parlé émerge peu à peu en un deuxième temps, fruit d'un *glissement* opéré dans le texte, par lequel certains éléments de la glose biblique "envahissent" le récit[17]: le texte ainsi tissé, mélange d'éléments exégétiques et de narration, relevé parfois par des bribes de discours coloriés, eux aussi, par des renvois en sourdine à tel ou tel texte emprunté aux Saintes Ecritures, consiste désormais en une espèce d'"'aparté''soutenu et *virtuellement* ironique[18] qui fournit un contrepoint sourd et trouble à la narration "additive" des faits sur laquelle il vient se greffer.

Le deuxième épisode que nous nous proposons d'analyser – séjour du comte de Flandre dans l'humble demeure d'une femme de Bruges, après la défaite du Beverhoutsveld – se développe d'une façon analogue, tout en enrichissant le dispositif textuel que nous venons d'évoquer par l'adjonction du niveau de la description (rudimentaire, mais description tout de même). Nous trouverons, cette fois-ci, que ce sont les objets décrits (ou plutôt privilégiés) qui semblent porter un surplus de sens. A mesure qu'on parcourt ces textes, cependant, la perception des éléments et de leurs relations possibles – interférences aux niveaux du récit, du discours et de la description – semble permettre au lecteur d'amorcer un mouvement d'*intégration*[19] qui finira par constituer une *isotopie*[20] sémantique et, croyons-nous, littéraire. En un mot, le texte cesse de *parler de ce dont il parle*, pour *parler de ce dont il ne parle pas*.[21]

(i)　　*Sermons et paraboles: l'Exode et l'Evangile*

Au tournant de 1379-80, Louis de Mâle avait essayé d'apaiser les Gantois, et de les faire rentrer dans l'ordre, en les haranguant d'une fenêtre qui dominait la place du marché de leur ville:

> (...) là leur remonstra il comment un sires devoit estre amés, cremus, servis et honnerés de ses gens; là remonstra il comment il avoient fait tout le contraire; là remonstra il comment il les avoit tenus, gardés et deffendus contre tout homme; là leur remonstra il comment il les avoit tenus en paix et en pourfit et en toutes prosperités (etc.).[22]

Deux ans plus tard, cependant, la situation n'a fait qu'empirer: les tentatives de réconciliation ont périclité après bien des développements sanglants, et Louis, installé cette fois dans la ville de Bruges, se prépare à écraser la population de Gand au terme d'un blocus prolongé qui a réduit hommes, femmes et enfants à la disette. Des négociations de paix, qui viennent d'avoir lieu à Tournai, n'ont produit d'autre résultat que le durcissement de la résistance des Gantois à un seigneur qui "a respondu par ceulx de son conseil que il a envoiiet à Tournai" qu'il "ne prendera en la ville de Gand nullui à merchi". Dans un concile privé, Philippe d'Artevelde, capitaine des Gantois, et Pieter van den Bossche, ancien disciple de Jan Hyoens, décident qu'il faut "prendre le frain as dens" et jouer le tout pour le tout. Il s'agira peut-être de mourir, mais ils ne mourront pas seuls:

> 'En dedens briefs jours, la ville de Gand sera la plus honnourée ville des crestiiens ou li plus abatue. A tout le mains, se nous mourons en ceste querelle, ne morons nous pas seulx (...) i morons ou viverons à honneur'.[23]

Cette fois-ci, c'est d'Artevelde qui monte *as phenestres* pour haranguer la foule dans la place du marché. Son discours est un modèle de rhétorique persuasive; il réduit d'abord l'assistance aux larmes en leur présentant une première alternative: les Gantois se livreront entièrement à la "miséricorde" du comte:

> 'Et, quant il nous vera en ce parti tout en genoulx et mains jointes

crians merchi, il ara pité et compasion de nous, se il li plaist; mais je ne puis pas veoir ne entendre par le relation de son conseil que il n'en conviengne morir honteussement, par pugnition de justice et de prisons, la grigneur partie dou peuple qui là sera venu en ce jour. Or regardés se vous vollés venir à pais par ce parti'.[24]

Après avoir calmé les sanglots (''ce tourment de noisse''), Philippe énonce les modalités de cette soumission collective et abjecte, en s'offrant lui-même à l'immolation (''et je tous premiers, pour li oster de sa felonnie, presenterai ma teste et voel bien morir pour l'amour de Gand''), avant de passer tout de suite à l'énonciation de sa deuxième alternative: le combat à outrance. Le courage des Gantois éveillera la compassion de Dieu et du monde entier, car les milices de Gand agiront comme cette *preuse* de la Bible qui vint à bout des forces armées de Nebucadnetsar, Judith.[25]

Une troisième alternative, qui consiste à mourir *confès et repentans* – mais brûlés – dans les églises de Gand après l'arrivée des troupes de Louis, n'est pas plus propre à séduire la foule des habitants affamés que la première, et les Gantois se préparent donc à affronter la puissance armée de Louis de Mâle sur le champ de bataille. Les provisions, après tout, sont presque épuisées (il ne leur reste, nous dit Froissart, que ''*set* chars seullement de pourveances'', à savoir ''*cinc* chars chergiés de pain quit et *deus* chars de vins'': nous reviendrons sur ces chiffres ...); si l'expédition échoue, ce sera l'hécatombe.[26]

Avant de partir, les cinq mille hommes choisis pour combattre reçoivent la bénédiction et les prières de leurs amis et parents; la première nuit est passée sur les champs, à une lieue environ de Bruges. Le lendemain, un samedi, tous assistent à la messe, ''enssi que gens qui atendoient la grace et la mesericorde de Dieu'', et écoutent un sermon fort peu flatteur à l'égard de Louis de Mâle. Nebucadnetsar devient Pharaon:

Et là leur fu remonstré par ces clers, Frères Menours et autres, comment il se figuroient au peuple d'Israël que li rois Faraon d'Egipte tint lonc tamps en servitude, et comment depuis, par la grace de Dieu, il en furent delivret et menet en tère de promision par Moïse et Aaron, et li rois Pharaon et li Egiptiien mort et peri. 'Enssi, bonnes gens, dissoient chil Frère Preceur en leurs sermons, estes vous tenu en servitude par vostre signeur le conte et vos voisins de Bruges, (...)'[27]

Le sens de ce sermon est plus qu'évident. N'oublions pas, pourtant, que l'histoire de l'Exode avait aussi, pour les croyants du Moyen Age, son sens typologique: la délivrance des Israélites et le passage de la mer Rouge figurent la rédemption de l'ancien Homme par le sang du Christ. De même, la nourriture miraculeuse envoyée aux Hébreux dans le désert – la manne – figure le vrai pain du ciel. Pris ensemble, ces deux épisodes de l'histoire sainte annoncent la Cène, célébrée pour la première fois à la Pâque des Juifs. C'est lors du miracle de la multiplication des pains, cependant, que Jésus explique à la foule le véritable sens de la manne mangée dans le désert:

> En vérité, en vérité, je vous le dis, Moïse ne vous a pas donné le pain du ciel, mais mon Père vous donne le vrai pain du ciel; car le pain de Dieu, c'est celui qui descend du ciel et qui donne la vie au monde.[28]

L'exégèse que nous venons de faire n'est pas contenue dans le sermon des Frères, mais nous allons la retrouver, bientôt, dans un discours de Philippe d'Artevelde, et dans le récit des préparatifs de bataille. Après le sermon, Philippe monte sur une charrette et s'adresse aux cinq mille Gantois armés. Ses paroles[29] font penser au discours de Jésus dans Luc IX ("Quiconque met la main à la charrue, et regarde en arrière, n'est pas propre au royaume de Dieu" – v.62) qui, dans cet évangile, termine le récit de la multiplication des pains. Il ne s'agit plus, cependant, du royaume de Dieu, mais plutôt de l'honneur des Gantois, et la conclusion du discours est toute séculière:

> 'Biaulx seigneurs, vous veés devant vous toutes vos pourveances; si les vuelliés bellement departir l'un à l'autre, ensi que frères sans faire nuls outraiges, car, quant elles seront passées, il vous fault conquerir des nouvelles, se vous voulés vivre'.[30]

Séculière, oui; mais le repas qui suit est, précisément, un déjeuner sur l'herbe assez remarquable. En tout premier lieu, notons que les propos de d'Artevelde rappellent étrangement l'avertissement de saint Paul sur la manière convenable de célébrer le repas du Seigneur.[31] Remarquons aussi que les *pourveances* apportées au camp pour nourrir ces cinq mille hommes sont: "cinc chars chergiés de pain quit et deus chars de vins". Le récit du déjeuner qu'on va lire fond ensemble, paraît-il, la multiplication des pains et le repas du Seigneur (mais aussi la manne du désert):

> A ces paroles se ordonnèrent il mout humblement, et furent les chars deschargiés et les sachiées de pain données et departies par connestablies et li tonnel de vin tourné sus le fons. Là desjeunèrent il de pain et de vin raisonnablement et en heurent pour l'eure chascuns assés, et se trouvèrent après le desjunner fors et en bon point et plus aidables et mieux aidant de leurs membres que se il eussent plus mengié.[32]

Le récit de cette deuxième "messe" semble frôler le blasphème; il

st en tout cas extraordinaire, et on est en droit de se demander pourquoi Froissart l'a glissé dans sa narration des préparatifs de la bataille
du Beverhoutsveld. Il est tout à fait possible qu'il ait voulu expliquer
ainsi la défaite imminente du seigneur de Flandre par des ouvriers
textiles: le repas-miracle aurait donné des forces extraordinaires à ces
hommes, qui bénéficiaient en tout cas de la faveur divine. Bien plus
probable, à notre avis, est l'hypothèse suivante : le "commentaire"
théologique implique une certaine sympathie de la part de Froissart
à l'égard des Gantois; davantage encore, il prépare et justifie l'humiliation d'un seigneur qui n'a pas su gouverner ses états, et qui ne les
a pas maintenus dans une situation de paix et de prospérité. Dans cette
perspective, les rebelles de Gand sont pour ainsi dire le fléau de Dieu.
Mais cette "explication" ne nous paraît pas entièrement satisfaisante
non plus, justement parce que l'épisode ne cherche pas à
"expliquer".[33] Disons, au bout du compte, qu'il paraît soulever des
doutes quant à la responsabilité morale de chacun des partis, qu'il semble exprimer un certain malaise de la part du chroniqueur, qu'il com-
munique, enfin, une note discrète de pathétique (et même de poésie)
à un récit historique qui a traité, d'abord, de la résistance confraternelle
mais – ne l'oublions pas – *orgueilleuse* de la communauté de Gand à la
puissance d'un seigneur extrêmement impopulaire, et qui procèdera
bientôt à la description des circonstances fort piteuses dans lesquelles
tombera celui-ci à la suite d'une bataille (pour lui) désastreuse[34].

(ii) *Le Lit d'une pauvre femme et le berceau d'un comte*

L'espace nous manque pour une analyse détaillée de l'épisode qui
décrit la fuite de Louis de Mâle par les rues de Bruges, et dans lequel,
comme le dit F.-L. Ganshof, "les couleurs, les oppositions de lumière
et d'ombre, le mouvement, sont rendus avec une extrême netteté"[35].
Complètement isolé, déguisé dans la *hoppelande* de son page, Louis se
trouve dans une situation extrêmement périlleuse, évoquée par
Froissart dans une phrase essoufflée dans laquelle les subordonnées
se suivent et s'emboîtent pêle-mêle:

> Ensi demora li contes de Flandres tout seul, et pouoit bien adont dire
> que il se trouvoit en grant aventure, car, à celle heure, [se] par aucune
> infortunité, il fust escheus ens es mains des routes qui aval Bruges
> estoient et alloient et qui les maisons serchoient et les amis dou conte
> occisoient ou ens ou marchié les amenoient, et là tantost devant Philippe
> d'Artevelle et les cappitaines il estoient mort et esservelé, sans nul moien
> ou remède il eust esté mort. Si fu Dieu proprement pour lui, quant de
> ce peril il le delivra et saulva (etc).[36]

Cette fois-ci, c'est Louis qui bénéficie de la protection de Dieu; la suite de l'épisode, pourtant, renoue avec la glose analysée plus haut, et fait du sort du comte de Flandre un document à la fois moral, didactique et profondément poétique, sorte de *miroir aux princes* en miniature – et en négatif. La "scène" exceptionnellement et exagérément "réaliste" de l'arrivée de Louis de Mâle dans *l'ostel d'une pauvre femme* est bien connue[37]:

> Ce n'estoit pas hostel de seigneur, de sales, de cambres ne de manandries, mais une povre maisonnette enfumée, ossi noire que arremens [*sc.* matière dont on produit l'encre] de fumiere de tourbes, et n'i avoit en celle maison fors le bouge devant et une povre tente de vièle toille enfumée pour esconser le feu, et pardessus un povre solier ouquel on montoit à une eschelle de set eschellons. En ce solier avoit un povre litteron ou li povre enfant de la femmelette gisoient.[38]

Le contraste marqué entre l'*hostel de seigneur* et la *povre maisonnette* de la *femmelette* et des *povre enfant*, avec son *povre tente de vièle toille,* son *povre solier* et son *povre litteron* n'échappera à personne; il dépasse sans doute un peu les bornes du bon goût. Ce qui retient notre attention dans cet épisode, au contraire, c'est la façon dont l'impression très forte créée par cette image de la *maisonnette* s'estompe éventuellement, ou plutôt se rétrécit pour ne comprendre, enfin, que le lit.

Tout d'abord, le *litteron* est privilégié par rapport aux autres éléments descriptifs de l'humble demeure de cette femme, et cela pour au moins trois raisons: (i) la progression même de la description "homérique"[39] qui s'élabore à mesure que nous "faisons la visite" de la maison et qui se termine avec la mention du lit; (ii) l'importance qu'assume celui-ci dans la narration même de l'épisode – Louis s'y cachera pour échapper aux *routiers* de Gand; (iii) la précision apportée par les détails supplémentaires suivants:

> Li contes de Flandres entra en ce solier et se bouta, au plus bellement et souef que il pot, entre la coute et l'estrain de ce povre literon; (...)[40]

Ensuite, faisons remarquer que le *litteron* n'a pas, comme les autres éléments du décor, son pendant *noble*; ceux-ci, au contraire, s'ordonnent selon une série oppositive et métonymique: *maisonnette, bouge, solier/hostel de seigneur, sales, cambres,* etc. Or, le lit, c'est un lieu de sécurité et de repos. Froissart nous dit que le lit de la pauvre femme contient déjà des enfants qui dorment, mais il ajoute que "la femme se essonia en son hostel entour le feu et à *ung autre petit enfant qui gisoit en ung repos*" (espèce de berceau? Le terme est fort évocateur). Le repos, la sécurité de ces enfants miséreux (ils ne se réveillent pas, même pendant la "perquisition" des *routiers*) contrastent donc vivement avec la sécurité précaire et menacée du grand seigneur; voilà ce qui donne tout son prix à l'observation suivante:

(...) et là se quati et *fist le petit: faire li convenoit.*[41]

C'est pendant que Louis se cache sous ce lit que Froissart s'inter-roge sur les pensées qui ont dû traverser son esprit au cours de ces instants périlleux:

> Quel chose pouoit il là, Dieux, penser ne imaginer? Quant au matin, il pouoit bien dire: 'Je suis li uns des grans princes dou monde des cres-tiens,' et la nuit ensuivant il se trouvoit *en telle petitesse,* il pouoit bien dire et imaginer que les fortunes de ce monde ne sont pas trop estables. Encores grant heur pour lui, quant il s'en pouoit issir saulve sa vie. Toutesfois ceste perilleuse et dure aventure lui devoit bien estre ung grant *mirouer* et *doit estre toute sa vie.* (C'est nous qui soulignons ici)[42]

Les derniers mots cités semblent impliquer que cet épisode fut écrit très tôt après les événements racontés, et surtout avant le 30 janvier 1384, car la suite du Deuxième livre nous réserve une nouvelle ironie: ce jour-là, Louis de Mâle mourut, et la narration fort détaillée des obsèques[43] – processions, *destriers* du défunt, bannières et armoiries –, qui ne contient aucune expression de regret ou de sympathie de la part de Froissart ou des assistants à la cérémonie, ne peut que nous faire rappeler le passage dont il est question ici. Ce qui donne tout leur piquant aux propos supposés de Louis, cependant, c'est que ceux-ci viennent compléter un motif que nous n'avons pas encore isolé, dans l'épisode de la *maisonnette,* et qui réintroduit la glose théologique "filée" amorcée dans le récit des préparatifs de la bataille du Beverhoutsveld.

A l'instant même où Louis pénètre dans la maison de la femme de Bruges ("Femme, sauve moi! Je suis tes sires le conte de Flandres, mais maintenant il me fault repourre et mussier, car mes ennemis me chassent, et dou bien que tu me feras *je t'en donrai bon guerdon*"), celle-ci le reconnaît:

> (...) car elle avoit esté plusieurs fois *à l'aumosne à sa porte:* si l'avoit veu aller et venir, ensi que ungs sires va en ses deduis.

Ce fragment est une sorte de variation sur la parabole du mauvais riche et du pauvre Lazare; ici, pourtant, le "mauvais riche" de Flandre se voit accorder une deuxième chance, pour se racheter, car les rôles sont renversés. Louis tient ici le rôle de Lazare et cherche abri auprès de la femme, en échange d'un *guerdon* promis mais fort hypothétique (notons que Froissart ne nous dit pas si la femme avait jamais reçu l'aumône demandée à la porte de son seigneur), alors que la femme assumera le rôle du riche et donnera partant à Louis de Mâle une jolie leçon de charité.[44]

Revenons maintenant, et pour une dernière fois, au *litteron.* Nous avons vu comment, dans la description de la maison, cet élément se signale par l'absence de son "pendant" noble. Nous avons souligné aussi l'importance narrative du lit – détail motivé – dans son contexte immédiat. Or, la motivation[45] de cet élément déborde le cadre restreint de l'épisode de Bruges: par un nouvel avatar, il sert de foyer d'intégration aux niveaux de la description et du discours (théologique, sur les *fortunes de ce monde* – aux. deux sens de l'expression, d'ailleurs – qui "ne sont pas trop estables").[46]

Philippe d'Artevelde célèbre son triomphe en mettant à sac le château préféré du comte (et qui porte son nom – le château de Mâle); la nouvelle de ce pillage scandaleux parvient à Louis qui s'est réfugié dans sa résidence à Hesdin. Dans le récit qu'en donne le texte du Deuxième livre, Froissart insiste beaucoup sur le destruction de tous les objets associés à la naissance et à l'enfance du comte (y compris les objets blasonnés) dans le château éponyme:

> En che tamps se tenoit li contes de Flandres à Hesdin. [Si] li fu recordé comment li routier de Gand avoient esté à Malle et abatu l'ostel ou despit de lui, et le cambre ou il fu nés arse, et les fons ou il fu batissiés rompus, et *le repos ou il fu couchiés enffes, armoiiés de ses armes, qui estoit tout d'argent*, et la cuvelette ossi ou on l'avoit d'enffanche bagniet, qui estoit d'or et d'argent, toute deschirée et aporté[e] à Bruges, et là fait leurs galles et leurs ris; [ce] li vint et tourna à grant desplaissance.[47]

Et le lecteur (sinon Louis lui-même) de se souvenir de la pauvre maison enfumée de Bruges où dormait "ung autre petit enfant qui gisoit en ung repos", pendant que son seigneur au premier étage – "se bouta, au plus bellement et souef que il pot, entre la coute et l'estrain de ce povre literon".[48] Louis de Mâle trouvera bientôt d'ailleurs le repos (?) de la mort, sur une bière entourée de ses armoieries et de sept cent chandelles :

> (...) il ot en l'eglise, à l'obsecque, ung traveil auquel il avoit set cens candeilles u environ, cascune candeille de une livre pesant, et sus ledit traveil avoit cinc banières: chelle dou milieu estoit de Flandres [et la destre d'Artois, et la senestre] au desous, de la conté de Bourgongne, et la quatrime apriès, de la conté de Nevers, et la cinquime, de la conté de Rethel. Et estoit li travaux armoiés d'un lés d'escuchons de Flandres, et au lés senestre de madame, d'escuchons de Flandres et de Braibant. (...) Et i fist on ung très biau disner, et furent delivret de tous coustenges et frais, tant de bouce comme as hostels, tous chevaliers et escuiers qui la nuit et le jour de l'obsecque i furent ensonniiet, et leur furent envoiiet tout li noir drap de coi il furent vesti à ce jour.[49]

134

Dans les textes que nous avons considérés ici, la présence de gloses accompagnant le récit historique ainsi que l'organisation de paradigmes d'éléments descriptifs créent comme une concurrence des voix du texte. Cette espèce de configuration textuelle (en puissance) ne représente pas un effort d'*interprétation* des causes et des responsabilités, mais plutôt une *invitation* (émise par le texte et non par l'auteur) à la réflexion morale. Le thème de *Fortune,* à la base de ces développements textuels et méta-textuels, n'épuise pas en tout cas le sens de ces épisodes qui nous semblent manifester le trouble profond du chroniqueur devant le spectre de la tyrannie (au sens de ''despotisme'', mais aussi au sens de ''renversement de l'ordre établi, du dessous''). Sur la position morale de Louis de Flandre, Froissart ne *prononce* pas; il se limite (au niveau cette fois du *commentaire,* non de la glose) à reproduire les avis d'autrui, sans les endosser lui-même:

Quant pape Clement oït les nouvelles, il pensa ung petit et puis dist que celle desconfiture [*sc.* Beverhoutsveld] avoit esté une verge de Dieu pour exempliier le conte, et que il lui envoioit celle tribulacion pour la cause de ce qu'il avoit esté rebelles à ses oppinions. Aucun autre grant seigneur disoient en France et ailleurs que li contes ne faisoit que ung peu à plaindre, se il avoit ung petit à porter et à souffrir, car il avoit esté si presumptueux que il n'amiroit nul seigneur voisin que il eust, ne roi de France ne aultre, se il ne venoit bien à point audit conte; pour quoi il le plaindoient mains de ses persecutions. Ensi avient, et que li proverbes soit voirs que on dist, car, à cellui à qui il meschiet, chascuns lui mesoffre.⁵⁰

L'équivoque de ce commentaire s'allie donc à l'ambivalence de ce que nous avons appelé la *glose.* De même, il est assez difficile de juger de la tonalité expressive du paragraphe suivant, prélude à la bataille de Roosebeke (remarquons l'essoufflement de la syntaxe, les emboîtements de construction, et le mélange des temps verbaux où domine un futur ''triomphal'', épique ... ou peut-être *ironique*?):

Or a li contes de Flandres, qui se tient ens ou chastel de Lisle, assés à penser et à muser, quant il voit tout son païs plus que onques mais rebelle à lui, et ne veoit mie que de sa poissance singulière il le puist recouvrer, car toutes les villes sont si en unité et d'un accord que on ne les en puet jamais roster, se ce n'est par trop grant puissance, ne on ne parle par tout son païs de Flandres de lui non plus en lui honnourant ne recongnoissant à seigneur, que dont que il n'eust oncques esté. Or lui reviendra l'aliance que il a au duc de Bourgongne, liquels a sa fille madame Marguerite en mariage, dont il a des biaux enfans, bien à point. Or est il heureux que li rois Charles de France est mort et que il i a un jeune roi en France ou gouvernement de son oncle de Bourgoigne, qui le menra et ploiera du tout à sa voulenté, car, ensi comme de l'osier que on ploie jeune autour de son doi, et, quant elle est aagée, on n'en peut faire sa voulenté, ensi est il dou jeune roi de France et sera, sicomme je croi, car il est de si bonne voulenté, et si se desire à faire et à armer si croira son oncle de Bourgoingne, quant il lui remonstrera l'orgueil de Flandres et comment il est tenus de aidier ses hommes, quant leurs gens veullent user de rebellion.[51]

Anticipation surexcitée de la némésis de l'orgueil de Gand, soulagement vif dû à la pensée du rétablissement prochain de l'ordre – ou cynisme moqueur et amer?

Si Froissart approuve la destruction de Philippe d'Artevelde, utilisé naguère comme *verge de Dieu* pour châtier l'orgueil d'un prince (Cf. les Assyriens employés par Dieu pour punir les Israélites[52]), c'est le sort des verges de Dieu de périr à leur tour, ce qui explique peut-être l'espèce de *sic et non* des rôles remplis par ce personnage. Quant à Louis de Mâle, la lecture de ces épisodes étrangement poétiques ne nous permet pas de conclure; c'est là, sans doute, le gage de la *littérature*.

NOTES

1. Nous achevons en ce moment même, sous la direction de M. Jean DUFOURNET (Paris-III), une thèse de 3ème cycle qui, nous l'espérons, contribuera modestement à l'étude de ce que nous appelons ici "la valeur proprement littéraire" de l'oeuvre en prose de Froissart: *Le Manteau troué: étude littéraire des "Chroniques" de Jean Froissart* (soutenance, janvier 1984). La présente étude est une version abrégée d'un chapitre de cette thèse, intitulé "Le Récit et sa glose: Louis de Mâle et Philippe d'Artevelde en 1382". On pourra consulter aussi, éventuellement, un chapitre intitulé "Littérarité et littérature au Moyen âge" qui propose d'étudier la notion de *spécificité littéraire* appliquée à nos textes anciens et, bien sûr, à l'oeuvre de Froissart. Parler des aspects littéraires d'un ouvrage historique est une entreprise fort délicate: c'est pourquoi nous nous réservons ici, quitte à examiner sérieusement le problème dans notre thèse.
2. A consulter: S.G. Nichols (Jr.), "Discourse in Froissart's 'Chroniques'," *Speculum* XXXIX (1964), pp. 279-287; L. Chalon, "La Scène des bourgeois de Calais chez Froissart et Jean le Bel," *Cahiers d'analyse textuelle* X (1968), pp. 68-84; M. Zink, "Froissart et la nuit du chasseur," *Poétique* XLI (1980), pp. 60-77.
3. F.S. Shears, *Froissart, Chronicler and Poet* (London: Routledge, 1930) (voir surtout le chapitre XI, "A Master of Fair Language," pp. 171- 192). Notre ami et collègue de l'Université de Swansea, M. Diverres, prépare en ce moment même un livre sur Froissart, l'homme et l'oeuvre: *Froissart, his Life and Works* (titre provisoire).
4. Sur le texte de connotation, v. R. Barthes, *S/Z* (Paris) Seuil (coll. "Tel Quel"), 1970), pp. 14-15. Dans ce genre de textes, la relation du signifiant au signifié n'est plus la même que celle qui opère dans les textes de "pure" communication. Le *sens* de ces textes n'est pas celui du monde extérieur, mais celui du "langage second" – du nouveau système de signifiés organisés mis en jeu par la configuration particulière des signifiants. Cf., à ce sujet, les propos de G. Genette: "Le discours consiste apparemment en une chaîne de signifiés absents. Mais le langage, et spécialement le

langage littéraire, fonctionne rarement d'une manière aussi simple: l'expression n'est pas toujours univoque, elle ne cesse au contraire de se dédoubler, c'est-à-dire qu'un mot, par exemple, peut comporter à la fois deux significations, dont la rhétorique disait l'une littérale et l'autre figurée, l'espace sémantique qui se creuse entre le signifié apparent et le signifié réel abolissant du même coup la linéarité du discours" *Figures II* (Paris: Seuil (coll. "Tel Quel")) 1969): "La littérature et l'espace", pp. 46-47).

5. J. van Herwaarden, "The War in the Low Countries," dans *Froissart : Historian,* éd. J.J.N. Palmer (Woodbridge, Suffolk: Boydell Press Ltd., et Totowa, N.J.: Rowman & Littlefield, 1981)(recueil d'articles de Palmer, Barber, Henneman, Sherborne, Jones, Russell, van Herwaarden, Tucoo-Chala, Contamine et Diller), pp. 101-117.

6. On sait que Froissart rédigea d'abord une version suivie de ces événements (*Chronique de Flandre,* terminée en 1386) qu'il corrigea ensuite avant de l'insérer, sous forme d'épisodes intégrés au récit du conflit entre France et Angleterre, dans son Deuxième livre (terminé avant son départ pour le Béarn, donc en 1387). Voir à ce sujet, et sur une version en néerlandais, aujourd'hui incomplète, des *Chroniques* – Livres II et III, mss. Bibl. Univ. de Leyde, BPL 3 I,II et Bibl.roy., La Haye, 130B2I - Palmer, *op. cit.,* p. 175 note 17, et les pp. 101-2 de l'article de van Herwaarden. La version néerlandaise contiendrait des développements qu'on ne trouve pas dans les mss. français, d'après celui-ci. Voir aussi, enfin, l' *Introduction* au Deuxième livre de G. Raynaud, SHF 9, pp. I et sq. Nous renvoyons à l'édition de la Société de l'Histoire de France, éd. S. Luce, G. Raynaud et A. Mirot, Paris, 1869-1975. 15 vol. parus (le Deuxième livre occupe les tomes 9, 10 et 11). Nos références à cette édition seront signalées par l'abréviation "SHF" suivi du numéro du tome en chiffres arabes, et de l'indication des pages, toujours en chiffres arabes (accompagnée d'une indication portant sur les lignes citées, ainsi: SHF 7, pp. 11-12 (ll. 28-32/1-5)).

7. Van Herwaarden, *loc. cit.,* p. 102: "His account of the events of the years 1379-85 in Book II (...), is the work of a mature and independent historian"; p. 105: "His narrative is vivid and dramatic and although modern research has uncovered much more about the causes and consequences of these events, Froissart himself has some shrewd insights to offer. For although he recorded his opinion that the persistent state of war in these years was the work of the devil, he did not allow this pious conclusion to prevent him from observing the faults and responsibilities of the parties involved."

8. Sur l'affaire Hyoens-Mayhuus, v. la p. 106; sur la *poorterie,* les pp. 103 et 108.

9. v. surtout SHF 9, pp. 218-219 (ll. 23-32/1-9); SHF 10, p. 80 (ll. 7- 25), où Froissart blâme la faiblesse de sa propre classe: celle-ci accepte l'usurpation du pouvoir seigneurial par les éléments les moins propres à l'exercer.

10. J. van Herwaarden, *op. cit.,* pp. 105 et 108 (Franc de Bruges). Sur d'autres aspects de la valeur historique du témoignage de Froissart, *cf.* les pp. 114-115 (l'empire croissant – et menaçant, pour la France et pour l'Angleterre - de la maison de Bourgogne).

11. Scandalisé, il en énumère les conséquences économiques ("et je vous pri que vous i voelliés entendre", nous dit-il): "Proprement li Turc, li paiien et li Sarrasin s'en doloient, car marcandisses par mer en estoient toutes refroidies et toutes perdues. Toutes les bendes de la mer, de soleil levant jusques à soleil esconsant, et tout le septentrion s'en sentoient, car voirs est que de dis et set roiaulmes crestiiens li avoirs et les marcandisses viennent et arive[n]t à l'Escluse en Flandres, et tout ont la delivrance ou au Dam ou à Bruges"(SHF 11, pp. 283-284 (ll. 28-31/1- 5)).

12. SHF 11, p. 33 (ll. 12-27): "Or regardés la grant deablie que ce euist esté, se li rois de France euist esté desconfis en Flandres et la noble chevalerie qui estoit avoecques lui en che voiage. On puet bien croire et imaginer que toute gentillèce et noblèce euist esté morte et perdue en France et tant bien ens es autres païs; ne li Jaquerie ne fu onques si grande ne si orible que elle euist esté, car parellement à Rains, à Caalons en Campaigne et sus la rivière de Marne, li villain se reveloient et manechoient ja les gentils [hommes] et dames et leurs enfans qui estoient demoret derière; otretant bien à Orliiens, em Blois, à Roem, en Normendie et en Biauvesis. Et leur estoit li diables entrés en la teste pour tout ochire, se Dieux proprement n'i euist pourveu de remède, enssi que vous orés recorder ensieuant en l'istoire."

13. Van Herwaarden, *op. cit.,* p. 115: "His conception of proper social order was peace, maintained by a just prince who watched over the general good, in harmony with his subjects (so too the – good – representatives of towns). Precisely that stratum of society from which Froissart himself came identified itself most with princely authority; (…)" et la p. 116: "The peace which Froissart wished see (*sic*) retained was civil peace, whereby the prosperity of his subjects would allow the prince and his knights to carry out their function in just wars." *Cf.* les idées de Christine de Pisan, dans le *Livre du corps de policie,* rédigée vers 1407; sa conception de la société ne diffère pas sensiblement de celle de Froissart: *v.* Christine de Pisan, *Le Livre du corps de policie,* édition critique par Robert H. Lucas (Genève: Droz (T.L.F.), 1967), pp. 14-15 et 168, ainsi que le chapitre IX, "Comment le bon prince doit ressembler le bon pasteur" (pp. 23-28). Sur l'ensemble de ces questions on consultera désormais l'étude de Jacques Krynen, *Idéal du prince et pouvoir royal en France à la fin du Moyen Age (1380-1440).* Étude de la littérature politique du temps (Avant-propos de Bernard Guenée) (Paris: Editions A. et J. Picard, s.d. (impression: quatrième trimestre 1981)).
14. Avant la journée néfaste de Roosebeke, d'Artevelde (écrit Froissart) "se glorefioit si en la belle fortune et victore que il ot devant Bruges, que il li sambloit bien que nuls ne li poroit fourfaire, et esperoit bien à estre sires de tout le monde" SHF 11, p. 39 (ll. 8- 11) .
15. C'est l'avis aussi de van Herwaarden, qui voit en Froissart l'avocat de la *mesure*: "Froissart chose the side neither of the count nor of his subjects: he chose moderation, *mesure,* personified in the actions of Philip of Burgundy. This made him an enemy of the rebels and a supporter of those who tried to bring an end to the conflict by negotiation. It was the Flemish *orgueil* which he condemned, which first led to rebelliousness, and then to the destruction of many. This did not blind him to the courage of those of Ghent and Flanders, but it was a courage which led to the unnecessary spilling of blood" (*op. cit.,* p. 116).
16. SHF 10, p. 221 (ll. 3-5).
17. Ajoutons que la glose "envahit" aussi certaines répliques de d'Artevelde: c'est ce qui arrive quand celui-ci harangue ses troupes avant la bataille. L'*instance de discours* n'est plus, à ce moment, d'interprétation (biblique). C'est comme si d'Artevelde prenait en charge un discours dont il ne devine pas la résonance ironique. *Cf.,* à ce propos, notre étude "Style direct et peinture des personnages chez Froissart," *Romania* XCIII(1972), pp. 498-522, ainsi que l'analyse détaillée que nous présentons ci-dessous, sous la rubrique *Sermons et paraboles: l'Exode et l'Évangile.*
18. Nous entendons par *"virtuellement* ironique" que l'ironie du texte est disponible à quiconque en reconnaîtra la présence et saura en déchiffrer le ou les sens possible(s); – mais n'est-ce pas là, en tout cas, la fonction même de l'ironie, fonction primordiale: demeurer virtuelle? *Cf.,* à ce propos, l'étude remarquable de V. Jankélévitch, *L'Ironie* (Paris: Flammarion, 1964).
19. *Cf.,* R. Barthes, "Introduction à l'analyse structurale des récits, *Communications* VIII (1966), pp. 1-27; 2. "Les niveaux de sens." Dans les textes littéraires, "(…) aucun niveau ne peut à lui seul produire du sens: toute unité qui appartient à un certain niveau ne prend de sens que si elle peut s'intégrer dans un niveau supérieur" (p. 5).
20. Terme d'A. Greimas explicité par J. Batany dans "Paradigmes lexicaux et structures littéraires au Moyen Age," *Revue d'histoire littéraire de la France* LXX, no. 4 (1970), pp. 819-835. P. 831: c'est, précisément, "ce qui fait l'homogénéité d'un texte." *Cf.* R. Barthes, *art. cité,* p. 5, et W. Iser, *The Implied Reader: Patterns of Communication in Prose Fiction from Bunyan to Beckett* (Baltimore & London: John Hopkins University Press, 1974),p. 284 (sur la création par le lecteur de la *Gestalt* du texte, et sur le sens "configuratif", etc.).
21. Nous empruntons cette expression au livre de M. Marghescou, *Le Concept de littérarité; essai sur les possibilités théoriques d'une science de la littérature* (La Haye et Paris: Mouton, 1974). En ce qui concerne les deux épisodes qu'on va lire ici, il serait peut-être plus juste de dire qu'ils *parlent d'autre chose tout en parlant de ce dont ils sont censés parler.*
22. V. la p. 216 du tome 9 de l'édition SHF. Nous donnons ci-dessous, en intégral, le texte de ce discours. Faisons remarquer comment la répétition, le martèlement du même élément syntaxique de présentation – *là leur remonstra il* (série fermée par un imparfait "de résumé", *remonstroit*) – semble figurer la mine sévère (et sardonique?) ainsi que l'impatience à peine contenue de ce prince *merancolieus*:

"Li contes, en fendant le marchiet, jettoit communement ses ieulx sus ces blans capprons qui se mettoient en sa presence, et ne veoit autres gens, che li estoit avis, que blans capprons: si en fu tous merancolieus. Si descendi de son cheval, et ossi fissent tout li autre, et monta sus à unes phenestres, et s'apoia là, et avoit on estendu un drap vermeil devant lui. Là commencha li contes à parler mout sagement. Tout se teurent, quant il parla. Là leur remonstra il de point en point l'amour et l'affeccion que il avoit à iaulx, avant que il l'euissent courouchié; là leur remonstra il comment uns sires devoit estre amés, cremus, servis et honnerés de ses gens; là remonstra il comment il avoient fait tout le contraire; là remonstra il comment il les avoit tenus, gardés et deffendus contre tout homme; là leur remonstra il comment il les avoit tenus en paix et en pourfit et en toutes prosperités, depuis que il estoit venus à tière, ouviers les passages de mer qui leur estoient clos en son jone avent. Là leur remonstroit il pluiseurs poins raisonnables que li sages concevoient, et entendoient bien clerement que de tout il dissoit verité" (SHF 9, p. 216 (ll. 6- 28).

23. SHF 10, pp. 213-214 (ll. 30-32/1-3 et 21-22).
24. *Ibid.*, p. 216 (ll. 15-22).
25. *Ibid.*, pp. 217-218 (ll. 24-32/1-2): "'Se nous sommes mort en che voiage, che sera honnerablement, et ara Dieux pité de nous et li mondes ossi; et dira on que loiaument et vaillanment nous avons soustenu et parmaintenu nostre querelle. Et, se en celle bataille Dieux a pité de nous, qui anchiennement mist poissance en le main de Judith, ensi (que) nos pères le recordent, qui ochist Olifernès qui estoit desous Nabugodonosor du et maistres de sa chevalerie, par quoi li Asseriien furent desconfit, nous serons li plus honnourés peuples qui ait resgné puis les Roumains'." *Cf.* aussi, *Apocryphes*, Livre de Judith, chapitres 4, 7, et 8-13 (siège de Bethulie; défaite du général assyrien).
26. "N'aiiés nulle esperance de retourner", disent les habitants à ceux qui partiront pour combattre, "se ce n'est à vostre honneur, car vous ne trouveriés riens, et, sitos que nous orons nouvelles se vous estes mort et desconfi, nous bouterons le feu en la ville, et nous destruirons nous meîsmes, ensi que gens desesperés" (*Ibid.*, p. 219, ll. 21-26).
27. *Ibid.*, pp. 221-222 (ll. 29-32/1-6).
28. Jean VI, 28-33.
29. Rapportées, en partie, SHF 10, p. 223, ll. 8-14: "Or estoient il si avant trait et venut que reculler il ne pooient, et aussi au retourner, tout considéré, riens il ne gaigneroient, car nulle cose derière fors que povreté et tristrèce laissiet il n'avoient. [Si] ne devoit nuls pensser après Gand ne à femme ne [enfans] que il eusist, fors que tant faire que li honneurs fust leur."
30. *Ibid.*, ll. 18-22.
31. I Corinthiens 11, vv. 20-26, et plus partic. les vv. 20-21: "Lors donc que vous vous réunissez, ce n'est pas manger le repas du Seigneur; car, quand on se met à table, chacun commence par prendre son propre repas, et l'un a faim, tandis que l'autre est ivre."
32. SHF 10, p. 223 (ll. 23-30). *Cf.* Jean VI, vv. 8-13 et les récits parallèles, Matt. XIV, vv. 15-21; Marc VI, vv. 35-44; Luc IX, vv. 12-17; ainsi que Exode XVI, vv. 17-18, et I Corinthiens 11, vv. 20-26. Ce n'est guère ici, nous semble-t-il, le viatique des mourants auquel pense Froissart. D'ailleurs, les Gantois ont déjà assisté à une messe proprement dite. *Cf.* la note 1, p. lxii de l'édition de Raynaud (SHF 10): "D'après une chronique (*Ist. et chr.*, t. II, p. 204), les Gantois n'étaient que 4,000 'et avoit avec yauls pluiseurs carios qui menoient trebus et espingalles.' D'après Olivier de Dixmude, cité par Kervyn (t. X, p. 458), l'armée de Philippe d'Artevelde s'élevait à 8,000 hommes."
33. Dans un article récent, G.T.Diller a pu écrire que, chez Froissart, "l'explication fictive tend à traduire un rapport causal historique" et que – dans la dernière rédaction du Premier livre – "bon nombre des scènes et des discours inventés par le chroniqueur dénotent non pas une indifférence pour la vérité historique, mais une vraie intention – sinon un système – d'explication causale" ("Robert d'Artois et l'historicité des *Chroniques* de Froissart," *Le Moyen Age* LXXXVI (1980), pp. 217-231. Pp. 229-231. *Cf.*, du même auteur, "Froissart: Patrons and Texts", dans *Froissart: Historian*, éd. Palmer, pp. 145-160: "(...) may it not be the case that his re-ordering of events, his factual deformations, reflect another level of historical reality, that of beliefs generally held among his noble patrons? In some cases, fictional reconstruction in the *Chronicles* may even correspond to a particular method employed by the chronicler

for explaining historical causality." – p. 145). Le critique américain répond ici, en effet, à des idées que nous avions ébauchées dans une étude parue en 1972: "Style direct et peinture des personnages chez Froissart," *Romania* XCIII (1972), pp. 498-522. Pour notre part, nous croyons toujours qu'il faut être plus prudent en ce qui concerne la caractérisation de *l' historicité* de Froissart. La verité, chez lui, est sanctionnée par l'éthique chevaleresque; il s'agit d'enregistrer (sans parti-pris aucun) ce qui s'est "réellement" passé sur le champ de bataille ou ailleurs: "(...) sans faire fait, ne porter partie, ne coulourer plus l'un que l'autre, fors tant que li biens fais des bons, de quel pays qu'il soient, qui par proèce l'ont acquis, y est plainnement veus et cogneus, car de l'oubliier ou esconser, ce seroit pechiés et cose mal apertenans, car esploit d'armes sont si chierement comparet et achetet, che scèvent chil qui y travaillent, que on n'en doit nullement mentir pour complaire à autrui, et tollir le glore et renommée des bienfaisans, et donner à chiaus qui n'en sont mies digne" (SHF 1, *Prologue*, pp. 1-2). L'interprétation proprement dite (et au sens moderne) est de moindre importance pour lui, même s'il parle quelquefois des *suites* économiques, sociales ou politiques, de certaines actions. Ce qui, pour Froisart, distingue l'*hystoire* de la *cronique non pas historiée*, c'est l'impartialité, mais c'est aussi la précision qu'exige celle-ci: "Se je disoie: 'Ainsi et ainsi en avint en ce temps', sans ouvrir ne esclarcir la matere qui fut grande et grosse et orrible et bien taillie d'aler malement, ce seroit cronique non pas historiée, et se m'en passeroie bien, se je vouloie; or ne m'en vueille pas passer que je n'esclarcisse tout le fait ou cas que Dieu m'en a donné le sens, le temps, le memoire, et le loisir de cronissier et historier tout au long de la matiere" (SHF 13, p. 222, ll. 20-28). Notons bien le contexte de ces propos: Froissart s'apprête à raconter des événements impliquant des parents de son patron. Il enchaîne, par conséquent: "(...) et tout ce qui est escript est veritable. On ne dye pas que je aye la noble hystoire corrompu par la faveur que je aye eu au conte Guy de Blois, qui le me fist faire (...) etc." (*Ibid.*, pp. 223-224, ll. 26-33/1-6). Bref, la "causalité" l'intéresse bien moins que ne le fait l'examen du sens moral et exemplaire de certains événements ou comportements: "There is much truth in Tucoo-Chala's assertion that Froissart should be viewed more as moralist than historian. And of course, his determination to see and interpret events so that they fitted into his view of a society dominated by chivalry implied imposing on history an aesthetic vision that also pulled him constantly towards the action-packed, incurious superficialities of romance, towards literature" (P.E. Russell, "The War in Spain and Portugal," dans *Froissart: Historian,* éd. Palmer, pp. 83-100. P. 99. *Cf.* la p. 118 pour les remarques de Tucoo-Chala). Notons toutefois que – dans les épisodes que nous analysons ici – ce n'est pas à proprement parler *Froissart* qui moralise; il serait plus juste de dire que *son texte* donne matière à une réflexion à la fois esthétique et morale. Si Froissart est moraliste, il l'est parfois sans le savoir.

34. Lors du Colloque de Manchester, Mlle Madeleine Blaess du département de français de l'université de Sheffield nous a fait remarquer combien malencontreuse était la journée choisie pour cette bataille. D'après Froissart (et l'éditeur de la Chronique des règnes de Jean II et Charles V, R. Delachenal, t. 2, p. 380, note 1, ainsi que H. Pirenne, *Histoire de Belgique,* t. II, pp.191-195), d'Artevelde avait choisi (à dessein?) le samedi, 3 mai, jour de la fête et procession du Saint-Sacrement de Bruges (v. Raynaud, SHF 10, *Sommaire,* pp. lxii-lxiii) et fête de l'Invention de la Sainte Croix. Ces faits ont pu influencer le chroniqueur en ce qui concerne la "messe" des Gantois et, d'après Mlle Blaess, l'humiliation de Louis de Mâle (qui n'hésite pas à combattre ce jour-là) ainsi que la destruction de Ph. d'Artevelde à Roosebeke, seraient pour ainsi dire présagées par ce double blasphème. Mme Marie Collins, de Westfield College, université de Londres, nous a rappelé l'importance, chez Chaucer, du 3 mai; il s'agit cette fois-ci, pourtant, d'une réminiscence plus païenne que chrétienne (v. John P. McCall, "Chaucer's May 3," *Modern Language Notes* LXXVI (1961), pp. 201- 205). Nous tenons à remercier nos deux collègues de Londres et de Sheffield.
35. F.-L. Ganshof, "Jean Froissart," *Annales de la Soc. Arch. de Bruxelles* XLII (1938), pp. 256-272. p. 266.
36. SHF 10, p. 230 (ll. 23-32).
37. Ph. Contamine s'en sert, par exemple, pour évoquer l'habitat modeste d'une bonne part des citadins au quatorzième siècle, dans *La Vie quotidienne pendant la guerre de Cent ans* (Paris: Hachette, 1976), pp. 112-113.
38. SHF 10, p. 231 (ll. 8-16).

39. Sur la description "homérique" (qui se greffe sur une narration), *cf.* l'ouvrage remarquable de Ph. Hamon, *Introduction à l'analyse du descriptif* (Paris: Classiques Hachette, (coll. "Langue, linguistique, communication" dirigée par Bernard Quemada), 1981), pp. 22-23: "(...) c'est une description 'dramatisée', une description-récit où les données simultanées du réel ou les éléments accumulés d'une nomenclature passent, sur la scène du texte, par un mouvement de personnage qui les prend en charge dans la successive 'naturelle' d'un ordonnancement motivé. Cela consiste par exemple en ce que, au lieu de passer directement en revue les différentes pièces de l'armement d'un guerrier, l'auteur nous présente ce guerrier s'habillant pour partir au combat et revêtant, successivement, les différentes pièces de son armement, conformément à l'ordre 'naturel' de n'importe quel programme d'habillement (le baudrier, par exemple, viendra *après* la cuirasse)." Dans le cas qui nous concerne ici, nous "faisons la visite" de la maison, avec le narrateur.

40. SHF 10, p. 232 (ll. 1-4).

41. *Ibid.,* (ll. 4-5). C'est nous qui soulignons.

42. SHF 10, pp. 232-233 (ll. 31-2/1-8). Il est fort possible que Froissart se soit souvenu ici de l'emprisonnement et de la fuite du jeune comte de Flandres, en 1347 (*v.* Jean le Bel, *Chronique,* éd. J. Viard et E. Déprez, SHF, Paris, 1904-5, 2 vol. Tome 2, pp. 138-9; Froissart, SHF 4, pp. 34-37, et 252-256 (ms. de Rome; *voir* aussi l'édition de Diller: *Chroniques.* Dernière rédaction du premier livre. Edition du manuscrit de Rome Reg. lat. 869 (Paris et Genève: Droz, coll. "Textes littéraires français", 1972, pp. 800-806); *Chronique Normande du XIVe siècle,* éd. A. et E. Molinier (Paris: S.H.F., 1882), pp. 85-86.

43. Chose assez rare chez Froissart que la description d'obsèques. Nous reproduisons le texte ci-dessous en Appendice (SHF 11, pp. 157-164; Froissart le fait mourir le 28 janvier ...) La "revanche" de Roosebeke est donc suivie par la mort du vainqueur, et par la transmission du comté à Philippe de Bourgogne. S'il est tout à fait possible que l'épisode fût écrit avant la mort de Louis, nous acceptons, avec Raynaud, que la rédaction des mss. contenant celui-ci doit être datée de 1387 (SHF 9, *Introduction,* p. vi).

44. *Cf.* Luc XVI, vv. 19-31. Raynaud (SHF 10, *Sommaire,* p. lxiv, note 5) observe que "Froissart a donné dans sa *Chronique de Flandre (Bibl. nat.,* ms. fr. 5004, fol. 105v°-108r°) une rédaction plus détaillée qui nous apprend que ce fut à un bourgeois de Gand, nommé Renier Campion, que le comte dut son salut. La vieille femme qui le cacha chez elle était la veuve Bruynaert (Kervyn, *Hist. de Flandre,* t. III, P. 486)." Or, Raynaud propose, pour les mss. de la *Chronique de Flandre,* un *terminus ad quem* de 1385 (novembre 1386 au plus tard); celle-ci a été "intercalée dans son deuxième livre" et Froissart a corrigé et supprimé beaucoup (SHF 9, *Introduction au Deuxième livre des Chroniques de J. Froissart,* pp. i-vi). Froissart a donc *travaillé* le texte dont il s'agit ici, au niveau surtout de la forme (nous reproduisons le texte de la *Chr. de Fl.,* fol. 105v°-108r°, dans notre thèse – rubrique "Choix de textes" – en Appendice).

45. *Cf.,* à ce sujet, pour la motivation des "faits de réel" chez Chrétien de Troyes, le livre de Faith Lyons, *Les Eléments descriptifs dans le roman d'aventure au XIIIe siècle* (Genève: Droz (Publications romanes et françaises), 1965). A la page 1, l'auteur oppose, aux "descriptions plaquées sur le récit, superposées en quelque sorte à la narration" et même prescrites par les arts poétiques du temps, les objets décrits par Chrétien "*qui ont de l'importance pour l'évolution du* récit" (c'est nous qui soulignons). Voir aussi la p. 88, sur le "bliaut de Sire" dans l'*Escoufle* de Jean Renart.

46. Paradoxalement, Froissart ne réussit guère à motiver – de façon convaincante – les détails descriptifs utilisés dans le *Meliador,* oeuvre romanesque. Il réussit fort bien, pourtant, la motivation thématique et narrative des *poésies* de Wenceslas de Brabant insérées (toujours à propos) dans la trame de son roman. *Cf.,* à ce sujet, de M. Zink, "Les Toiles d'Agamanor et les fresques de Lancelot," *Littérature* XXXVIII (1980), pp. 43-61 (et surtout la p. 52) et de Jeanne Lods, "Les Poésies de Wencelas et le *Meliador* de Froissart", *Mél. Ch. Foulon* (1980) tome I, pp. 205-216 (surtout la p. 207 et la p. 216: il s'agit, pour Froissart, de "lier si étroitement ces pièces au roman qu'il serait impossible de les supprimer sans déchirer la trame du récit; (...) etc.").

47. SHF 10, pp. 250-251 (ll. 27-31/1-5); et *cf.* la p. 240 (ll. 16-26), et la p. 249 (ll. 13-22).

48. Mlle Blaess nous a fait part de sa méfiance concernant le rapprochement que nous faisons des deux berceaux (de Bruges et de Mâle). Admettons volontiers avec elle

que les lecteurs contemporains ne se seraient pas souciés de rapprocher (comme nous le faisons ici) les deux berceaux – qui sont mentionnés, d'ailleurs, dans l'édition de Raynaud, à la page 232 et à la page 249, respectivement – ; mais n'oublions pas que, pour un lecteur moderne, ce rapprochement devient possible, dans le cadre d'un *régime de lecture* plus proche de nos sensibilitiés actuelles. Nous ne croyons pas que ce soit là une déformation (par "anachronisme") du texte de Froissart. Les *Chroniques* peuvent être lues selon des perspectives distinctes et différentes (lecture "archéologique" ou lecture "transhistorique"; *cf.*, à ce sujet, le ch. 2 de notre thèse). Quant à la reconnaissance (par un lecteur du Moyen Age) de la *glose,* et de sa contribution à la "couleur morale" du récit, Mlle Blaess convient cette fois avec nous que ce phénomène était sans aucun doute "à la portée" des lecteurs contemporains de Froissart.

49. SHF 11, pp. 163-164 (ll. 30/1-9; 14-18). Si les passages examinés ci-dessus ne constituent pas en eux-mêmes un *memento mori,* ils en fournissent du moins, peut-être, les éléments – pour un lecteur tant soit peu attentif ...

50. SHF 10, pp. 238-239 (ll. 24-31/1-6).

51. *Ibid.,* pp. 243-244 (ll. 27-31/1-19). Relevons en passant la comparaison presque machiavélique de l'osier. *Cf.,* enfin, SHF 11, p. 57 (ll. 17-28): soulagement de Froissart après la défaite des rebelles à Roosebeke.

52. *Cf.* Quatrième livre, édition Kervyn de Lettenhove (*Oeuvres complètes de Froissart,* 28 vol., Bruxelles 1867-1877), tome XV, pp. 38-39: "Et on a veu en l'Anchien Testament et ou Nouvel moult de figures et d'exemples. N'avons-nous pas de Nabugodonosor, roy des Assiriens, lequel ung temps régna en telle puissance que dessus luy il n'estoit nouvelle de nul autre, et soubdainement en sa greigneur force et règne le souverain roy, Dieu, souverain sire des cieulx et de la terre et fourmeur de toutes choses, l'appareilla tel que il perdy sens et règne, et fut sept ans en tel estat que il vivoit de glans et de pommes sauvages, et avoit le goust et l'appétit d'un pourcel? [*sic*] et quant il ot fait celle pénitance, Dieu luy rendi sa mémoire, et adont dist-il à Daniel, le prophète, que dessus de Dieu d'Israel n'avoit nul autre Dieu."

Il est intéressant de constater que, quand Froissart rapporte la naissance de Philippe d'Artevelde dans la dernière rédaction du Premier livre (composée vers 1400), il écrit: "Chils enfes, nonmés Phelippes, fu depuis moult sages et bacelereus, et obtint tout le pais de Flandres a l'encontre dou conte et des signeurs et dou roi de France, ensi que vous orés recorder avant en l'istore" (édition Diller du ms de Rome, p. 415).

SUMMARY

Only two years before his death in 1384, Louis de Mâle, Count of Flanders, was to suffer a crushing (though temporary) reverse at the hands of Ghentish rebels at the battle of the Beverhoutsveld. Pursued by the Ghenters, he finds himself obliged to seek refuge in the miserable dwelling of a townswoman of Bruges.

The account of these events as it is given in Book II of Froissart's *Chronicles* offers the reader more than a purely historical interest. The text unexpectedly brings together a curious mixture of conventional elements – historical narrative, "novelistic" description, direct speech and biblical gloss, to the extent that it comes to resemble what might be described as an ironical *miroir du prince.* Unlike such works, however, Froissart's narrative does not moralise but rather *invites* moral reflexion on the part of the reader. No definitive statement is offered concerning the moral predicament of Count Louis, so suddenly reduced to the lowliest circumstances after a life of seigneurial pomp. Instead, the episodes considered in this paper appear to exhibit certain characteristics normally associated with literary texts. That is to say, the text – and the moral issues it raises – remain "open".

APPENDIX I

Prélude à la bataille du Beverhoutsveld; la bataille; fuite de Louis de Mâle, etc.
(Froissart, *Chroniques,* SHF 10), pp. 216-233)

Quant Phelippes ot parlé, ce fut grans pités de veoir hommes, femmes, et enffants plorer et tordre leurs poins pour l'amour de leurs maris, de leurs pères, de leurs voisins, de leurs frères. Après ce tourment de noisse, Philippes reprist la parolle et dist: "Or paix! paix!" Et on se teut tout, sitretos comme il recommencha à parler et dist: "Bonnes gens de Gand, vous estes en ceste place la grigneur partie dou peuple de Gand chi assamblé. [Si] avés oï che que jou ai dit: [si] n'i voi autre remède ne pourveance nulle que brief (*217*) conseil, car vous savés comment nous sommes menet et astraint de vivres; et il i a tels trente mille testes en ceste ville qui ne mengièrent de pain, passet a quinse jours: [si] nous faut faire des trois coses l'une. La première si est que nous nos encloons en ceste ville et entièrons toutes nos portes, et nous confessons à nos loiaux pooirs et nous boutons en eglises et en moustiers, et là morons confès et repentans, comme gens martirs de qui on ne voelt avoir nulle pité. En cel estat, Dieux ara merchi de nous et de nos ames, et dira on, partout où les nouvelles en seront oïes et sceues, que nous sommes mort vaillanment et comme loial gent. Ou nous nos mettons tout en tel parti que hommes, femmes et enffans alons criier merchi, les hars ou col, nus piés et [nus] chiefs, à monsigneur de Flandres: il n'a pas le coer si dur ne si oscur que, quant il nous vera en cel estat, que il ne se doie humelier et amoliier et de son povre peuple il ne doie avoir merchi; et je tous premiers, pour li oster de sa felonnie, presenterai ma teste et voel bien morir pour l'amour de ceulx de Gand. Ou nous nos eslissons en ceste ville cinc ou sis mille hommes les plus aidables et les mieux armés, et l'alons querir hastéement à Bruges et l'i combatre. Se nous sommes mort en che voiage, che sera honnerablement, et ara Dieux pité de nous et li mondes ossi; et dira on que loiaument et vaillanment nous avons soustenu et parmaintenu nostre querelle. Et, se en celle bataille Dieux a pité de nous, qui anchiennement mist poissance en le main de Judith, ensi [que] nos pères le nous recordent, qui ochist Olifernès qui estoit desous Nabugodonosor dus et maistres de sa chevalerie, par quoi li Asseriien (*218*) furent desconfit, nous serons li plus honnourés peuples qui ait resgné puis les Roumains. Or regardés laquelle des trois coses vous vollés tenir, car l'une faut il faire."

Adont respondirent cil qui plus prochain de lui estoient et qui le mieux sa parolle oï avoient: "Ha! chiers sires, nous avons tout en Gant grant fiance en vous que vous nous consillerés: si nous dites lequel nous ferons." – "Par ma foi! respondi Phelippes, je conseille que nous alons tout à main armée devers Monsigneur. Nous le trouverons à Bruges, et, lorsque il sara nostre venue, il istera contre nous et nous combatera, car li orgoes de ceux de Bruges, qui nous het, est avoec lui; et cil qui nuit et jour l'enfourment sur nous li consilleront de nous combatre. Se Dieux ordonne par sa grace que la place nous demeure et que nous desconfissons nos ennemis, nous serons recouvré à tousjours mais et les plus honnerées gens dou monde; et, se nous sommes desconfi, nous morons honnerablement, et ara Dieux pité de nous. Et parmi tant li demorans de Gand se passera, et en ara merchi li contes nos sires."

A ces parolles respondirent il tout d'une vois: "Et nous le volons, ne autrement nous ne finerons." Lors respondi Phelippes: "Or, [beaulx] signeur, puisque vous estes en celle volenté, or retournés en vos maissons, et apparilliés vos armeures, car demain dou jour je voel que nous partons de Gand, et en alons vers Bruges, car li sejourners ichi ne nous est point pourfitables. Dedens cinc jours, nous sarons se nous viverons à honneur ou nous morons à dangier, et je envoiierai les connestables des parosces de maison en (*219*) maison pour prendre et eslire à cues les plus aidables et les mieux armés."

Sus cel estat se departirent en la ville de Gand toutes gens qui à ce parlement avoit estet dou marchiet des devenres, et retournèrent en leurs maisons; et se apparillièrent, cascuns endroit de li, de ce que à lui appertenoit, et tinrent che merquedi leur ville si close que onques homs ne femme n'i entra ne n'en issi jusques au joedi à heure de relevée, que cil furent tout prest qui partir devoient. Et furent environ cinc mille hommes et non plus, et cargièrent environ deus cens chars de canons et d'artellerie, et set chars seullement de pourveances, cinc chars chergiés de pain quit et deus chars de vins; et tout partout n'en i avoit que deus tonniaulx, ne riens n'en demoroit en la ville. Or regardés comment il estoient astraint et menet. Au departement et au prendre congiet, che estoit une pités de veoir ceulx qui demoroient et ceuls qui s'en aloient, et dissoient li demorant: "Bonnes gens, vous veés bien à vostre departement que vous laissiés derrière. N'aiiés nulle esperance de retourner, se ce n'est à vostre honneur, car vous ne trouveriés riens, et, sitos que nous orons nouvelles se vous estes mort et desconfi, nous bouterons le feu en la ville, et nous destruirons nous meïsmes, ensi que gens desesperés." Chil qui s'en aloient dissoient, en iaulx reconfortant: "De tout che que vous dites, vous parlés bien. Priiés pour nous à Dieu: nous avons espoir que il nous aidera et vous ossi avant nostre retour." Enssi se departirent cil cinc mille hommes de Gand et leurs petites pourveances; et s'en vinrent ce (220) joedi logier et jesir à une heure et demie de Gand, et n'amenrirent de riens leurs pourveances, mais se passèrent de ce que il trouvèrent sus le pás. Le venredi tout le jour il ch[e]minèrent, et encores n'atouchièrent il de riens à leurs pourveances, et trouvèrent li fourageur sus le pás aucunes coses, dont il passèrent le jour; et vinrent che venredi logier à une grande lieue de Bruges, et là s'arestèrent, et prisent place à leur avis et pour atendre leurs ennemis, et avoient au devant d'eus un grant plachiet plain d'aighe dormant. De che lés là se fortefiièrent il à l'une des pars, et à l'autre lés de leur charroi, et passèrent enssi la nuit.

Quant che vint le samedi au matin, il fist moult bel et moult cler, car che fu le jour Sainte Elaine et le tierch jour dou mois de mai. Et che propre jour siet la feste et le pourcession de Bruges, et à che jour avoit plus de peuple en Bruges estragniers et autres, pour la cause de la solempnité de la feste et pourcession, que il n'eust en toute l'anée. Nouvelles avolèrent à Bruges en dissant: "Vous ne savés quoi? Li Gantois sont venu à nostre pourcession." Dont veïssiés en Bruges grant murmure et gens resvillier et aler de rue [en rue] et dire l'un à l'autre: "Et quel cose atendons nous que ne les alons nous combatre?" Quant li contes de Flandres, qui se tenoit en son hostel, en fu enfourmés, [si] vint à grant mervelle, et dist: "Velà folle gent et outrageus! La male mescance les cache bien. De toute le compaignie jamais piés n'en retournera. Or arons nous maintenant fin de guerre." Adont oï li contes sa messe; et toudis venoient chevalier de Flandres, de Hainnau et d'Artois, qui le servoient, (221) devers li, pour savoir quel cose il voroit faire. Enssi comme il venoient, il les requelloit bellement, et leur dissoit: "Nous irons combatre ces mesceans gens; encores sont il vaillant, disoit li contes: il ont plus chier à morir par espée que par famine."

Adont fu consilliet que on envoiieroit trois hommes d'armes chevaucheurs sour les camps, pour aviser le convenant de ceux de Gand et comment il se tenoient ne quelle ordonnance il avoient. Si furent dou mareschal de Flandres ordonné troi vaillant homme d'armes escuier, pour les aler aviser: Lambert de Lambres, Damas de Bussi [et] Jehans du [Beart]; et partirent tout troi de Bruges et prissent les camps, montés sus fleurs de coursiers, et chevauchièrent vers les ennemis. Entrues que chil troi fissent che dont il estoient cargiet, [s'ordonnèrent] en Bruges toutes manières de gens en très grant volenté que pour issir et venir combatre les Gantois, desquels je parlerai un petit et de leur ordenance.

Che samedi au matin, Phelippes d'Artevelle ordonna que toutes gens se meïssent envers Dieu en devotion, et que messes fuissent en pluiseurs lieux cantées, car il avoient là en leur compaignie des Frères Religieux, et que ossi cascuns se confessast et adrechast à son loial pooir et [mesist] en estat deu, enssi que gens qui atendoient la grace et la mesericorde de Dieu. Tout che fu fait: on celebra en l'ost en set lieux messes, et à cascune messe ot sermon, liquel sermon durèrent plus de heure et demie. Et là leur fu remonstré par ces clers, Frères Menours et autres, comment il se figuroient au peuple d'Israël que li rois Faraon d'Egipte tint lonc tamps en servitude, et comment depuis, par la

(*222*) grace de Dieu, il en furent delivret et menet en tère de promision par Moïse et Aaron, et li rois Pharaon et li Egiptiien mort et peri. "Enssi, bonnes gens, dissoient chil Frère Preceur en leurs sermons, estes vous tenu en servitude par vostre signeur le conte et vos voisins de Bruges, devant laquelle ville vous estes venu et arresté, et serés combatu, il n'est mie doubte, car vostre ennemi en sont en grant volenté, qui petit amirent vostre poissance. Mais ne regardés pas à cela, car Dieux, qui tout puet, tout set et tout congnoist, ara merchi de vous; et ne penssés point à cose que vous aiiés laissiet derière, car vous savés bien que il n'i a nul recouvrier ne restorier, se vous estes desconfi. Vendés vous vaillanment, et morés, se morir convient, honnerablement, et ne vous esbahissiés point, se grans peuples ist de Bruges contre vous; car la victoire n'est pas ou [grant] peuple, mais là où Dieux l'envoie et maint par sa grace; et trop de fois on a veu, par les Macabiiens ou par les Roumains, que li petis peuples de boine volenté et qui se confioit en la grace de Nostre Signeur, desconfissoit le grant peuple. Et en ceste querelle vous avés bon droit et juste cause par trop de raisons: si en devés estre plus hardi et mieux conforté." De telles parolles et de pluiseurs autres furent [par] les Frères Preceurs che samedi au matin li Gantois prechiet et remonstré, dont moult il se contentèrent; et se acumeniièrent les troi pars des gens de l'oost, et se missent tout en grant devotion, et monstrèrent tout grant cremeur avoir à Dieu.

Appriès ces messes, tout se missent ensemble (*223*) en un mont, et là monta Phelippes d'Artevelle sur un char pour li monstrer à tous et pour estre mieus oïs. Et là parla de grant sentement, et leur remonstra de point en point le droit que il penssoient à avoir en ceste querelle, et comment par trop de fois la ville de Gand avoient requis et priiet merci envers leur signeur le conte, et point n'i avoient peut venir sans trop grant confusion et damage de ceulx de Gand. Or estoient il si avant trait et venut que reculler il ne pooient, et aussi au retourner, tout consideré, riens il ne gaigneroient, car nulle cose derière fors que povreté et tristrèce laissiet il n'avoient. [Si] ne devoit nuls pensser après Gand ne à femme ne enfans que il eusist, fors que tant faire que li honneurs fust leur. Pluseurs belles parolles leur remonstra Phelippes, car bien fut enlangaigiés et mout bien sçavoit parler, et bien lui avenoit, et, sur la fin de sa parole, il leur dist: "Biaulx seigneurs, vous veés devant vous toutes vos pourveances; si les vuelliés bellement departir l'un à l'autre, ensi que frères, sans faire nuls outraiges, car, quant elles seront passées, il vous fault conquerir des nouvelles, se vous voulés vivre."

A ces paroles se ordonnèrent il mout humblement, et furent les chars deschargiés et les sachiées de pain données et departies par connestablies et li tonnel de vin tourné sus le fons. Là desjeunèrent il de pain et de vin raisonnablement et en heurent pour l'eure chascuns assés, et se trouvèrent après le desjunner fors et en bon point et plus aidables et mieux aidant de leurs membres que se il eussent plus mengié. Quant [ce] disner fu passés, il se mirent en ordonnance de bataille et se catirent entre leurs ribaudiaux. (*224*) Ces ribaudiaux sont brouettes haultes, bendées de fer, à longs picos de fer devant en la pointe, [qu'il] font par usage mener et brouetter avoec eulx; et puis les arroutèrent devant leurs batailles, et là dedans s'[encloïrent]. En cel estat les veïrent et trouvèrent les trois chevaucheurs dou conte, qui i furent envoiié pour aviser leur couvenant, car il les approchièrent de si près que jusques à l'entrer en leurs ribaudiaux, ne oncques les Gantois ne s'en esmeurent, et monstrèrent par samblant que il feussent tout   resjoï de leur venue.

Or retournèrent chil coureux à Bruges devers le conte, et le trouvèrent en son hostel à grant fuison de chevaliers qui là estoient, qui attendoient leur revenue pour oïr nouvelles. Il rompirent la presse et vinrent jusques au conte, et puis parlèrent tout hault, car li contes volt que il fussent oï des circonstans qui là estoient, et remonstrèrent comment il avoient chevauchié si avant que jusques ou trait des Gantois, se traire (pour édition S.H.F. *trairent*) volsissent, mais tout paisiblement il les avoient laissié approuchier, et comment il avoient veu leurs banières et comment il s'estoient repeus et quatis entre leurs ribaudiaux. "Et quel quantité de gens, dist li contes, puent il estre par advis?" Ceulx respondirent, selon leur advis au plus justement qu'il peurent, que il estoient de cinc à sis mille. Adont dist li contes: "Or tost, faittes apparillier toutes gens; je les vueil aller combatre, ne jamais dou jour ne partiront sans estre combatu.'' A ces parolles sonnèrent trompettes parmi Bruges, et s'armèrent toutes gens et se assemblèrent sur le marchié. Et ensi comme il (225) venoient, il se traioient tous et mettoient dessoubs les banières, ensi que par ordonnance et connestablies il avoient eu de usaige. Pardevant l'ostel dou conte se assembloient barons, chevaliers et gens d'armes. Quant tous furent apparilliés, li contes vint ou marché et veï grant fuisson de peuple rengié et ordonné, dont il se resjoï: adont commenda il à traire sus les champs, [A son commandement nuls ne desobeï, mais se departirent tous de la place et se mistrent au chemin par ordonnance et se traïrent sus les champs] et gens d'armes après.

Au vuider de la ville de Bruges, ce estoit grant plaisance dou veoir, car bien estoient quarante mil testes armées. Et ensi tout ordonnéement à cheval et à piés il s'en vinrent assés près dou lieu où li Gantois estoient, et là se arrestèrent. A celle heure, quant li contes de Flandres et ses gens vinrent, il estoit haulte remontée et le souleil s'en alloit tous jus. Bien estoit qui disoit au conte: "Sires, vous voïés vos ennemis; il ne sont au regard de nous que une pungnée de gens. Il ne puent fuir; ne les combatons meshui. Attendés jusques à demain que le jour venra sur nous; si verrons mieux quel chose nous devrons faire et se seront plus affoiblis, car il n'ont riens que mangier.'' Li contes s'acordoit assés à ce conseil, et oust voulentiers veu que on eust ensi fait, mais chil de Bruges par grant orgueil estoient si chaulx et si hastifs de eulx combatre que il ne vouloient nullement attendre, et disoient que tantost les aroient desconfis, et puis retourneroient en leur ville. Nonobstant ordonnance de gens d'armes, car li contes en avoit là grant fuison, plus de uit cens lances, chevaliers et escuiers, ceulx (226) de Bruges approchèrent et commencèrent à traire et à jetter de canons. Adont ceulx de Gand se misent tous en ung mont et se recueillirent tous ensemble et fisent tous à une fois desclicquer plus de trois cens canons, et tournèrent autour de ce plasquier, et misent ceulx de Bruges le souleil en l'ueil, qui mout les greva, et entrèrent dens eulx en escriant: "Gand!'' Sitost que ceulx de Bruges oïrent la voix de ceulx de Gand et les canons desclicquer, et que il les veïrent venir de front sur eulx et assaillir asprement, comme lasches gens et plains de mauvais convenant, il se ouvrirent tous et laissièrent les Gantois entrer dens eulx sans deffence, et jettèrent leurs bastons jus, et tournèrent le dos.

Les Ganthois, qui estoient fors et serrés et qui congneurent bien que leurs ennemis estoient desconfis, commencèrent à abatre devant eulx à deux costés et à tuer gens, et tousjours aller devant eulx, sans point desrouter, le bom pas, et crier: "Gand! Gand!'' et à dire entr'eux: "Avant! avant! suivons chaudement nos ennemis, il sont desconfis, et entrons en Bruges avoecq eulx. Dieu nous a ce soir regardés en pitié.'' Et ensi fisent il tous. Il poursuivirent ceulx de Bruges asprement, et, là où il les raconsuivoient, il les abatoient et occisoient, ou sus eulx il passoient, car point il n'arrestoient ne de leur chemin il n'issoient; et ceulx de Bruges, ensi que gens mors et desconfits, fuioient. Si vous di que en celle chace il en i ot mout de mors et de desconfits et d'abatus, car entr'eux point de deffence il n'avoient, ne onques si meschans gens que ceulx de Bruges ne furent ne qui plus recreanment se maintinrent scelon le grant bobant que (227) au venir sus les champs fait il avoient. Et veulent li aucun dire et supposer par imagination que il i avoit traïson, et les autres disent que non heut, fors povre deffence et infortunité qui cheï sur eulx.

Quant li contes de Flandres et les gens d'armes qui estoient sus les champs veïrent le povre arroi de ceulx de Bruges et comment d'eulx meïsmes il estoient desconfi ne point de recouvrer il n'i veoient, car chascuns qui mieux mieux fuioient devant les Gantois, si furent esbahis (pour édition S.H.F. *eshahis*) et eshidé de eulx meïsmes, et se commencèrent ossi à desrouter et à saulver et à fuir l'un sà et l'autre là. Il est bien vrai que, se il eussent point veu de bon convenant ne d'arrest de retour à ceulx de Bruges sur ceulx de Gand, il eussent bien fait aucun fait d'armes et ensonniet les Gantois, par quoi, espoir, il se fussent recouvrés; mais nennil, il n'en i veoient point, mais s'enfuioient chascuns qui mieux mieux vers Bruges, ne le fils n'attendoit mie le père ne le père le fils. Adont se desroutèrent ossi ces gens d'armes et ne tinrent point d'arroi, et n'eurent li pluseurs talant de traire vers Bruges, car la foule et la presse estoit si très grande sus les champs et sur le chemin en venant à Bruges que c'estoit grant hideur à veoir et de oïr les navrés et les blechiés plaindre et crier, et les Gantois aux talons de ceulx de Bruges crier: "Gand! Gand!" et abatre gens et passer oultre sans arrester. Ces gens d'armes le plus ne se fussent jamais boutés en ce peril. Meïsmement li contes fu conseilliés de retraire vers Bruges et de entrer premiers en la porte, et de faire garder la porte ou clorre, par quoi les Gantois ne l'esforchassent et feus(228)sent seigneurs de Bruges. Li contes de Flandres, qui ne veoit point de recouvrer de ses gens sus les champs et que chascuns fuioit et que ja estoit toute noire nuit, creï ce conseil et tint ce chemin et fist sa banière chevaucher devant lui, et chevaucha tant qu'il vint dedans Bruges, et entra en la porte auques des premiers, espoir, lui quarantime, ne plus ne se trouva il. Adont ordonna il ses gens pour garder la porte et pour clorre, se les Gantois venoient, et puis chevaucha li contes vers son hostel et envoia par toute la ville gens, et [fist] commandement que chascuns sus la teste perdre se traisist vers le marché. L'intention dou conte estoit telle de recouvrer la ville par ce parti, mais non fist, sicomme je vous recorderai.

Entretemps que li contes estoit en son hostel et que il envoioit les clers des doiens des mestiers de rue en rue, pour traire sur le marché et [recouvrer] la ville, li Gantois qui entrèrent en la ville de Bruges en poursuivant asprement leurs ennemis, le premier chemin qu'i fisent sans tourner chà ne là, il s'en allèrent tout droit sus le marchié, et là se rengièrent et arrestèrent. Messires Robert Mareschaux, ung chevalier dou conte, avoit esté envoié à la porte pour sçavoir comment on s'i maintenoit, entretemps que li contes faisoit son commandement qui cuidoit recouvrer la ville, mais il trouva que la porte estoit volée hors des gons et que li Gantois en estoient maistre; et proprement il trouva de ceulx de Bruges qui lui disent: "Robert, Robert, retournés et vous sauvés, car la ville est conquise de ceux de Gand." Adont retourna li chevaliers au plus tost qu'il peut devers le conte, qui se partoit (229) de son hostel tout à cheval et grant fuison de falots devant lui, et s'en venoit sus le marchié. Si lui dist ce chevalier ces nouvelles. Nonobstant, li contes, qui vouloit tout recouvrer, s'en vint vers le marchié; et, ensi comme il i entroit à grant fuison de falots, en escriant: "Flandres au lion au conte!" ceulx qui estoient à son frain et devant lui regardèrent et verent que la place estoit toute chargée de Gantois; si lui disent: "Monsigneur, pour Dieu, retournés. Se vous alés plus avant, vous estes mors, ou pris de vos ennemis au mieux venir, car il sont tous rengiés sus le marchié et vous attendent." Et ceulx lui disoient verité, car li Gantois disoient ja, si trestost comme il le verent naistre d'une ruelle: "Veci Monsigneur, veci le conte! Il vient entre nos mains." Et avoit dit Phelipes d'Artevelle et fait dire de renc en renc: "Se li contes vient sus nous, gardés bien que nuls ne lui face mal, car nous l'enmenrons vif et en sancté à Gand, et là arons nous paix à nostre voulenté." Li contes, qui venoit et qui cuidoit tout recouvrer, encontra, assés près de la place où li Gantois estoient tous rengiés, de ses gens qui lui disent: "Ha! Monsigneur, pour Dieu, n'alés plus avant, car li Gantois sont seigneurs dou marchié et de la ville; et, se vous entrés ou marchié, vous estes mort; et encores en estes vous en aventure, car ja vont grant fuison de Gantois de rue en rue, querant leurs ennemis, et ont mesmement assés de ceulx de Bruges, qui les mènent querir d'ostel en hostel ceulx qu'i veullent avoir; et estes [tous] ensonniés de vous sauver, ne par nulles des portes de Bruges ne vous poués [issir ne partir que vous ne soiés ou mors ou pris, car] li Gan(230)tois en sont seigneur, ne à vostre hostel ne poués vous retourner, car il i vont une grant route de Gantois."

Quant le conte entendi ces nouvelles, si lui furent très dures, et bien i ot raison, et se commença grandement à eshider et à imaginer le peril où il se veoit, et creut conseil de non aler plus avant et de lui saulver, se il pouoit. Et fu tantost de lui meïsmes conseilliés: il fist estaindre tous les falots qui là estoient, et dist à ceulx qui dalés lui estoient: "Je voi bien qu'il n'i a point de recouvrer. Je donne congiet à tout homme, et chascuns se saulve qui puet ou scet." Ensi comme il l'ordonna, il fu fait; les falots furent estaints et gettés dedans le[s] russiaux, et tantost s'espardirent et demuchièrent ceulx qui là estoient. Si se tourna li contes en une ruelle, et là se fist desarmer par ung sien varlet et jetter toutes ses armeures aval, et vesti la hoppelande de son varlet, et puis li dist:"Va t'an ton chemin, et te saulve, se tu pues. Aies bonne bouche: se tu eschiés es mains de mes ennemis et on te demande de moi, garde bien que tu n'en dies riens." – "Monsigneur, respondi chil, pour mourir ossi ne ferai je." Ensi demora li contes de Flandres tout seul, et pouoit bien adont dire que il se trouvoit en grant aventure, car, à celle heure, [se] par aucune infortunité, il fust escheus ens es mains des routes qui aval Bruges estoient et alloient et qui les maisons serchoient et les amis dou conte occisoient ou ens ou marchié les amenoient, et là tantost devant Phelippe d'Artevelle et les cappitaines il estoient mort et esservelé, sans nul moien ou remède il eust esté mort. Si fu Dieu proprement pour lui, quant de ce peril il le delivra et saulva, car (231) onques en si grant peril en devant n'avoit esté ne ne fu depuis, sicomme je vous recorderai presentement.

Tant se demucha, à icelle heure, environ mienuit ou ung peu oultre, li contes de Flandres par rues et par ruelles que il le convint entrer de nécessité, autrement il eust esté trouvé et pris des routiers de Gand et de Bruges ossi qui parmi la ville aloient, en l'ostel d'une pouvre femme. Ce n'estoit pas hostel de seigneur, de sales, de cambres ne de manandries, mais une povre maisonnette enfumée, ossi noire que arremen de fumiere de tourbes, et n'i avoit en celle maison fors le bouge devant et une povre tente de vièle toille enfumée pour esconser le feu, et pardessus un povre solier ouquel on montoit à une eschelle de set eschellons. En ce solier avoit un povre litteron où li povre enfant de la femmelette gisoient.

Quant li contes fut, tout seul et tout esbahi, entré en celle maison, il dist à la femme, qui estoit toute effreé[e]: "Femme, sauve moi! Je suis tes sires le conte de Flandres, mais maintenant il me fault repourre et mussier, car mes ennemis me chassent, et dou bien que tu me feras je t'en donrai bon guerdon." La povre femme le recongneut assés, car elle avoit esté plusieurs fois à l'aumosne à sa porte: si l'avoit veu aller et venir, ensi que ungs sires va en ses deduis, et fu tantost avisée de respondre, dont Dieu aida au conte, car elle n'eust peu si petit detrier que on eust trouvé le conte devant le feu parlant à elle: "Sire, montés amont en mon solier, et vous bout[és] dessoubs un lit où mes enfans dorment." Il le fist, et entretemps la femme se essonia en son hostel entour le feu et à ung (232) autre petit enfant qui gisoit en ung repos. Li contes de Flandres entra en ce solier et se bouta, au plus bellement et souef qu'il pot, entre la coute et l'estrain de ce povre literon; et là se quati et fist le petit: faire li convenoit.

Evous ces routiers de Gand qui routoient, qui entrent en la maison celle povre femme, et avoient, ce disoient aucuns de leur route, veu un homme entrer ens. Il trouvèrent celle povre femme seant à son feu, qui tenoit son enfant. Tantost il lui demandèrent: "Femme, où est uns homs que nous avons veu entrer seans et puis reclorre l'uis?" – "Et, par ma foi, dist elle, je n'i veï de celle nuit entrer homme ceans; mais j'en issi, n'a pas granment, et jettai hors un pou d'eaue, et puis recloï mon huis. Ne je ne le sçaroie où mussier; vous veés toutes les aisemences de ceans; velà mon lit, là sus gisent mes enfans." Adont prist li uns une chandelle, et monta amont sus l'eschellette et bouta sa teste ou solier, et n'i veï autre chose que le povre litteron des enfans qui dormoient. Si regarda il bien partout hault et bas. Adont dist il à ses compaignons: "Alons! alons! nous perdons le plus pour le mains. La povre [femme si] dist voir: il n'i a ame ceans fors elle et ses enfans." A ces parolles issirent il hors de l'hostel de la femme et s'en allèrent router autre part. Onques puis nuls n'i rentra qui mal i voulsist.

Toutesfois ces paroles avoit oïes li contes de Flandres, qui estoit couchés et catis en ce povre litteron. Si poués bien imaginer que il fu adont en grant effroi de sa vie. Quel chose pouoit il là, Dieux, penser ne imaginer? Quant au matin, il pouoit bien dire: "Je (233) suis li uns des grans princes dou monde des crestiens," et la nuit ensuivant il se trouvoit en telle petitesse, il pouoit bien dire et imaginer que les fortunes de ce monde ne sont pas trop estables. Encores grant heur pour lui, quant il s'en pouoit issir saulve sa vie. Toutesfois ceste perilleuse et dure aventure lui devoit bien estre ung grant miruer et doit estre toute sa vie.

Nous lairrons le conte de Flandres en ce parti, et parlerons de ceulx de Bruges et comment les Gantois perseverèrent.

APPENDIX II

Obsèques de Louis de Mâle (SHF 11, pp. 157-164)

Et li contes de Flandres vint à Saint Omer, et là se tint; et lui prist une maladie, de laquelle il morut assés tost après. Si fu ordonné que il giroit en l'eglise Saint Pierre à Lille. Et trespassa de cest siècle l'an de (*158*) grace mil trois cens quatre vins et trois, le vint et witime jour dou mois de jenvier, et fu apportés à Los l'Abeïe dalés Lille; et ossi i fu apportée la contesse sa femme, qui trespassée estoit, cinc ans avoit, en la conté de Rethés; et furent ensevé ensamble en l'eglise Saint Pière de Lille.

Or vous voel jou recorder l'ordenance.

Chi s'ensieuwent les ordonnances dou conte de Flandre et de la contesse sa femme, dont les corps furent aportés à Los l'Abeïe dalés Lille; et, quant il deurent entrer en Lille, grant fuison de seigneurs de France, de Flandres, de Hainnau et de Braibant i furent la vesprée, au venir de la porte des Malades et à porter les corps parmi la ville jusques à l'eglise Saint Pierre.

Chil qui i furent armet pour la guerre et les escuiers qui les menoient:

Et premiers, messire Jehan de Halluwin, le plus prochain dou corps, mené de Engherran de Walenne et de Rogier de l'Espière; le seigneur de Marcq, devant le seigneur de Halluwin, mené de Henri de l'Aubiel et de Jehan de Gommer; le seigneur de Mamines, devant le seigneur de Marcq, mené de Jehan de l'Espière et de Sausset de Fretin; messire Jehan dou Molin, devant le seigneur de Mamines, mené de Godefroid de Noiielle et de Henri de le Vacquerie.

Item s'ensieuwent chil ordonné pour le tournoi:

Messire Pierre de Bailloel prochain dou corps, devant messire Jehan dou Molin, menet de Jehan de Quinghien et de Lambequin le Marescal; messire Sohier de Gand, devant messire Pierre de Bailloel, menet de Guiot de Loncpret et de Jehan Loeuïs; le seigneur de Bethen(*159*)court, devant messire Sohier de Gand, menet de Gerart de Quinghien et de Rolant d'Isenghien; monseigneur l'Aigle de Sains, devant le seigneur de Bethencourt, menet de Huart de Quinghien et de Michiel de le Bare.

Apriès s'ensieuwent les banières de la bière:

Et premiers, messire François de Havesquerque; et puis messire Gossuin le Sovage, devant messire François; messire Lancelot la Personne, devant messire Gossuin; messire Jehan de Helle, devant messire Lancelot.

Item s'ensieuwent cil qui portèrent les banières de le bière et du tournoi:

Messire Mahieux de Humières, devant messire Jehan de Helle; le seigneur des Abiaux, devant le dessus dit sire Mahieu; messire Tiercelet de le Bare, devant le seigneur des Abiaux; messire Jehan de Paris, devant messire Tiercelet.

Item chi après s'ensieuwent les noms des barons, qui aidièrent à porter le corps dou conte de la porte des Malades mouvant, en venant parmi la ville de Lille, jusques à l'eglise Saint Pierre:

Et premiers, messire Jehans de Viane, amiraus de France, au destre, et li seigneur de Ghistelle, au senestre; messire Waleran de Raineval après, au destre, et le castelain de Disquemue, au senestre; le seigneur d'Escornais après, au destre; messire Ansel de Salins, au senestre.

Item chi s'ensieuwent li baron, qui aidièrent à porter le corps de la contesse de Flandres, mouvant de la porte Saint Ladre en venant, jusques à l'eglise Saint Pière:

Et premiers, le seigneur de Sulli, au costé destre, (*160*) et le seigneur de Castillon, au costé senestre; messire Guis de Pontaliers, marescal de Bourgongne après, au costé destre, et monsigneur Gerart de Ghistelle, au costé senestre; et puis, messire Henri d'Antoing, au destre, et le castellain de Furnes, au senestre.

Item chi après s'ensieuwent les ordonnances dou jour de l'obsecque, lequel on fist en l'eglise Saint Pierre à Lille, et comment les corps furent enterés, et li seigneur qui i furent, et les escus; ossi les noms des escuiers qui tinrent les escus toute la messe durant jusques à l'ofertoire:

Le duc de Bourgongne tout seul; et le premier escut fist porter devant lui de messire Raoul de Raineval et dou seigneur de la Grutuse; et fu soustenu l'escut de Lambequin de la Coustre et de Jehan de Pontaliers, frère au mareschal de Bourgongne.

Après, le second escut, devant monseigneur Jehan d'Artois, conte d'Eu, et messire Philippe de Bar: l'escut fu tenus de Waleran de la Sale et de l'Esclave d'Anechin.

Après, le conte de la Marce et messire Phelippe d'Artois: l'escut fu tenus de Gillion de le Brest et de Robin de Floregni. Après, Robert, monseigneur de Namur, dalés lui messire Guillaume de Namur, sen nepveu: l'escut fu tenus de Cambernart et de Gerart d'Estervaille.

Item pour les escus dou tournoi:

Le seigneur d'Enghien, dalés lui messire Jehan de Namur: l'escut fu tenus de Eulart de Poucres et de Hervi de Mouci.

Après, messire Hue de Chalon et le seigneur de Fère: (*161*) l'escut fu tenus de Jehan de Halluin et de Oudart de [Caserom].

Après, le seigneur d'Antoing et le seigneur de Ghistelle: l'escut fu tenus de Tristran de Lambres et de Jehan dou Beart.

Après, le seigneur de Moriamés et le seigneur de Sulli: l'escut fu tenus de Jehan de Fressinghem et de Damas de Bussi.

Item s'ensieuwent chil qui offrirent les destriers de la guerre:

Et premiers, le seigneur de Chastillon et messire Simon de Lalaing, bailli de Hainnau, et estoient li seigneur à piet, et li cheval armet et couvert; pour le second, messire Waleran de Raineval et le castelain de Disquemue; pour le tierch, messire Hue de Melun et le seigneur d'Aussi; pour le quart, le seigneur de Briffoel et le seigneur de Brimeu.

Item s'ensieuwent chil qui offrirent les destriers dou tournoi:

Et premiers, messire Henris d'Antoing et messire G[e]rart de Ghistelle pour le premier; pour le second, le seigneur de Montegni et le seigneur de Rassenghien; pour le tierch, le seigneur de le Hamaide et le castelain de Furnes; et pour le quart, le seigneur de Fagnoelles et messire Rolant de le [Clite].

Item s'ensieuwent chil qui offrirent les glaives de la gherre:

Premiers, monseigneur l'amiral de France; [le] second, le seigneur de[Rai]; le tierch, le mareschal de Bourgogne; et le quart, le seigneur de Sempi.

Item s'ensieuwent les noms de ceux qui offrirent les espées dou tournoi:

(*162*) Premiers, messire Guillaume de Ponthieu; le second, messire Guillaume de la Tremouille; le tierch, le castellain d'Ippre; et le quart, messire Ghuis de Honcourt.

Item s'ensieuwent cil qui offrirent les hiaumes de la gherre:

Pour le premier, le seigneur de Villers, et dalés lui le seigneur de Mailli; pour le second, messire Guillaumes de Hornes et messire Ansiel de Salins; pour le tierch, messire Jehan d'[Ophem] et le castelain de Saint Omer; et pour le quart, messire Ghuis de Ghistelle et le Galois d'Aulnoi.

Item pour les heaumes dou tournoi:

Premiers, messire Josse de Halluwin et messire Olivier de Gussi; pour le second, le seigneur de la Capelle et le seigneur de Mornai; pour le tierch, le seigneur de [Hollebeque] et le seigneur de Lalaing; et pour le quart, messire Tristran dou Bois et Messire Jehan de Jeumont.

Item s'ensieuwent chil qui offrirent les banières de guerre:

Pour le premi[è]re, le seigneur de [Lichtervelde]; pour le seconde, messire Lionel d'Araines; pour le tierce, messire Gille de la Grutuse; et pour le quarte, messire Jehan de Linseillon.

Item s'ensieuwent chil qui offrirent [les banières] dou tournoi:

Pour la première, messire Orengois de Rilli; pour la seconde, messire Jehan de Chevreuses; pour la tierce, messire Jehan de Disquemue; et pour la quarte, messire

Guillaume de la [Clite].

Item s'ensieuwent les noms des seigneurs qui, après *(163)* l'obsèque fait, misent le corps dou conte de Flandres en terre: messire Jehan de Viane, amiral de France, le seigneur de Ghistelle, messire Walleran de Raineval, le castellain de Disquemue, le seigneur de [Rai] et messire Ansiau de Sallins.

Item s'ensieuwent les noms de ceux qui enterrèrent le corps de la contesse, femme qui fu au conte: monseigneur Ghuis de la Tremouille, le seigneur de Sulli, le seigneur de Castillon, le mareschal de Bourgoingne, monseigneur Gerard de Ghistelle, monseigneur Henri d'Antoing et le castellain de Furnes. Et est assavoir que tous ceux qui furent en office à l'entrer en l'eglise de Saint Pierre de Lille, quant les corps i furent aportés la vesprée, il demorèrent en l'office à l'endemain à la messe, tant des chevaliers armés comme de ceux qui portoient banières, et ossi des escuiers qui menèrent les chevals.

Item i eut à l'aporter les corps dou conte de Flandres et de la contesse sa femme, parmi la ville de Lille, venant jusques à l'eglise Saint Pierre, quatre cens hommes, ou environ, tous noirs vestus. Et porta cascuns desdis hommes une torse, pour convoier les corps jusques à le dite eglise Saint Pierre; et ces quatre cens hommes dessus dis tinrent les torses l'endemain en l'eglise durant la messe, et tout chil qui les tenoient estoient eschevin de bonne villes ou officier de son hostel; et dist la messe li archevesques de Rains, et estoit acompaigniés de l'evesque de Paris, de l'evesque de Tournai, de l'evesque de Cambrai et de l'evesque d'Arras, et si i furent avoecq eux cinc abbés.

Item, il est assavoir que il ot en l'eglise, à l'obsecque, *(164)* ung traveil auquel il avoit set cens candeilles u environ, cascune candeille de une livre pesant, et sus ledit traveil avoit cinc banières: chelle dou milieu estoit de Flandres, [et la destre d'Artois, et la senestre] au desous, de la conté de Bourgongne, et la quatrime après, de la conté de Nevers, et la cinquime, de la conté de Rethel. Et estoit li travaus armoiés d'un lés d'escuchons de Flandres, et au lés senestre de madame, d'escuchons de Flandres et de Braibant. Et aval l'eglise avoit douse cens candelles ou environ, pareilles à celles dou traveil, et n'i avoit dame ne damoiselle de par monseigneur de Bourgongne ne de par madame sa femme, fors la gouverneresse de Lille, femme au gouverneur. Et i fist on ung très biau disner, et furent delivret de tous coustenges et frais, tant de bouce comme as hostels, tous chevaliers et escuiers qui la nuit et le jour de l'obsecque i furent ensonniiet, et leur furent envoiet tout li noir drap de coi il furent vesti à ce jour.

APPENDIX III

Obsèques de Louis de Mâle (Chronique des règnes de Jean II et de Charles V, éd. R. Delachenal, Paris, SHF, 1910-1920; tome 3, pp. 62-64.

Item, le penultime jour de janvier l'an mil CCCIIII``et troiz dessus dit, trespassa messire Loys, conte de Flandres, d'Arthois, de Bourgoigne, de Nevers et de Rethel, et fut enterré à Lille, le derrain jour de fevrier l'an dessus dit, et sa femme aveques lui, en l'eglise Saint-Pierre et fut fait l'obseque moult solennelment par la maniere qui s'ensuit: Premierement, le duc de Bourgoigne, qui avoit espousé la fille du conte, et son heritiere seule et pour le tout, ala au devant jusques à l'abaie d'Alos, à une lieue de Lille, où les diz corps estoient, et les fist admener en deux chars couvers de noir, à une croix vermeille en chascun char où ilz estoient, à grant compaignie de gens tous armez et leurs lances après eulx avec leurs bacinez, et y en avoit grant foison de vestuz de noir, de l'ostel dudit duc de Bourgoigne, sans les gens et officiers du feu conte. Et, quant ilz furent arrivez à la porte de Lille, les diz corps furent deschargiez des dis chars et furent chargiez sur deux autres petiz et bas charios, sur lesquelx ilz furent assés hault troussez sur tresteaux, qui y furent ordenez pour les mener plus seurement jusques en la dite eglise de Saint-Pere, le long de la *(63)* chaussée de ladite ville, qui est moult mauvaise, escrillant et perilleuse, et ne les eust on peu bonnement porter à gens, consideré le mauvais pavement et que leurs corps, ainsi qu'ilz estoient, pesoient chascun de IIII à V^e livres. Et lors dessendi le dit duc de Bourgoigne et toutes ses gens à pié, et aussi V ou VI dames et damoiselles, vestues de noir, qui estoient emprès le corps de ladite contesse, et furent menez les diz corps sur les diz petiz charioz au long de la dite ville, depuis la porte jusques à la dite eglise de Saint-Pierre, par la maniere qui ensuit, c'est assavoir qu'il y avoit devant les diz corps XVI destriers ou autres chevaux, touz sellez de haultes [selles?], et sur les VIII premiers estoient VIII chevaliers, qui portoient VIII banieres des armes de Flandres, dont il y avoit IIII de bateure pour le tournay et IIII pour la guerre, et sur les autres VIII chevaulx avoit VIII autres chevaliers, qui portoient escus des dites armes de Flandres aveques espées, dont les [quatre] estoient semblablement pour le tournay et les autres IIII pour la guerre.

Et après iceulx chevaulx, entre eulx et les diz charioz, avoit seulement un religieux, qui portoit devant les diz corps une petite croix de bois painte et basse, sanz hault baston. Et, quant ilz furent en la dite eglise de Saint-Piere, furent faites incontinent, ce jour mesmes, les vegilles moult solennelles, et landemain, c'est assavoir le dit lundi derrain jour de fevrier, la messe à (64) moult grant luminaire, par l'ordenance qui s'ensuit: Premierement s'ensuivent les seigneurs qui offrirent les escuz de la guerre: le dit duc de Bourgoigne offrit le premier escu, et furent au dit escu atachées XIII chandelles, et fut porté l'escu du seigneur de Royneval et du seigneur de Gruthuse, le quel escu les diz deux seigneurs receurent de Lammequin de la Cousture et de Jehan de Pontalier, escuiers. Et aveques ce offri icellui duc de Bourgoigne XIII frans, et au retour de la dite offrande s'agenoilla une espasse de temps devant le corps du dit conte.

DEUX POETES DU MOYEN AGE EN FACE DE LA MORT : RUTEBEUF ET VILLON

Jean Dufournet

Tout mot me fait mal. Combien pourtant il me serait doux d'entendre des fleurs bavarder sur la mort!

J'ai journellement des apartés avec mon squelette, et cela, jamais ma chair ne me le pardonnera.

(E.M. Cioran, Syllogismes de l'amertume)

Rutebeuf, dans la seconde moitié du 13ème siècle, se situe à un moment de changement où, selon Philippe Ariès[1], on passe de la *mort apprivoisée* à la *mort de soi*, plus dramatique et plus personnelle, dont les traits distinctifs auront tendance à s'accentuer jusqu'au 16ème siècle: représentation du Jugement dernier, suppression du temps eschatologique, apparition du cadavre, individualisation des sépultures. Aussi retrouvons-nous d'abord, de Rutebeuf à Villon, les mêmes lieux communs, avec des variantes dues à la manière propre aux deux poètes.[2]

I

La mort nous guette, bête sauvage qui mord et dévore, prête à nous assaillir à chaque instant, sans que personne puisse prévoir sa venue. Chaque moment peut être fatal. Pour Rutebeuf,[3] elle est derrière chacun, la massue levée ou les filets en mains. Ainsi dans la *Disputaison du Croisé et du Décroisé* (vers 177-182)

> Laz! ti dolant, la mors te chace
> Qui tost t'avra lassei et pris;
> Dessus ta teste tient sa mace:
> Viex et jones prent a un pris,

Tantost a fait de pié eschace.

L'image de la massue présente deux variantes, que la Mort brise les jambes de sa victime[4] ou qu'elle la plonge dans la nuit.[5] Villon, plus concis, utilise l'image du couteau suspendu sur la tête de chaque homme:

Ce monde n'est perpetuel,
Quoi que pense riche pillard:
Tous sommes sous mortel coutel (T. XLIII).

La mort frappe sans avertir, *jusqu'au fort ne menace*[6], l'homme qui est à la merci d'un funeste accident[7], et tout se déroule avec une effrayante rapidité:

Et il muert si soudainement
C'on ne veut croire qu'il soit mort.[8]

Rien ne peut l'empêcher de survenir, ni la beauté, ni la force, ni la sagesse. Rutebeuf le répète dans la *Voie de Tunis* (vers 105-107) à grand renfort de lieux communs:

Foulz est qui contre mort cuide troveir deffence:
Des biax, des fors, des sages fait la mors sa despanse:
La mors mort Absalon et Salomon et Sanse.[9]

La richesse ne sert à rien[10], mais pas davantage la sagesse ni la piété:

En la mort a felon passage,
Passer i estuet fol et sage;
Qui cel pas cuide trespasser
En fol cuidier se puet lasser.
Tout li estuet lessier, tout lesse.
La mort ne fet plus longue lesse
A ceste dame ci endroit.

(*La Vie sainte Elysabel*, vers 1967-1973).

Aussi peut-elle sembler déloyale, cruelle, ignoble, quand elle arrache au monde un prudhomme:

> Mors desloauz, qui riens n'entanz,
> ...
> Mors desloiaux, mors deputaire,
> De toi blasmeir ne me puis taire
> Quant il me sovient des bienz faiz
> Que il a devant Tunes faiz ...
>
> *(La Complainte du Roi de Navarre*, vers 43 et 51-54)[11]

Villon a repris le *topos* dans un huitain qui suggère le mouvement de la danse macabre, et qui fait une place particulière aux femmes:

> Je congnois que pauvres et riches,
> Sages et fous, prêtres et lais,
> Nobles, vilains, larges et chiches,
> Petits et grands, et beaux et laids,
> Dames à rebrassés collets,
> De quelconque condition,
> Portant atours et bourrelets,
> Mort saisit sans exception (T. XXXIX).[12]

De toute façon, la vie est courte, car, le répète Rutebeuf, ''nous n'avons point de demain''.

> Et nous n'avons point de demain,
> Quar li termes vient et aprouche
> Que la mort nous clorra la bouche.
>
> *(La Complainte d'Outremer*, vers 146-148)[13]

Nous portons le trépas en nous-mêmes, et Rutebeuf s'est complu à illustrer un lieu commun vulgarisé par les poésies pieuses: ''Quant li hons naist, lors commence a morir, et quant plus vit, et moins a a durer''.[14] La seule certitude est que l'on doit mourir:

> Mais je vos puis par droit proveir
> Que, quant li hons commence a nestre,
> En cest siecle a il pou a estre

Ne ne seit quant partir en doit.
La riens qui plus certeinne soit
Si est que mors nos corra seure;
La mains certainne si est l'eure.

(Nouvelle Complainte d'Outremer, vers 190-196)

En ce monde-ci transitoire, dira Villon (T.VIII), les jours s'en vont, aussi vite emportés que les bouts de fil d'une pièce de toile que brûle le tisserand:

Lors, s'il y a un bout qui saille,
Soudainement il est ravie (T. XXVIII).

L'on ne peut rien emporter, il ne reste, au mieux, que l'amour de Jésus-Christ:

Mout est fols qu'en son cors se fie,
Quar la mort, qui le cors desfie,
Ne dort mie quant li cors veille,
Ainz li est toz jors a l'oreille.
N'est fors que prez li granz avoirs;
Tout va et biauté et savoirs:
Por c'est cil fols qui s'en orgueille,
Quant il les pert, vueille ou ne vueille.
Folie et orgueil sont parent;
Sovent i est bien apparent.
Tout va, ce trovons en escrit,
Fors que l'amors de Jhesucrist.

(La Vie sainte Elysabel, vers 1935-1947)

Villon rappelle que Jacques Coeur pourrit *sous riche tombeau* (T. XXXVI) sans qu'il subsiste aucune trace de lui:

Qu'avoir esté seigneur! Que dis?
Seigneur, lasse! ne l'est-il mais?
Selon ce que David en dit,
Son lieu ne connaîtra jamais (T. XXXVII).

Mourir est douloureux, au physique d'abord. Pour suggérer le *pas de la mort*, Rutebeuf, tout au long de sa carrière poétique, a joué sans se lasser sur la *mort qui mord*. En voici les principales variations, de la plus simple à la plus complexe:

1.   Voici la plus élémentaire:

> Que feras se la mors te mort?
>> (*Disputaison du Croisé et du Décroisé*, vers 207)

> (Dieu) por nos ot le mors amer
> De la mort vilaine et amere.[16]

2.   Le jeu s'étoffe par répétition et par adjonction d'*amordre* ou de *remordre*, en parlant de la conscience:

> Vous vous moqueiz de Dieu tant que vient a la mort,
> Si li crieiz merci lors que li mors vos mort,
> Et une consciance vos reprent et remort;
> Si n'en souvient celui tant que la mors le mort.
>> (*Voie de Tunis*, vers 117-120)[17]

3.   Nous atteignons à la plus grande ampleur avec la succession *remordre + mort + mordre + morceau*:

> Mort en fait la mors a remordre
> Qui si gentil morcel a mors:
> Piesa ne mordi plus haut mors.
>> (*Complainte du Roi de Navarre*, vers 32-34)[18]

4.   Une variation intéressante introduit le thème de la mort de la mort par Dieu:

> C'est cil qui por nos reçut mort,
> C'est li sires qui la mort mort,
> C'est cil par qui la mort est morte
> Et qui d'enfer brisa la porte.
>> (*La Vie sainte Marie l'Egiptianne*, vers 1063-1068)

Ailleurs, il s'agit de la *mort amère*.[19] Mais chez Rutebeuf, rien de réaliste, aucune description de l'agonie, aucun macabre, hormis une furtive allusion dans l'*Ave Maria Rutebeuf* (vers 25-26):

> Trop par sont les morsiaus divers
> Dont la char manjuent les vers.

Nous sommes loin de Lothaire de Segni[20] et de la fin du Moyen Age qui se complaît à montrer le cadavre grouillant de vers. Quant à Villon qui reprend le lieu commun de la mauvaise morsure (*Eschevez le, c'est un mal mors*, vers 1724), il ne consacre que deux strophes aux affres de l'agonie; encore la seconde se termine-t-elle par l'évocation du corps féminin dans toute sa beauté (XL-XLI):

> Et meure ou Pâris ou Hélène,
> Quiconque meurt, meurt à douleur:
> Celui qui perd vent et haleine,
> Son fiel se crève sur son coeur,
> Puis sue, Dieu sait quel sueur!
> Et qui de ses maux si l'allège?
> Car enfant n'a, frère ne soeur
> Qui lors vousît être son pleige.
>
> La mort le fait frémir, pâlir,
> Le nez courber, les veines tendre,
> Le col enfler, lâcher, mollir,
> Jointes et nerfs croître et étendre …
> Corps féminin, qui tant est tendre,
> Poli, souef, si précieux,
> Te faudra-il ces maux attendre?
> Oui, ou tout vif aller ès cieux.

II

Mais maintenant Villon et Rutebeuf vont s'éloigner l'un de l'autre. Car, pour le second, le *mourir* est douloureux aussi d'un point de vue moral. L'on éprouve le sentiment d'avoir gaspillé sa vie à ne rien faire, de l'avoir dépensée en jeux futiles, d'arriver devant Dieu les mains vides:

> Au siecle ne sons que prestei
> Por veoir nostre efforcement;

Nos n'avons yver ne estei
Dont aions asseurement;
S'i avons jai grant piece estei,
Et qu'i avons nos conquestei
Dont l'arme ait nule seurtei?
Je n'i voi fors desperement.

(Chanson de Pouille, vers 17-24)[21]

Il faut donc mériter le Paradis quand il est encore temps:

Que n'entendeiz a vostre afaire
Tant com de vie aveiz espace?
N'atendeiz pas que la mors face
De l'arme et dou cors desevrance.

(Nouvelle Complainte d'Outremer, vers 68-71)

Ce sentiment, Rutebeuf le reprend à son compte dans la Repentance Rutebeuf (vers 4-9):

Bien me doit le cuer lermoier,
C'onques ne me poi amoier
A Dieu servir parfetement,
Ainz ai mis mon entendement
En geu et en esbatement,
Qu'ainz ne daignai nes saumoier.[22]

Villon, s'il regrette le temps de sa jeunesse folle où il a plus qu'un autre galé, fait la noce (T. XXII et XXVI), c'est surtout en raison de son échec social, du manque de biens matériels: J'eusse, dit-il, maison et couche molle (vers 204), et, comme les grands maîtres:

Bons vins ... souvent embrochés,
Sauces, brouets et gros poissons,
Tartes, flans, oeufs frits et pochés,
Perdus et en toutes façons (T. XXXII).

Pour Rutebeuf, la mort surtout débouche sur le Juise, le Jugement, qui, selon la vie que l'on aura menée, nous vaudra une éternité de bonheur au Paradis ou de malheur en Enfer:

Li fel, li mauvés, li cuivers
....
Doit bien avoir le cuer plain d'ire
Quant du siecle doit departir;
De duel li doit li cuers partir
Quant il voit bien sans sejorner
Que il n'en puet plus retorner;
Perdre li estuet cors et ame
Et metre en perdurable flame.
Més li bons qui a Dieu servi
Et qui a le cors asservi
Au siecle por l'ame franchir,
Cil ne puet cheoir ne guenchir
Que s'ame n'ait isnel le pas
Paradis aprés le trespas;
Liement le passage passe.

(*Vie de sainte Elysabel*, vers 1952-1965)

Si le règne de l'injustice est si proche de son écroulement terrible, ses représentants auront à se justifier devant la justice impitoyable de Dieu: *Si covient a Dieu reson rendre (Repentance Rutebeuf*, vers 71). Il s'agit alors d'une nouvelle justice, contrepoint à celle du monde, d'un nouveau renversement cette fois dans le sens du Bien. Atmosphère du Dies Irae. La peur frappera les plus hardis:

Li plus hardi seront si qoi
C'on les porroit prendre a la main.

(*Complainte d'Outremer*, vers 144-145)

.... au Jugement,
Quant il fera si aigrement
Tout le monde communement
Trambler com fueille.

(*Ave Maria Rutebeuf*, vers159-162)

Honteux, incapables de se justifier, même les justes se tairont:

Comment oseroie tentir,
Quant nés li juste avront doutance?

(*Repentance Rutebeuf*, vers 17-18)[24]

Tous ces thèmes, cent fois traités, se regroupent autour de la vision du Christ en croix, montrant ses plaies (*Complainte d'Outremer*, vers 140), séparant les justes des méchants, redressant le monde et remettant l'échelle des vraies valeurs en place:

C'est cil qui au jour du Juise
Fera des pecheors justise:
Les siens fera avoec lui estre
Et li autre iront a senestre.

(*La Vie sainte Marie l'Egiptianne*, vers 1073-1076)

– c'est-à-dire en enfer dont les images matérielles s'organisent autour des thèmes d'obscurité, de flamme, de claustration et d'impureté. C'est la fournaise d'*enfer le bouillant* (*Miracle de Théophile*, vers 392), *punaise, laide et obscure* (*Ave Marie*, vers 136), la flamme se doublant d'obscurité (*en la flame d'enfer le noir, Miracle de Théophile*, vers 108), dans le monde clos de ce *mal hosté* (*Dit de Notre Dame*, vers 116), puits, prison, maison à la porte obstinément fermée:

Et lor mesons rest si obscure
C'on n'i verra ja soleil luire,
Ainz est uns puis toz plains d'ordure:
        La irai gié.

(*Miracle de Théophile*, vers 118-120)

Marais infernaux qui véhiculent l'idée de souillure et d'ordure: *enfer l'entoié* (*Dit de sainte Eglise*, vers 71), *palu d'enfer qui est vils et obscure* (*Vie de sainte Marie l'Egiptianne*, vers 270-272) De là un certain pathétique destiné à émouvoir et à effrayer pour convaincre. Faut-il y retrouver un écho des bûchers de l'Inquisition?

L'on retrouve, dans deux ballades de Villon, certaines formules et évocations, les *infernaux palus* (vers 874) où *damnés sont boullus* (vers 897); mais l'une de ces ballades, la *Ballade pour prier Notre Dame*, au coeur du *Testament*, Villon l'a mise dans la bouche de sa mère; l'autre, celle des *Pendus*, est demeurée exclue du *Testament*. Pour faire bref, jugement dernier et enfer sont absents de son oeuvre, sinon sous forme d'allusions, souvent burlesques, puisque, selon lui, parlant des patriarches et des prophètes, *onques grand chaud n'eurent aux fesses* (vers 808), et qu'en enfer,

Pions y feront mate chere,
Qui boivent pourpoint et chemise.

> Puisque boiture y est si chère,
> Dieu nous garde de la main mise!

(vers 821-824)

En revanche, pour Villon, la mort est liée au vieillissement, présence de la mort dans la vie, qu'il observe chez les *pauvres femmelettes/qui vieilles sont ... pauvres vieilles sottes*, dont *la Belle qui fut heaumière* est le porte-parole, et chez le *pauvre vieillard*, autrefois un *plaisant raillard*. La vieillesse, qui survient d'un coup, écarte de la vie, contraint de vivre dans le seul univers des vieux, incapable de susciter l'attention et *a fortiori* l'amour:

> Car vieilles n'ont cours ni être
> Ne que monnaie qu'on décrie.

(vers 539-540)

Elle apporte avec elle la laideur, la léthargie, la paralysie: tel est le sinistre avertissement des vers 958-962. Elle est encore plus redoutable pour un poète qui, usé, est dépossédé de ce qui le distinguait, de sa drôlerie et de sa verve satirique. Sa jeunesse évanouie, il n'a plus de génie, il déplaît, parce qu'il est triste et qu'il se répète, vieux singe débitant des bouffonneries ressassées qui, loin de faire rire, excèdent (huitain XXXXV).[25]

III

Comment donc échapper à l'obsession, voire aux tortures de la mort?

De nouveau, les positions des deux poètes diffèrent considérablement. Pour Rutebeuf, il faut se préparer à la mort en se pénétrant de ces tragiques vérités et en les répandant autour de soi, en se conciliant Dieu et la Vierge, en méritant l'intercession de celle-ci par une vie de sacrifice et le service de Dieu selon sa classe sociale: pour le clergé, ne penser qu'à l'âme et secourir les autres au double point de vue spirituel et matériel; pour les chevaliers, opter pour un nouvel idéal qui passe par la croisade où l'on peut trouver la palme du martyre; pour le poète, dénoncer le mal, dire la vérité sans se soucier des risques, indiquer des modèles, prêcher la croisade.

Ainsi est-il possible d'atteindre à la sainteté qui apporte une mort apaisée et douce, et sur ce point comme sur d'autres Rutebeuf retrouve l'idéal de la première chanson de geste. Témoin sainte Elisabeth de Hongrie, qui chante (vers 1982-1994), met en fuite le démon (vers 1999-2001), parle de Dieu, *li purs, li fins, li afinez* (vers 2008), semble e pas souffrir ni perdre ses couleurs:

> Au parler de Dieu deïssiez,
> Se vous el vis la veïssiez,
> Qu'ele n'avoit mal ne dolor,
> Que lors ne perdist ja sa color.

(vers 2015-2018)

Elle connaît l'heure de sa mort, ce qui la remplit de joie (vers 2019-2022). Bref,

> Cele qui si douce fin a
> Fu tout aussi comme endormie,
> Qu'au trespasser n'est point finie.

(vers 2024-2026)

Son cadavre répand une très douce odeur (vers 2029-2032); on se disputa les reliques de son corps, et de nombreux miracles se produisirent. Il en alla de même pour Marie l'Egyptienne, la prostituée réconciliée avec Dieu par trente ans de pénitence (vers 1121-1141): sa chair ne se décomposa pas, protégée contre les oiseaux et les vers jusqu'à son ensevelissement, et c'est un lion qui creusa sa tombe.

En filigrane, il est possible de découvrir un autre type de consolation, que suggère la *Pauvreté Rutebeuf*, qui célèbre la naissance divine de la poésie à travers le manque et le dépouillement, la découverte de la richesse spirituelle et poétique dans une misère de plus en plus atroce qui est une véritable mort au monde. La troisième strophe où le poète se proclame *mors* et *maubailliz*, la plus chargée de négativité, où la pauvreté se creuse jusqu'à la béance de l'être, constitue un sommet par la densité poétique et la richesse symbolique: on passe d'un jeu sur la *faille*, le manque, à une image simple qui éclate et rayonne, celle de la paille.[26]

Pour Villon, il s'agit avant tout d'écarter toute vision horrible de la mort, de l'oublier plutôt que de s'y préparer. Aussi utilise-t-il, pour l'essentiel, trois moyens.

1. Il procède par *allusions* plutôt que par *descriptions*. La mort n'est nommée que de façon détournée. Chr. Martineau-Génieys, dans des pages remarquables, a bien indiqué la pudeur et la discrétion de Villon quand il évoque le vieillissement et l'agonie, elle a noté l'absence du macabre de la décomposition et de l'intervalle, elle a remarqué avec acuité que la *Ballade des Pendus* n'a rien de réaliste et que le huitain LXXXVI (*Item mon corps j'ordonne et laisse/A nostre grand mere la terre ...*)

utilise un contre-thème, puisque l'on affirmait que plus le corps aura été bien nourri, plus sa putréfaction sera horrible: Villon est ainsi rangé parmi les ascètes et les austères dont la charogne sera "perle fine", pour parler comme Pétrarque, au milieu de l'universelle putréfaction de ceux qui, en ce monde, voulaient lui dicter leur loi. Ce qui le distingue, c'est son élégance, son respect de la chair qui le coupent radicalement de son temps dont il présente en creux les thèmes favoris.

Il reste que le *Testament* contient de nombreuses allusions à la mort, qu'il faut souvent deviner, d'autant plus qu'elles se compliquent de doubles sens, et qui ont trait à toutes ses formes.

Mort par pendaison, que pouvait redouter particulièrement un marginal comme Villon[27], à travers un serment traditionnel (*Mais pendu soit-il, que je soie,/Qui lui laira écu ne targe*, vers 916-917) ou une locution équivoque comme *faire un* (ou *le*) *saut*, au v.926, qui peut signifier: "se rendre d'un endroit à un autre", "avoir des relations sexuelles", "faire le saut de la mort au bout d'une corde". Le *Maubue* où Villon convie Jean Raguier pour arroser sa gorge (vers 1076) n'est pas seulement la fontaine où se rafraîchir le gosier, mais le gibet où, pendu par la gorge, on est "mal lessivé", à rapprocher de la *Ballade des Pendus*: la pluie nous a *débués* et *lavés*. A Denis Richier et Jean Vallette (T. CVII), le poète donne *une grand cornette pour pendre ... à leurs chapeaux de feutre*, à la fois la bande de velours pour orner leur chapeau et la longue corde qui servira à les pendre.[28] Pour Maître François de la Vacquerie (T. CXXIII) ce sera un *haut gorgerin d'Ecossais sans orfèvrerie*, tout autant une pièce d'armure pour bien protéger le cou qu'une cravate de chanvre pour le suspendre au gibet et ainsi le châtier de sa sévérité de promoteur.[29] Villon ne demande rien au *tyran séant en hault* de peur qu'il ne tende ses filets, c'est-à-dire au roi René qui recommandait le retour à une vie naturelle, loin de la cour, ou au bourreau assis sur les fourches patibulaires.[30] Evoquer Colin de Cayeux (vers 1674), c'est évoquer l'ami pendu à Montfaucon[31]. Toutes ces allusions ont, sur le mode du jeu, préparé, en la désamorçant, la vision du gibet:

> Gardez-vous tous de ce mau hâle
> Qui noircit les gens quant ils sont morts;
> Eschevez-le, c'est un mal mors.
> Passez-vous au mieux que pourrez (T. CLIX).

Mort sur le bûcher, insinuée dès le huitain V par la mention de Douai et de Lille en Flandre où venaient d'être brûlés des gens soupçonnés de vauderie.[32] Plus loin (XXI), le poète accepterait d'*être ars et mis en cendre*, s'il rencontrait un bienfaiteur comme Alexandre le Grand et que néanmoins il retombât dans le mal. Mais plutôt que de renoncer à l'amour des jeunes *bachelettes*, le jeune *bachelier*, qui lui ressemble comme un frère, préférerait qu'on le brûlât comme un *chevaucheur d'écouvettes* (vers 668), comme un sorcier qui chevauche les balais. Quand, enfin, Villon parle des *langues cuisantes, flambantes et rouges*, quand il souhaite que *soient frites ces langues ennuyeuses* (plutôt qu' *envieuses*), il s'agit tout à la fois des langues médisantes, des langues que portaient sur la poitrine et le dos certains condamnés de l'Inquisition et des flammes du bûcher, voire de l'Enfer.[33]

Ailleurs, ce seront les faux monnayeurs qui meurent bouillis (... *que tu soies/Tailleur de faux coins et te brûles/Comme ceux qui sont échaudés* ...), ou son barbier Colin Galerne à qui il souhaite une fluxion de poitrine et l'enfer par la suite en lui donnant

> Un gros glaçon (pris où? en Marne)
> Afin qu'à son aise s'hiverne.
> De l'estomac le tienne près:
> Se l'hiver ainsi se gouverne,
> Il aura chaud l'été d'après (T. CLIV),

ou encore les victimes d'une rixe dans une maison en ruine:

> Pour enseigne y mis un havet,
> Et qui l'ait pris, point ne m'en loue:
> Sanglante nuit et bas chevet (T. XCVI).[34]

Inutile de multiplier les exemples: dans ces nombreuses allusions, il s'agit souvent de la mort d'autrui, d'un ennemi, et l'auteur joue avec les mots, si bien que les doubles sens brouillent la vision du trépas.

Lorsque Villon interpelle cette redoutable puissance dans le très beau rondeau *Mort, j'appelle de ta rigueur*, légué à Y. Marchant qu'il n'aime pas, on est tout de suite amené à se demander si ce poème concerne son auteur, ou s'il souhaite à son légataire de connaître l'amertume de la mort et de la séparation.

D'autre part, la *Ballade des Seigneurs*, sorte d'antiballade par son côté prosaïque, entasse un certain nombre de morts récentes, survenues entre 1456 et 1461, le plus souvent dans des conditions affreuses ou dramatiques: Calixte III disparaissant après s'être parjuré, Alphonse d'Aragon trépassant au milieu d'inquiétants prodiges (le trône s'effondra dans la chambre royale), Charles VII se laissant mourir de faim de peur d'être empoisonné sur l'ordre de son fils, Jacques II d'Ecosse "tué ... de l'éclat d'un canon rompu" ... Mais Villon, qui se contente d'un nom, ne dit rien de la manière dont chacun mourut; de surcroît, ne surnagent que des éléments *positifs* en rapport avec la *vie* du défunt, le *gracieux* duc de Bourbon, Charles VII *le bon*, le roi d'Ecosse *Qui demi face ot, dit on,/vermeille comme une ématiste*, le roi de Chypre *de renom*; le *bon roi d'Espagne*, Du Guesclin *le bon Breton* et bien entendu le *preux Charlemagne*.[35]

2.   Il s'agit aussi d'une ballade, construite sur le modèle archiconnu de l'*Ubi sunt*, qui considère la mort comme un départ, et qui nous amène au deuxième moyen qu'utilise Villon, le recours à la poésie où "l'horreur du réel est subtilisée par la métaphore" pour reprendre une expression de Chr. Martineau. Dans la *Ballade des Dames*, bornons-nous à remarquer, sans reprendre le merveilleux commentaire de Léo Spitzer[36] que tous les moyens contribuent à la sublimation du réel: les personnages mythologiques et antiques, aux limites du rêve, se mêlent à des personnages plus proches, comme Héloïse et Abélard, la reine et Buridan, Jeanne d'Arc, la plupart saisis sous leur jour le plus éclatant, *Flora la belle Romaine*, Echo … *Qui beauté ot trop plus qu'humaine*, la très sage Héloïse, la *reine Blanche comme lis, qui chantait à voix de sirène*, Haremburgis *qui tint le Maine*, Jeanne *la bonne Lorraine*. Rythme et sonorités en *i* et *è* se combinent aux images et aux allusions (l'écho sur l'étang, le lis, la sirène …) pour créer un climat de douceur et d'apaisement qui culmine avec le refrain, *Mais où sont les neiges d'antan?* qui, à quatre reprises, ramène l'évocation de la blancheur, de la pureté, de la grâce fragile et du silence dans l'alternance naturelle des saisons.

La ballade en *vieil langage françois*, qui n'a rien d'archéologique ni de philologique, introduit un double sentiment de jeu qui distrait, d'irréalité et d'éternité quand elle passe en revue d'illustres personnages appréhendés non pas dans leur individualité, mais dans leurs fonctions, le pape en train d'exorciser le diable, l'empereur de Constantinople tenant sur son poing la pomme d'or symbole de sa toute-puissance, le roi de France bâtisseur d'églises et de monastères.

Le poète recourt à la poésie, à toutes les formes de poésie, dès que l'angoisse affleure. Le triptyque *Ubi sunt* suit l'évocation de la danse macabre et de l'agonie. Après le rappel de ses déboires à Bourges où peut-être risqua-t-il le bûcher, c'est la ballade imprécatoire des *Langues ennuyeuses*, inspirée d'E. Deschamps[37], où Villon s'est complu à imaginer les mixtures les plus immondes. Le gibet se profile-t-il au détour d'un double sens? Répond alors la ballade de la bonne vie, des ébats amoureux d'un gras chanoine et de dame Sidoine, *blanche, tendre, polie et attintée*, les *Contredits de Franc Gontier* dont le refrain constitue tout un programme pour oublier l'angoisse de la mort et la peur de l'au-delà: *Il n'est trésor que de vivre à son aise*.

3.   Mais déjà avec ces deux ballades, nous avons quitté le domaine de l'allusion et/ou de la poésie pour entrer dans le tohu-bohu carnavalesque, avec toutes les valeurs qu'il véhicule, et la volonté de jouir pleinement, immédiatement de la vie, pendant qu'il est temps, comme le poète le laisse entendre dès les vers 419-420:

Mais que j'aie fait mes étrennes,
Honnête mort ne me déplaît.

Le carnaval, c'est l'abolition de toutes les hiérarchies, de toutes les frontières, entre tous les règnes, céleste, humain, animal, entre la vie et la mort: l'on passe de l'un à l'autre, dans les deux sens, sans effort ni difficulté – *de mort à vie*, est-il précisé au vers 1862. Ce qui est inerte, immobile, s'anime. La vieillesse se métamorphose en jeunesse: Marle, un vieux banquier qui se meurt, redevient un mâle vigoureux, un merle gaillard, un amoureux généreux[38]; deux vieux chanoines de Notre-Dame se transforment en *povres clergeons, jeunes et esbattant*, "s'amusant bien", à qui l'on peut tirer les oreilles[39]; le vieux frère Baude, par la grâce de son nom et les dons du poète, apparaît sous les traits d'un guerrier redoutable, d'un amoureux robuste, voire d'une sorte de monstre vert, le diable de Vauvert qui terrorisait le quartier d'Enfer.[40]

Le carnaval, c'est la disparition de tous les tabous, le rire avec ses jeux et ses doubles sens, jusqu'à la grossièreté. Plus rien n'est sérieux, tout devient objet de plaisanteries. Même le cimetière des Innocents: Villon charge les aveugles des Quinze-Vingts de séparer *les gens de bien des déshonnêtes*, et, pour les aider dans leur tâche, il leur donne ses *grandes lunettes*, tout en se réservant l'étui (T. CLX). Même l'entrée en Paradis, habité surtout, pour le poète, de Noé, l'inventeur de la vigne et du vin dont il s'enivra, de Loth le père incestueux, de l'Architriclin qui présida aux noces de Cana et manifesta sa science oenologique: l'ivrogne Cotart, jamais las de boire, la démarche vacillante, se cognant aux étalages, hurle pour qu'on lui ouvre la porte.[41] Du coup, le carnaval, comme la mort, libère de l'engluement de la morale, du mépris des gens bien assis.

Le carnaval, c'est aussi le triomphe du bas corporel, du vin chanté tout au long – vin d'Aunis que prise Denis Hesselin, hypocras du gras chanoine, morillon "gros rouge" de la ballade finale – et des ivrognes qui boivent à pleins *barils et courges* (vers 1285), de la bonne chère, des *grasses soupes jacobines* et des *flans*, du sexe et des prostituées, des maris ou des amants trompés et des *hoirs Michaut qui fut nommé le bon Fouterre*, du jeune prêtre Thomas Tricot à qui Villon fait miroiter le *Trou Perrette* (vers 1959) et de Jacques Raguier à qui il interdit de boire sans lui au *Trou de la Pomme de Pin* (vers 1045); triomphe même de la scatologie, avec les *culs rogneux* des Auditeurs du Châtelet à qui Villon offre une chaise percée (T. CXXII) et les *pets* et les *rots* que Villon aimerait faire pour narguer ses persécuteurs (vers 1988) qu'il ne craint plus *trois crottes* (vers 1987).

Emporté par le rythme endiablé de cette fête débridée, le poète peut évoquer les réalités les plus tragiques, la pendaison de Colin de Cayeux, le destin de l'âme et la mort dans la honte (T.CLVI-CLVII):

Ce n'est pas un jeu de trois mailles
Ou va corps et peut-être l'âme.
Qui perd, riens n'y font repentailles
Qu'on n'en meure à honte et diffame;

Et qui gagne n'a pas à femme
Dido, la reine de Carthage.
L'homme est donc bien fol et infame
Qui, pour si peu, couche tel gage.

Mais aussitôt, dans la même *Belle leçon aux enfants perdus*, il revient aux valeurs qu'il a mises au premier plan et en particulier à la boisson, à la morale que chacun pratique et que lui-même recommande à la faveur d'un jeu morphologique (T. CLVIII):

Qu'un chacun encore m'écoute!
On dit, et il est verité,
Que charterie*se boit toute
Au feu l'hiver, au bois l'été,
S'argent avez, il n'est quitte,
Mais le dépendez tôt et vite.

*salaire du charretier

Dépendez, ''dépensez'', est à la fois un indicatif, ''vous le dépensez'', et un impératif, ''dépensez-le''. Double sens qui se retrouve dans la *Ballade de bonne doctrine à ceux de mauvaise vie*, où Villon, jouant sur le refrain, constate d'abord

Ou va l'acquêt, que cuidez?
Tout aux tavernes et aux filles

(vers 1698-1699)

....
Aussi bien va, or escoutez!
Tout aux tavernes et aux filles

(vers 1706-1707)

avant de conseiller:

Ains que vous fassiez pis, portez
Tout aux tavernes et aux filles.

Parle-t-il de sa sépulture? Ce sera à Sainte-Avoie, où la chapelle était au premier étage et dont les hôtesses n'étaient rien moins que chastes.[42] Et son épitaphe le représente en train de dormir, rasé, tête, barbe et sourcil, comme *un navet qu'on ret et pèle*, dans l'apaisement du *repos éternel* et de la *clarté perpétuelle*.

A relire le *Testament* dans cette optique, on découvre l'itinéraire du poète et celui qu'il recommande à son lecteur: de la mort tragique à la mort burlesque, de l'horreur du trépas à la gaieté de la fin, des affreuses persécutions de Thibaud d'Aussigny et des bûchers du nord de la France, du souci de l'au-delà et de la conscience pécheresse (T. XIII-XIV), de l'omniprésence de Dieu aux deux ballades carnavalesques qui terminent le *Testament* dans une absence totale de Dieu, l'évêque-bourreau et ses séides devenus de *traîtres chiens mâtins*: l'une, la *Ballade de Merci*, est un cortège de Mardi-Gras, microcosme de l'oeuvre, avec ses moines mendiants et ses badauds, ses filles de joie et ses godelureaux, ses mauvais garçons et ses montreurs de marmottes, ses fous et ses sots agitant des marottes et des vessies garnies de pois; l'autre, la *Ballade finale*, est l'enterrement burlesque du poète, martyr d'amour, Christ dérisoire[44], Christ goliard sur la croix de l'amour, vêtu d'un haillon, piqué d'un aiguillon, assoiffé, qui quitte la terre de son plein gré (*quant de ce monde vout partir*, dit le refrain) et que ses compagnons devront accompagner, dans le tintamarre des cloches, *vêtus rouge com vermillon*, à la gloire du sexe et de l'amour physique: il jure *sur son couillon* qu'

> ... en mourant mallement
> l'époignait d'Amour l'aiguillon;
> Plus aigu que le ranguillon
> D'un baudrier lui faisait sentir ...
>
> (vers 2014-2017)

– à la gloire du vin, puisque son dernier geste est de boire un verre de vin rouge, *Un trait but de vin morillon*, tout en faisant un ultime jeu de mots, dans la mesure où le mot *morillon*, qui désignait au 15ème siècle une sorte de pinot, était aussi le nom de l'abbé de Saint-Germain des Prés, Hervé Morillon, mort le 25 février 1460: Villon boit donc le vin que venait de boire l'abbé Morillon et qui rappelle peut-être la cigüe de Socrate.

Ainsi donc l'ordre du *Testament* n'est rien de moins que concerté: l'angoisse et la tristesse qui remontent sans cesse à la surface, Villon finit par les maîtriser par le jeu et la folie de la fête. Il mérite bien son nom de François Villon, le poète qui se libère, qui devient *franc*, par ses *villonies*, qui sont loin d'être toujours respectables.[45]

Est-il le seul à avoir adopté cette attitude à un moment où l'horreur de la mort semble atteindre à son maximum, si l'on en juge par les craintes de Louis XI et les vaines mesures qu'il prit pour en retarder l'échéance? Songeons à la *Farce de Maître Pierre Pathelin* dans laquelle l'épisode de la fausse mort, qui occupe 500 vers sur 1600, parodie le

cérémonial des *Arts de bien mourir*.[46] Pathelin, qui invoque divers
saints, prétend voir des créatures démoniaques, des gens en noir, des
moines noirs, un chat, des crapauds, contre lesquels il recourt à des
formules magiques (vers 612-613), à l'étole bénite du prêtre (vers 620),
mimant la fin négative de qui meurt en état de péché mortel, terrorisé
par celle qui veut le piquer de son aiguillon. Aucun châtiment ne
rétablit l'ordre des valeurs officielles; mais, tout au long, la volonté
de dédramatiser la mort: "la fausse mort de Pathelin est suivie d'une
fausse résurrection et d'une vraie récompense non pas dans l'au-delà,
mais en ce bas monde"[47], puisque Pathelin garde les étoffes qu'il a
extorquées à Guillaume. La mort est bafouée dans ses fastes et ses
tabous au nom de la morale de l'intérêt: ce n'est plus un art de bien
mourir, mais un art de simuler la mort pour s'enrichir et assurer son
mieux-être dans le quotidien temporel.

IV

Nous voilà loin de Rutebeuf auquel il est bon de revenir dans une
ultime comparaison.

Pour Villon, il faut jouir vite et violemment du temps de vie qui
nous est offert, et que Rutebeuf recommandait d'utiliser pour faire
pénitence et mériter le pardon divin.

Le trépas, aux yeux de Villon, n'est pas loin d'être seulement un
accident mauvais en soi, un terme après quoi il n'y a plus rien à
attendre; c'est, pour Rutebeuf, un passage pénible qui donne accès
à la possibilité d'un bonheur éternel, une ouverture sur un autre monde
où il s'agit de gagner une éternité de bonheur ou de malheur.

Si Villon découvre dans la mort une revanche sur les injustices
sociales puisque tout le monde est logé à la même enseigne, Rutebeuf
y discerne d'abord l'occasion d'un retour sur soi et d'une conversion.

NOTES

1. Dans ses deux ouvrages fondamentaux, *Essai sur l'histoire de la mort en Occident
du Moyen Age à nos jours* (Paris, 1975), et *L'Homme devant la mort* (Paris, 1977).

2. En dépit, ou plutôt à cause, de l'étendue de la matière et de l'importance du
sujet, eu égard au temps imparti, il s'agit bien entendu d'une esquisse qui ne
saurait faire oublier les deux grands livres d'I. Siciliano, *Villon et les thèmes poétiques
du Moyen Age*, nouveau tirage (Paris, 1967), et de Chr. Martineau-Génieys, *Le
Thème de la mort dans la poésie française de 1450 à 1550* (Paris, 1978) (*Nouvelle
Bibliothèque du Moyen Age*, VI).

3. Que nous citerons d'après l'édition d'E. Faral et de J. Bastin, *Oeuvres complètes
de Rutebeuf*, deuxième tirage (Paris, 1969), 2 vol. Pour la traduction, se reporter
à notre *Rutebeuf, Poèmes de l'Infortune et Poèmes de la Croisade* (Paris, 1979) (*Traductions
des Classiques français du Moyen Age*, XXVIII).

4. *Complainte de Constantinople*, vers 78-82: "Or du fuir! la mort les chace,/Qui lor
fera de pié eschace./Tart crieront: "Trahi! Trahi!,/Qu'ele a ja entesé sa mache".

5. *La Complainte du Comte Eudes de Nevers*, vers 142-144: "La mors ne fait nule atendue, /Ainz fiert a massue estandue;/Tost fait nuit de jor esclerci".

6. *Complainte de Constantinople*, vers 83.

7. *Ave Maria Rutebeuf*, vers 16-24: "Quar il ne cuident pas morir/Ne dedenz la terre porrir,/Mes si feront,/Que ja garde ne s'i prendront/Que tel morsel englou-tiront/Qui leur nuira,/Que la lasse d'ame cuira/En enfer, ou ja nel lera Estez n'yvers".

8. *Plaies du monde*, vers 60-61.

9. Cf. *Repentance Rutebeuf*, vers 61-69: "Puis que morir voi foible et fort,/Comment prendrai en moi confort/Que de mort me puisse desfendre?/N'en voi nul, tant ait grant esfort,/Que des piez n'ost le contrefort,/Si fet le cors a terre estendre./Que puis je, fors la mort atendre?/La mort ne lest ne dur ne tendre/Por avoir que l'en li aport …".

10. *Plaies du monde*, vers 53-59: "Toz jors aquiert jusqu'a la mort;/Més quant la mort a lui s'amort,/Que la mort vient qui le veut mordre,/Que de riens n'en fait a remordre,/Si ne li lest pas delivrer: /A autrui li covient livrer/Ce qu'il a gardé longuement …"; *Voie de Tunes*, vers 89-92: "Dites, aveiz pleges de vivre longuement? Je voi aucun riche home faire maisonnement:/Quant il a assouvi tres tout entierement,/Se li fait hon un autre, de petit coustement".

11. *Complainte du Comte Eudes de Nevers*, vers 1-2: "La mors, qui toz jors ceulz aproie/Qui plus sunt de bien faire en voie …"; *De Monseigneur Anseau de l'Isle*, vers 1-4: "Iriez, a maudire la mort/Me voudrai des or més amordre,/Qui adés a mordre s'amort,/Qui adés ne fine de mordre …".

12. Voir aussi les trois ballades traitant le thème *Ubi sunt* et les huitains qui suivent.

13. *Voie de Tunes*, vers 109-110: "Et vos, a quoi penceiz, qui n'aveiz nul demain/Et qui a nul bien faire ne voleiz metre main?"; *Nouvelle Complainte d'Outremer*, vers 79-82: "Queil part se porront elz repondre/Qu'a Dieu nes estuisse respondre,/Quant il at le monde en sa main/Et nos n'avons point de demain?".

14. *Dit de Pouille*, vers 13-16: "Or preneiz a ce garde, li groz et li menu,/Que, puis que nos sons nei et au siecle venu,/S'avons nos pou a vivre, ç'ai ge bien retenu;/Bien avons mains a vivre quant nos sommes chenu"; *Voie de Tunes*, vers 97-98: "Des lors que li hons nait, a il petit a vivre;/Quant il a quarante ans, or en a mains ou livre".

15. *Nouvelle Complainte d'Outremer*, vers 231-236: "Diex vos fait bien; faites li dont/De cors, de cuer et d'arme don,/Si fereiz que preu et que sage./Or me dites quel aventage/Vos puet faire votre trezors/Quant l'arme iert partie dou cors?".

16. *Complainte du Roi de Navarre*, vers 4-6: "Mais a teil bien ne vint mais hons/Com il venist, ne fust la mors/Qui en sa venue l'a mors …"; *Dit des Cordeliers*, vers 31: "Que s'ame vialt sauver ainz que la mors l'amorde …".

17. *Bataille des Vices contre les Vertus*, vers 180-181: "La mort qui a mordre s'amort,/Qui n'espargne ne blanc ne noir …".

18. Voir la première strophe de *Monseigneur Anseau de l'Isle*.

19. *Disputaison du croisé et du décroisé*, vers 236; *Complainte du Comte de Poitiers*, vers 16-17: " … Por Celui qui le fais pesant/Vout soffrir de la mort ameire."; *Complainte d'Outremer*, vers 27-29 : "…Dieu le Pere/Qui por souffrir la mort amere/Envoia en terre son Fil".

20. Voir l'ouvrage cité de Chr. Martineau-Génieys.

21. *Voie de Tunes*, vers 101-104: "Or est mors: qu'a il fait, qu'au siecle a tant estei?/Il a destruiz les biens que Dieux li a prestei;/De Dieu ne li souvint ne yver ne estei./Il avra paradix se il l'a conquestei".

22. Voir notre article paru dans les *Mélanges J. Stiennon* (Liège, 1982), "La Repentance Rutebeuf ou le poème de la fin".

23. A comparer avec *Le miroir de la Mort* de Chastelain qui songe autant à l'âme qu'au corps. Aucun développement moral ni religieux chez Villon, tandis que Chastelain, obsédé par les fins dernières, foncièrement chrétien, se met vite à prêcher ses lecteurs, et l'oeuvre passe du *je* au *nous*, puis au *tu*: "L'homme, enclos d'abord dans sa douleur, voit les autres, pour émerger enfin face à eux comme un guide dans la volonté de les aider à faire leur salut" (Chr. Martineau-Génieys, *op. cit.*). Du coup, son oeuvre devient consciemment un répertoire de tous les thèmes qui ont nourri le coeur et l'âme des gens de la fin du Moyen Age.

24. Cf. *Complainte d'Outremer*: "Devant Dieu, que porrez responde,/Quar lors ne

se porront repondre/Ne gent clergies ne gent laies'' (vers 135-137).

25. Voir notre analyse dans *Sur Philippe de Commynes* (Paris, 1982), pp. 97-98.

26. Pour des compléments, voir notre article "Sur trois poèmes de Rutebeuf: *La Complainte Rutebeuf, Renart le Bestourné* et *la Pauvreté Rutebeuf* " dans *Hommage à la mémoire de Gérard Moignet, Mélanges de linguistique et de philologie* (Strasbourg, 1980) pp. 421-428.

27. Voir les livres de Br. Geremek, *Les Marginaux parisiens aux XIVe et XVe siècles* (Paris, 1976), et J. Favier, *Francois Villon* (Paris, 1982).

28. Cf. Jean Dufournet, *Nouvelles Recherches sur Villon* (Paris, 1980) pp. 138-142.

29. Idem. *Recherches sur le Testament de François Villon*, 2e éd. (Paris, 1973), II, pp. 381-394.

30. Idem, *Nouvelles Recherches sur Villon* (Paris, 1980), pp. 217- 223.

31. A propos de Thibaud d'Aussigny, il est fait allusion à la mort par pendaison de Judas; voir nos *Recherches sur le Testament de Villon*, 2e éd. (Paris, 1971), I, pp. 188-189.

32. *Ibid.*, pp. 179-185.

33. Voir notre article à paraître sur "Les Formes de l'ambiguïté dans le Testament de Villon''.

34. Cf. *Nouvelles Recherches sur Villon* (Paris, 1980), pp. 51- 63.

35. *Ibid.*, pp. 29-46.

36 "Etude ahistorique d'un texte: Ballade des dames du temps jadis", *Modern Language Quarterly* (1940), 7-22. Voir aussi J. Frappier, "Les trois ballades du temps jadis dans le Testament de Villon'', *Bulletin de l'Académie royale de Belgique (Classe des Lettres)* (1971), 316-341, et D. Kada-Benoît, "Le Phénomène de désagrégation dans les trois ballades du temps jadis de Villon'', *Le Moyen Age* (1974), 301-318.

37. Cf. S.V. Spilsbury, "The Imprecatory Ballade: A fifteenth century poetic genre'', *French Studies* XXXIII (1979), 385-396.

38. *Nouvelles Recherches sur Villon*, pp. 144-148.

39. *Ibid.*, pp. 149-171.

40. *Recherches sur le Testament de François Villon* t. II, pp. 359-380.

41. *Ibid.*, pp. 405-420.

42. Voir notre article cité à la note 33.

43. *Recherches sur le Testament de François Villon*, t. II, pp. 529-553

44. Cf. J. Ch. Payen, "Le coup de l'étrier: Villon martyr et Goliard, ou comment se faire oublier quand on est immortel'', *Etudes françaises* XVIII, Villon testateur, pp. 21-34.

45. Voir notre article à paraître dans la revue *Europe*, "Villon-Merlin ou la permanence d'un mythe''.

46. Voir J.L. de Altamira, "La vision de la mort dans *Maître Pathelin''*, *Dissonances* (1977), 119-129.

47. Idem, *ibid.*, p. 125.

SUMMARY

This paper begins by looking at a number of contemporary commonplaces used by both Rutebeuf and Villon: the image of death lying in wait for his victim, whose beauty, strength or wisdom will give him no protection from sudden attack; the notion that, from the moment of birth, death is the only certainty in life; and the emphasis placed on the pain of death through variations on the wordplay of **la mort qui mord.** Attention then moves to differences in approach and emphasis. Whereas Rutebeuf gives a clear moral dimension to the pain of death, with the sense that life has been wasted, and views death as the gateway to the last Judgment, presenting us with descriptions of the torments and privations of Hell, these elements are largely absent from the works of Villon. For him any sense of failure is on the social and material level, and ideas of death are closely linked with his preoccupation with the ageing process. But how can man escape this obsession with death? For Rutebeuf he should prepare for it spiritually, through a life of sacrifice and service to God; social class will determine the right path to follow. In Villon's case it is more a question of putting death to the back of his mind: his plays on words, double meanings and use of ambiguity and metaphor blur the vision of death and soften the horrors of reality; his poems often convey a sense of carnival, of exuberance and wit, where old age can be transformed into youth, and man enjoys the pleasures of the flesh. Whereas for Villon life should be lived to the full, while there is yet time, and death is merely the last of life's accidents, the great leveller who compensates for social injustices, Rutebeuf feels that life should be used to merit divine forgiveness and sees death as an occasion for soul-searching and spiritual conversion.

★

SPIRITUALITY

A LITTLE KNOWN 'ART OF DYING' BY A BRIGITTINE OF SYON:
A Daily Exercise and Experience of Death by Richard Whitford

★

Marie Collins

Richard Whitford, author of the early sixteenth-century death-treatise, *A Daily Exercise and Experience of Death*[1], is known chiefly in two ways: as translator of *The Imitation of Christ* and as friend of More and Erasmus. He also produced several very readable works of spiritual instruction (both translations and original pieces).[2] His work reached out to devout laymen from his monastic home, the Brigittine house at Syon, by way of the printing-presses as well as in manuscript copies.[3] Yet the literary histories have passed him by. My attention was drawn to *A Daily Exercise* by Dr. Michael Tait, who suggested that I look at the literary productions of Whitford and his fellow-monks, as he had found a dearth of material about them in the course of his work on Syon Monastery.[4] I would like to record my gratitude to Dr. Tait for his generosity in entrusting Whitford to me for literary study and in sparing time to answer questions and discuss points as they arose.

Whitford was educated at Cambridge, where he was elected Fellow of Queen's College *circa* 1497.[5] His scholarly bent appears to have been combined with practical if socially elevated pedagogy; shortly after gaining his Fellowship, he gained his college's permission to travel abroad as chaplain-tutor to William Blount, son of Lord Mountjoy and future companion of the young Henry VIII. The educational headquarters of the party was Paris, where Whitford continued his own studies and won the friendship and intellectual respect of Erasmus. The Dutch scholar's esteem is clear from a letter in which he asks Whitford to compare a composition of his with the equivalent by More.[6] The same letter illuminates the triple friendship, which apparently extended beyond academic affinities; Roper's *Life of More* depicts Whitford as being consulted by More for political and tactical advice during a period of royal disfavour.[7] After Whitford's journey abroad, it looked as though he would progress comfortably through collegiate academic life, but shortly after the turn of the sixteenth century he abandoned Cambridge to become chaplain to the influential Bishop Fox of Winchester, also associated with the More circle. Subsequently, Whitford left the world for monastic life. The date of his entry at Syon is not recorded; Dr. Tait accepts the presumed date, 1507, as probable.

Whitford, the scholar turned monk, must have found Syon a congenial environment for the characteristics discernible from his work: austerity tempered by humanity; love of learning; love of doctrinal orthodoxy. Syon, despite the lateness of its foundation, quickly evolved a distinguished intellectual tradition whilst avoiding intellectual aridity.[8] (The Brigittine rule takes as its foundation the Augustinian rule, which is preoccupied with spiritual and practical essentials rather than with learning.) The organisation of the double house[9] at Syon probably fostered interest in producing vernacular works of instruction. The monks acted as confessors and spiritual directors to the nuns. There was a need for effective aids for teaching devout but comparatively unlearned female religious; by extension, Syon developed an interest in the spiritual education of devout, literate but comparatively unlearned laymen. Between about 1500 and the Dissolution of Syon in 1539 the monks produced and had printed a cluster of English instructional works, many suitable for lay use; some of them, like Whitford's *Daily Exercise*, started as treatises for the nuns and later reached a wider, lay audience. Apart from Whitford, Syon's literary figures were Thomas Betson, William Bonde and John Fewterer.[10]

Whitford's work shows an inclination towards the type of systematic vernacular instruction of the laity which we associate with the recommendations of the Fourth Lateran Council (1215) and later derivative ecclesiastical pronouncements. Whitford's *A Work for Householders*, which went into many editions in his lifetime[11], manifests this special interest. It is remarkable in being addressed, not to parish priests having the cure of souls, but to lay heads of households. The *paterfamilias* is enjoined to ensure that his household receives a proper grounding in the faith, but never permitted by Whitford to usurp the priestly sacramental function in penance. Put into practice, Whitford's instructions would produce a well-regulated household like that elsewhere ascribed to More[12]; chronology permits no conclusions, but one cannot help speculating whether More may have influenced Whitford, or *vice versa*. *A Work for Householders*, *A Daily Exercise and Experience of Death* and Whitford's treatise preparatory to communion, *A Preparation Unto Houseling*, show Whitford's concern to offer lay-people, as well as nuns, a spiritual framework, a system of examinations and exercises which a devout person can operate for himself to prepare for the great occasions of Christian life and death.

Syon had productive connections with the early sixteenth-century printing-houses; a great deal more work needs to be done on the nature of those connections.[13] The four named Syon authors of that period used at least nine[14] printers between them. (It is interesting to note that the mother house at Vadstena had one of the earliest printing-presses in Sweden[15]; were the Brigittines peculiarly alert to the 'New Technology' of their time?) In the 1530s, Whitford bitterly complains about pirating and heretical adulteration of his work, more from fear for the souls of people who may be led into error by them than from grievance about infringement of what moderns would regard as copyright.[16] The relations between Syon and the printers may have been informal and personal; Wynkyn de Worde appears in the list of donors to the men's library twice[17], and he also tells how the manuscript of *The Orchard of Syon*, which he printed in 1519, was entrusted to him by the lay Steward of Syon, who also piously provided a large subvention.[18]

Once professed at Syon, Whitford seems to have led a quiet, productive life as monk, confessor and spiritual author. Apart from treatises for, or usable by, laymen, he produced English works on monastic subjects for the benefit of the nuns. The peace of perhaps thirty years of retirement was shattered by the events leading to the monastic dissolution, in which Whitford showed tenacity and courage. He infuriated Thomas Bedyll, the Visitor who came to inspect Syon, by his intractable stance against the royal manoeuvres. In two angry letters to Cromwell, Bedyll denounces Whitford as a 'vauntperler' or ringleader, as an irreligious liver, as talking bawdily to the nuns, and as shameless.[19] All this one might expect, granted Bedyll's aim; he also describes Whitford as having 'but small learning' and as 'a great railer'. The absurdity of Bedyll's distorted portrait of the friend of More and Erasmus is reinforced by reading his works, which, while doctrinally uncompromising, are full of charity, humility and the simplicity achieved by long study. Despite Bedyll's hostility, Whitford survived the monastic dissolution without sharing the fate of his superior, the martyred Richard Reynolds[20], and ended his days peacefully back in the Mountjoy household, possibly saved from punishment by his powerful patron. He was able to continue publishing after leaving Syon, until his death, probably on 16th September 1543.

Whitford's death-treatise, *A Daily Exercise (etc.)*, cannot be precisely dated; it probably belongs to his earlier days at Syon, though it might predate them. It was printed several times in his lifetime. It cannot have been written, in its first form, after summer 1518. In the undated preface to the 1537 Waylande print to which I refer throughout, Whitford tells us that he wrote it more than twenty years previously at the request of Dame Elizabeth Gibbs, Abbess of Syon from 1461 until her death in August 1518.[21] The earliest surviving print of the work is by Redman, possibly in 1534, which could bring the date back to before 1514, but we cannot be sure that Redman's was the earliest edition. Internal evidence is not a great deal of help. Whitford refers to two earlier works of his, *A Work for Householders*[22] and *A Preparation unto Houseling*[23], but these are not datable. These retrospective references also highlight the question of how far Whitford adapted his treatise for a wider audience than the nuns for whom it was first written. He refers to the criticisms of a fellow-monk in the postscript[24], which suggests that he envisaged some degree of revision before printing. He refers in *A Daily Exercise* to *A Work for Householders*, a treatise which one would expect laymen rather than nuns to own.[25] Yet he retains addresses and references to his first audience of female religious.[26] Even as it stood before printing, the text seems to have appealed beyond Syon; one of the reasons Whitford gives for going into print is that so many 'devout persons' have wanted manuscript copies that he is weary of transcribing it.[27]

Whitford says that the abbess of Syon had several times entreated him to write a brief treatise on the proper preparation for death. The Syon nuns' library probably already possessed a copy of the English treatise *Disce Mori* (a work in the tradition of the death-chapter in *La Somme le Roi*).[28] The abbess's request for a death-treatise teaching 'how you should prepare and ordain yourself daily thereunto' suggests her feeling that existing available work was in some way unsatisfactory: if it implies criticism of the *Disce Mori*, an extensively-augmented compilation, it is probably of that work's unwieldiness. Whitford's stress on the brevity and accessibility of his work would support this interpretation of the abbess's request:

> Read this, I pray you, once over, and after as you like; it is but very short, and therefore have I not divided it into chapters, but only into two parts ... Reverend Mother, and good devout sisters, you have (many and oftentimes with great instance) required me to write unto you some brief or short lesson of death, and how you should prepare and ordain yourself daily thereunto.[29]

The later Middle English works generally called 'arts of dying' are of various types, often interrelated.[30] The main types found in English[31], according to Sister Mary Catharine O'Connor, are:

(i)   renderings of the short discussion of dying well in Friar Lorens's *La Somme le Roi*, such as that included in *The Book of Vices and Virtues*[32], a translation of the whole;
(ii)   renderings of the death-chapter by Henry Suso in his *Horologium Sapientiae*, a Latin translation of his *Büchlein der ewigen Weisheit*;
(iii) a rendering of Jean Gerson's *De Arte Moriendi*, the death-section in his *Opusculum Tripartitum*;
(iv)   renderings of the 'long' ('CP') text of the *Ars Moriendi* proper, such as *The Book of the Craft of Dying*.[33]

Suso, Gerson and the *Ars Moriendi* itself devote much attention to formulae to be applied to, by or on behalf of the dying man. *The Book of the Craft of Dying* offers some discussion of the proper attitude of the living towards death, but it is outweighed by five subsequent chapters on deathbed temptations, questions, entreaties and instructions to the dying man and prayers for the departing soul. By contrast, *The Book of Vices and Virtues* offers an 'art of living', albeit brief. It is bipartite: the first section demonstrates the transitory nature of life, which should foster a longing for death, the gateway to eternity, for living well is learning to die well, in Augustinian tradition[34]: the second section gives a threefold spiritual exercise to encourage desire for a good death by meditating daily on hell, purgatory and heaven. This bipartite structure, the first part a discussion, the second an exemplary meditation, is the closest amongst the arts of dying to Whitford's structure.

Whitford is at pains to make clear his structural divisions:

Part I	discusses the reasons for rejecting fear of death and for cultivating a desire for death.[35] This corresponds partially with the aim of the first section of the death-discussion in *The Book of Vices and Virtues*[36];
Part II	sets forth meditative exercises to train Christians daily for death.[37] Whitford's exercises have some affinity with, though they are more advanced than, those in *The Book of Vices and Virtues*[38];
The Postscript	seems to have been written a good while after the main text.[39] It attempts to meet the objections of an unnamed Syon brother who read the work before printing.

Though Whitford's bipartite structure in some ways resembles that of the discussion of death in *The Book of Vices and Virtues*, there are considerable differences in their themes and processes in each section. The *Vices and Virtues* discussion opens, as does Whitford, with the Augustinian commonplace that dying well and living well are inseparable processes. The discussions immediately diverge. *Vices and Virtues* persuades by both emotional manipulation and rational argument that life is transitory, itself an extended death, and that Christians, even more than the pagan philosophers, should despise it and long for eternal life. No attention is there paid to the natural qualms of frightened humans facing death. By contrast, Whitford's first part admits and treats human fear of death, using several *ars moriendi* commonplaces but weaving them skilfully into his own lucid argument, the structure of which is always spelled out for the benefit of less sophisticated minds. Two kinds of fear of death are distinguished[40]:

(i) a vain fear of the parting of body and soul;
(ii) a profitable fear, to be cherished by everyone, of the uncertainty of the hour of death and of the condition of the soul at that time.

The first type of fear is then taken up in detail and proved by the following three methods to be groundless[41]:

(a)   by authority;
(b)   by reason;
(c)   by experience.

In proof (a), by authority, Whitford, in the best English tradition of Aelfric, the *Ancrene Wisse* author, and Walter Hilton, manifests a subtle, learned mind making the fruits of scholarship accessible and spiritually profitable to devout but less learned minds. He calls on the authority often cited by those terrified of death, Aristotle's *Ethics*, which state that death is the most terrible of all terrible things (an *ars moriendi* commonplace). Like a well-trained humanist, though without any humanistic intent, Whitford stresses the proper *context* of Aristotle's observation[41a], to demonstrate that its use to justify fear is an extra-contextual *mis*use of it. Aristotle actually applied it to people doubtful of any life beyond this world, which by implication is not the case for Christians. Here Whitford imagines an objection: 'yet say they that every man doth abhor and loathe death and doth what he can to avoid death and to prolong life'. Whitford accepts this statement whilst denying that it proves there is pain in death. An example from the natural world acts as transition to a demonstration that what people really fear is not actually death, but rather, the sickness and pain that may precede it: green young fruit may be reluctant to fall from the tree, but ripe ones fall without violence; likewise death is 'hugsum' (dreadful, abhorrent) to the young because it normally involves major physical disruption, whereas the old die easily, even pleasantly. Two statements from different works of Aristotle and one from Cicero lend authority to this commonsense observation. The 'proof by authority' is well-structured and concretely illustrated, so that it is easy to digest. It also demonstrates Whitford's characteristic wish to induce analytic clarity in his audience, making them define and precisely understand any statement they may make or borrow from an authority.

A similar wish for clarity is apparent in proof (b), by reason, that death need not be feared. Logic is allied to lively concrete illustration and the seamless joining-in of *ars moriendi* commonplaces. The pain in death, says Whitford, must exist either in the body or the soul: but the dying body loses its faculties and therefore cannot register pain; as for the soul, it is as delighted to be free as a suddenly liberated prisoner, to use Ambrose's image of the imprisonment of the soul in the body, often found in death-treatises.[42] Another analogy for the glad parting of soul and body appears, a homely one which yet incorporates a Pauline death-treatise commonplace: body and soul are like two 'marrows', a North-country dialect word for 'workmates', delighted at the prospect of going home after being obliged to collaborate to finish a task in exile. Thus pain can exist neither for body nor soul in the actual process of dying, since the departing soul is as joyful as the dying body is insentient.

Proof (c), by experience, has a similar mixture of logic, concrete illustration and scriptural allusion, though in this section the logic appears spurious to the modern mind, being based on faulty premisses. Those who, like St. Paul, have experienced a death-like parting of body and soul in visionary trances, have reported no pain. Fainting and swooning or 'talming' (another 'Doricism'[43]), also death-like, produce relief of pain, not pain itself. The oddest 'proof' occurs with Whitford's statement that many have died painlessly in their sleep who would have been awakened by a painful experience then, such as a pinprick in the ear or the burning of a finger. The example of Lazarus is adduced to strengthen the case, since, on rising from the dead, he did not report any pain in dying. Whitford either does not know or chooses to overlook the tradition that Lazarus gave a grim report of the horrors of mortality on his return from the grave.[44] Whitford's culminating proof by experience is almost throwaway; he includes his own experience of a miraculously-revived person who reported no pain: 'I knew, and spake with one such myself'.[45]

The rest of Part I continues with a strengthening of Whitford's case for the painlessness of death, by admitting and answering his audience's doubts. In his creation of an internal audience apparently debating with him, Whitford develops an impression of genuine argument, interest and mutual rapport. This 'epistolary' style can be found earlier, in the 13th-century *Ancrene Wisse*[46] and in the 14th-century mystics, notably Walter Hilton[47] and the *Cloud of Unknowing* author.[48] Apart from Richard Rolle, Hilton is the only English mystical writer reasonably represented in the Syon men's library[49]; possibly Whitford consciously or unconsciously found a stylistic model in his controlled yet relaxed lucidity. Whitford allows repeated expression to his audience's anxieties in the rest of Part I[50], continuing to meet them with sweet reasonableness and the well-integrated selection of scriptural, classical and patristic authorities. For example, Cicero the pagan and Ambrose the Christian collaborate in suggesting that sin, not death, is the only thing to fear whilst living. Seneca, a favourite death-treatise authority, joins in to remind us that it is foolish to fear death which we cannot control. Cicero reminds us that wise men account death as nothing. Whitford, unlike his younger contemporary Thomas Lupset, also a friend of More and Erasmus and author of a humanistic death-treatise[51], uses his classical learning only to play down the fear of death, without suggesting a proud humanistic-Stoic defiance incompatible with Christian attitudes. In using Cicero, Whitford deftly distances his less learned audience from one whose advice is right only insofar as it goes:

Note here how great courage and comfort this pagan giveth men, to despise and nothing to fear death.[52]

In the immediately-following objection, we catch the tone of speaking voices:

'Well sir,' say you, 'this is soon said, or soon spoken. But yet is not death so soon despised ne so lightly set at nought. For we see and behold many men that should have strong hearts, and more boldness than we women, and such also that been taken and supposed for wise and well learned men that been much afraid of death.'

Ah good sisters you must consider and call unto mind that men been made of the same metal that women been and that among them some been as fainthearted as women and therefore take no heed unto them.[53]

Discussion of the fear of death is concluded by arguing that spiritual sources offer the Christian a higher comfort; fear can be transformed into fervent desire for death by the theological virtues, Faith, Hope and Charity. I can find no precise parallel to the structure of this argument in the other death-treatises I have read; however, the theological virtues figure large in repelling the devil's deathbed temptations in *The Book of the Craft of Dying*. Once more, Whitford is probably reshaping familiar material to suit a new argument and context.

Part I concludes by discussing the second, beneficial type of fear of death, the uncertainty of man's dying-day and of his spiritual condition then. Its entire argument is based on exposing commonly-held earthly views as fallacious, so that sound religious attitudes may be taken up instead. For example, man will die in God's good time, not his own; those who die young are fortunate, despite the popular view. A commonplace is brought to life by referring it to everyday experience: death, with which we can gain familiarity by its images, sleep and shadows, is no more to be feared for itself than are sleep and shadows in real life, especially since Christians can take comfort from having tried to live a good life.

Part II opens by defining 'exercise' and 'experience', in terms congruent with modern concepts, though Dr. Tait has already suggested that Whitford's use of 'exercise' is coloured by his reading in Mombaer.[54] Whitford then analyses various categories of death, so that the audience may follow the argument of Part II having clearly understood its terms:

(i)   In popular euphemistic idiom, bodily death is referred to as a 'change of life' (a gloss on Malory's idiom which Professor Vinaver would have relished);

(ii)   The process of exchange or reversal implicit in the phrase 'change of life' is apparent in the spiritual death involved in falling from virtue into sin;

(iii) the opposite process is the 'death to sin' when a soul rises from sin to salvation through grace, as St. Paul in Romans characterises baptism;

(iv)   the highest form of death is *meditatio mortis*, as scholars call it, the contemplation of death.

Part II is to give two exercises, a lower and a higher, to help his audience achieve *meditatio mortis*. Even when approaching these more rarified spiritual levels, Whitford does not lose touch with his accessible and homely style. Lack of exercise and experience, which his teachings will remedy, causes people to be afraid of death:

> As by example, children and some women, or such persons [that] never had experience ne knowledge of a bug (that is, a personage that in play doth represent the devil), at the first sight been much afraid thereof: in so much that some persons have been in jeopardy to lose their wit and reason thereby. But when they afterward have knowledge what it was and by use have experience thereof, they been then nothing afraid thereof, but rather doon take pleasure therein.[55]

The first, lower meditative exercise is to imagine oneself like a convict condemned to death, or a sick man on his deathbed. The devil is to be imagined perpetrating the traditional deathbed temptations, to which model replies are suggested. These are generally in accordance with the recommendations of the temptation-chapter in *The Book of the Craft of Dying*, though there are no detailed resemblances; perhaps the closest resemblance is in the recommendation to put Christ's Passion between the sinner and his sins[56]. Once again we see Whitford adapting traditional material for his own purposes, incorporating demonic deathbed temptation into a spiritual exercise. Ever practical, Whitford suggests bed-time as the most convenient hour for this exercise, referring to his previous treatise, *A Work for Householders*, for various model concluding pious gestures and prayers.

The second, higher form of exercise seems to owe something to the *Somme le Roi* type as in *The Book of Vices and Virtues*, in recommending the separation of soul and body in meditation as a daily exercise and experience of death, though there is considerable difference in their processes.[57] The meditator is to follow a model repeated from Whitford's previous treatise *A Preparation unto Houseling*, systematically considering a series of comparisons between human worthlessness and divine magnanimity. A formal meditation on the life and Passion of Christ is offered, more extended than the treatment of the Passion in chapter IV of *The Book of the Craft of Dying*, the more limited purpose of which is to show how the dying man should imitate Christ on the Cross. Like the meditation in *The Book of Vices and Virtues*, though by a different route, Whitford's meditation rises to delighted contemplation of heaven and the presence of God. He exhorts the meditator:

MARIE COLLINS

And here kneeling or rather lying down prostrate upon your face, remain, bide and dwell here still; here expire and die stark dead and utterly ... For in this death (for that time) your soul is departed from your body, so that you be not then yourself. For as the iron lying in the fire is by similitude all fire, so been you all one with God. *Qui adheret deo unus spiritus est.* Whosoever (saith Saint Paul) doth cleave and stick fast unto Our Lord is with him one spirit.[58]

Whitford's lesson here culminates in prose of sober dignity, uniting in homogeneous simplicity and strength his own instructions and his citation of authority in St. Paul. Whitford concludes in a lower key; just as the devil may be expected at the lower form of exercise, so he will attack at this higher meditation, but the saints will help the struggling soul. There is nothing in the earlier death-treatises quite like Whitford's contemplative heights: the priest in *The Book of the Craft of Dying* prays that the departing soul may see God face to face and in *The Book of Vices and Virtues* we are left with our eye on the joyous energy generated by meditating on heaven, which makes men run there like greyhounds, rather than on the mystical union with God achieved by the process.

Whitford's Postscript shows the unease felt by his unnamed Syon brother at his adventurous conclusion. This other Brigittine expressed concern about the dangers of misleading people into giving credence to bogus rapturous visions and trances. It is a matter on which we might expect a Brigittine to be peculiarly sensitive. The foundress of the order had, after all, been a visionary. Asserting the importance of distinguishing true from false visions seems to have sprung quickly to mind at Syon. Whitford meets his reader's objection by referring his audience to a discussion of the distinctions by a third Syon brother, the recently-dead William Bonde in *The Pilgrimage of Perfection.*[59] Two other small pieces of evidence point to Syon's preoccupation with or nervousness about distinguishing true from false visions and sensible experiences. Walter Hilton, as I said, is the only English mystical writer apart from Rolle to be reasonably represented in the Syon men's library. In *The Scale of Perfection* Hilton offers his famous *caveat* about visions and other sensible experiences[60] (a presumed comment on abuses of the 'heat, sweetness and song' of Rolle and his school). They are not to be valued for themselves, though Hilton does not deny that they may accompany genuine mystical experiences. Hilton's interest in promoting awareness of the right kind of visions and mystical experiences may well have commended him to an order proud of its foundress's special visionary gifts. The other piece of evidence for nervousness at Syon about matters connected with mysticism comes from Whitford himself at the end of his monastic treatise, *The Pipe or Tun of the Life of Perfection.*[61] There Whitford, saying that he has been asked to explain to the unlearned (i.e. the Syon nuns) the meaning of the terms 'active' and 'contemplative', declines to give more than

188

a brief outline because he doubts his own competence.

In assessing Whitford's qualities as a spiritual author as they appear in *A Daily Exercise*, it may be useful to recall the conflicting opinions of, on the one hand, More and Erasmus, and on the other, Thomas Bedyll. Even disregarding Bedyll's political and religious bias, it is, I think, possible to see how he arrived at his wrongheaded estimate of Whitford's 'small learning', not being himself a very learned man. Whitford's priestly training, as well as his classical education, would have taught him to consider the needs of his audience in tempering his style and argument. In *A Daily Exercise* he addresses the unlearned, first nuns, then laymen. He therefore bares the bones of his argument to an extent possibly offensively simplistic to anyone with a high opinion of himself such as Bedyll apparently cherished; Bedyll's comment was provoked by a sermon which may well have employed similar techniques. What Bedyll failed to notice, however, is Whitford's art which conceals art in weaving classical, scriptural and patristic learning into a seamless fabric of argument, in a manner which in earlier days would have done credit to Aelfric or the *Ancrene Wisse* author in the integration of sources. In Whitford's synthesis of authorities, the fruits of his rigorous training are apparent in a more subtle way, in his scholarly concern not to use allusions without due regard for their original contextual meaning. His independence and mental agility are apparent in the assurance with which he weaves new arguments, or arguments with new emphases, out of art-of-dying commonplaces. Bedyll's scorn of Whitford's 'small learning' is in a perverse way a tribute to his skill in conveying it painlessly to others; Bedyll's letters give the impression of a self-important *parvenu* functionary who would have been easily impressed by an incomprehensible firework-display of learning. That is not Whitford's way; for him, Lady Study is God's handmaiden. Here a brief comparison with Thomas More is illuminating (though it would take another paper at least to substantiate it in detail): if we knew More only from the death-discussion in his unfinished treatise on *Memorare novissima*, we would have very little idea of the range and depth of his scholarship, which it is not his purpose to display there.[62]

Whitford's style, for the most part easy, relaxed yet controlled, helps to integrate his wide range of authorities, so that in his paraphrases, translations and allusions, they have the effect of additional voices contributing to an exploratory discussion between teacher and pupil. An affinity has already been suggested between Whitford and Hilton in their 'epistolary discussions'[63], though it may be simply the case that they belong to the same tradition of clear, unpretentious vernacular instructional prose. Where I feel Whitford to be an innovator is in his adaptation of the 'epistolary discussion' to the death-treatise; true, we find dialogue in other death-treatises, as between the Disciple and the Image of Death in Suso's chapter[64], but it is not of the ostensibly free-structured kind where the pupil is permitted objections and requests for clarification which become part of the didactic process and which are expressed in informal, conversational style. Whitford belongs to the main-stream of English religious prose with his unpretentious style, in which homely diction, natural conversational syntax and vivid concrete imagery, analogy and illustration figure large. The natural-seeming dignity and strength of Whitford's prose bears comparison with that of More in the *Memorare novissima* treatise. Clarity is Whitford's aim: thus his frequent use of near-synonymous doublets and triplets, a favourite contemporary stylistic trick, becomes functional. Above all he wants his meaning to be understood: if a trick of style offers a built-in gloss to the text, so much the better.

Whitford's independence of mind, already apparent from the structure and argumentative processes of his death-treatise, shows most clearly in its unusual content, especially in Part II. Not only has he adapted a method learned from his reading in the *devotio moderna*, with its stress on orderly and systematic spiritual exercises, for the use of simpler souls, but he has also given it a peculiarly Brigittine direction in its contemplative goal. The aim of the higher *meditatio mortis* is to achieve a state not only very like death but also a form of contemplative union with God. To my knowledge this is unique amongst the death-treatises.

In sum: Whitford is that paradoxical being, an original traditionalist, a bee rather than a spider, taking his materials from many sources but creating a final product with its own distinctive flavour.

NOTES

1. Printed texts survive as follows: R. Redman (? 1534: imperfect: STC 25413.7); J. Waylande (1537: STC 25414); R. Redman (? 1538: STC 25415) as part of a Whitford anthology; R. Redman (? 1537: STC 25413). All STC references are to A.W. Pollard and G.R. Redgrave, *A Short Title Catalogue of Books Printed in England, Scotland and Ireland (etc.), 1475-1640* (2nd edition, London, 1976, rev. W.A. Jackson, F.S. Ferguson and Katharine F. Pantzer).

2. Whitford's works fall into two main categories: (i) works on monastic subjects, mainly for the Syon nuns and (ii) works of spiritual direction suitable for laymen.
    (i) This category includes: An English version of the Rule of Saint Augustine; *The Martiloge; The Pipe and Tun of the Life of Perfection.*
    (ii) This category includes: *A Work for Householders*; the *Dialogue for Preparation unto Houseling; A Daily Exercise and Experience of Death; Divers Instructions Necessary for the Health of Man's Soul* (an anthology of shorter pieces); translations of *The Imitation of Christ* and *The Golden Pistle.* For further details see Whitford's entry in STC and the unpublished Oxford D. Phil. thesis by Michael Beckwith Tait, *The Brigittine Monastery of Syon (Middlesex) with Special Reference to its Monastic Usages* (Trinity Term, 1975), p. 290.

3. No manuscript copy of Whitford's work is known to me. He refers to making copies himself for the use of 'divers devout persons' (e.g. in Waylande's 1537 edition of *A Daily Exercise*, A.iᵛ). Printers known to have been used by Whitford are Redman; Waylande; Myddylton; Coplande; de Worde; P. Treueris.

4. See note 2 above. Dr. Tait and I hope to collaborate in further work on the Syon spiritual authors.

5. On this, and on subsequent stages of Whitford's career, see Tait, *op. cit.,* pp. 289-294.

6. See P.S. and H.M. Allen, eds., *Opus Epistolarum Desiderii Erasmi Roterodami* (Oxford, 1906 etc.), i, no. 191.

7. E.V. Hitchcock, ed., *The Life of Sir Thomas More, by William Roper*, EETS, O.S. 197 (London, 1935), p. 8.

8. See Tait, *op. cit.*, especially ch. 6.
9. See Tait, *op. cit.*, chs. 1-4 (pp. 3-192) and especially ch. 5 (pp. 194-238); Mary Bateson, ed., *Catalogue of the Library of Syon Monastery, Isleworth* (Cambridge, 1898), p. xi.
10. Surviving instructional works by these authors are:
    (i)   Thomas Betson, *A Right Profitable Treatise to Dispose Men to be Virtuously Occupied* (de Worde, 1500).
    (ii) William Bonde, *A Devout Treatise for them that been Timorous and Fearful in Conscience* (Fawkes, ?1534), (Fawkes, ?1535), and *A Devout Treatise Called the Pilgrimage of Perfection* (Pynson, 1526), (de Worde, 1531);
    (iii) John Fewterer, *The Mirror or Glass of Christ's Passion* (Redman, 1534).
11. I know of ten prints during Whitford's life: see Whitford's entry in STC for details.
12. For example, in Roper's *Life (ed. cit.), passim*.
13. As has previously been observed: see A.I. Doyle, "Thomas Betson of Syon", *The Library*, 5th ser., XI (1956).
14. The STC records the printers of Betson, Bonde, Fewterer and Whitford as including: de Worde; Redman; Pynson; Waylande; Fawkes; Myddylton; Coplande; and Treueris.
15. See *The New Catholic Encyclopedia* s.v. *Brigittines*.
16. E.g. in the Preface to Waylande's 1537 print of *A Work for Householders*, Whitford refers to a 'much vicious and faulty' edition, which numbers amongst its blemishes the fact that '… instead of my work is another heretic or heretical work set in place' (spelling modernised).
17. See the Syon library catalogue, *ed. cit.*, Appendix I, p. xxvii, for the list of donors. De Worde gave items A75 (*Ortus Vocabulorum*) and M30 (*Nova Legenda Anglie*).
18. *Ibid.*, p. xiii. The Steward was Richard Sutton, who 'finding this ghostly treasure, these dialogues and revelations of the new seraphical spouse of Christ, S. Katherine of Siena in a corner by itself willed of his great charity it should come to light' and had it printed at great personal expense.
19. Bedyll's letters are printed from MS Cotton Cleopatra E.IV in G.J. Aungier, *The History and Antiquities of Syon Monastery* (London, 1840), the relevant passages being pp. 87-8 and 435-8.
20. See Adam Hamilton, O.S.B., *The Angel of Syon* (Edinburgh and London, 1905).
21. *A Daily Exercise* (Waylande, 1537), A.i^v. On Elizabeth Gibbs see Aungier, *op. cit.*, p. 108).
22. *Exercise*, D. iii^v.
23. *Ibid.*, D.vi^v.
24. *Ibid.*, E.vi^v-F.iii^v.
25. *Ibid.*, D.viii^v.
26. E.g. *ibid.*, A.ii^r, B.i^r.
27. *Ibid*, A.i^v. Similar 'devout persons' appear to have been instrumental in the printing of *A Work for Householders*: see de Worde's 1533 edition, A.i^v.
28. This MS of the *Disce Mori* is now Jesus College Oxford MS 39. See N.R. Ker, *Medieval Libraries of Great Britain* (2nd edn., London, 1964), p. 186. On the *Somme le Roi* affiliation of the *Disce Mori*, see Sister Mary Catharine O'Connor, *The Art of Dying Well: the Development of the Ars Moriendi* (New York, Columbia U.P., 1942) p. 180.
29. *Exercise*, A.ii^{r-v}. Spelling and punctuation in all Whitford quotations are my own modernisations.
30. The inter-relation of the types in most cases probably preceded rendering into the vernacular. On the complex evolution of the *Ars Moriendi*, see O'Connor, *op. cit.*, p. 17 ff.
31. *Ibid.*, especially pp. 101, 179-89 (including the early modern period).
32. W. Nelson Francis, ed., *The Book of Vices and Virtues*, EETS, O.S. 217 (London, 1942).
33. In C. Horstman, ed., *Yorkshire Writers: Richard Rolle of Hampole and his Followers* (London, 1896), ii, pp. 406-420.
34. 'Si bene vixeris, male mori non poteris': Augustine, *Sermo* CCXLIX, Migne, *PL* XXXVIII, 1162.
35. *Exercise*, A.ii^r-C.iii^v.
36. *Ed. cit.*, pp. 68-71.

37. *Exercise*, C.iv^r-E.vi^v.
38. *Ed. cit.*, pp. 71-74.
39. *Exercise*, E.vi^v-F.iii^v.
40. *Ibid.*, A.iii^v.
41. *Ibid.*, A.iii^v-viii^r.
41a. Tait, *op. cit.*, p. 293, makes this point in a general way.
42. E.g. *The Book of the Craft of Dying, ed. cit.*, p. 407.
43. Whitford's occasional Northern dialect words might be explicable by a family connection with Lancashire, though I have been as yet unable to verify it. Aungier, *op. cit.*, p. 535, records a tradition that the Whitfords held land in two places in Lancashire as well as their Flintshire property. The dialect-words would have given little trouble to a south-east Midland audience because the early Tudor stylistic trick of using doublets and triplets builds in a gloss. 'Marrows' is glossed marginally on A.vi^r.
44. See George England and Alfred W. Pollard, eds., *The Towneley Plays*, EETS, E.S. 71 (London, 1897, reprinted 1952), pp. 390-393. Admittedly, Lazarus is describing the horrors of being dead, rather than of the moment of dying, strictly speaking.
45. *Exercise*, A.viii^r.
46. See J.R.R. Tolkien, ed., *Ancrene Wisse*, EETS, O.S. 249 (London, 1962 for 1960), e.g. in the discussion of patience as a remedy for wrath.
47. See L. Sherley-Price, transl., *Walter Hilton: The Ladder of Perfection* (Harmondsworth, 1957), e.g. in the discussion of appropriate and inappropriate administration of reproof, Bk. 1, ch. 17, pp. 18-19.
48. See Phyllis Hodgson, ed., *The Cloud of Unknowing*, EETS, O.S. 218 (London, 1944), e.g. on quelling the keen promptings of intellect, pp. 33-35.
49. See Bateson, *op. cit.*, indices, for details.
50. *Exercise*, A.viii^r-C.iii^v.
51. See John Archer Gee, ed., *The Life and Works of Thomas Lupset* (New Haven, 1928), pp. 263-290, for *A Treatise of Dieyng Well*.
52. *Exercise*, B.i^r-v.
53. *Ibid.*, B.i^v.
54. See Tait, *op. cit.*, p. 294.
55. *Exercise*, C.vii^r-v.
56. *Ibid.*, D.ii^v.; *Craft, ed. cit.*, p. 410; but even this resemblance is general.
57. Compare *Exercise*, D.iv^v and *Vices and Virtues, ed. cit.*, p. 73, ll. 7-8.
58. *Exercise*, E.iii^v-iv^v.
59. *Ibid.*, E.vii^v-viii^r, referring to Bk. II, ch. vii and Bk. III, chs. iii and iv of the *Pilgrimage*, which survives in two prints given in note 10 above.
60. *Scale, transl. cit.* (as *Ladder*), pp. 10-12 (Bk. I, chs. 10 and 11).
61. *Pipe, ccxxxvi* ^v in Redman's 1532 print.
62. See W.E. Campbell and A.W. Reed, eds., *The English Works of Thomas More* (London and New York, 1931), vol. I, pp. 459-499.
63. For helpful discussion of the 'epistolary' style in Middle English religious prose, see Roger Ellis, "A Literary Approach to the Middle English Mystics" in Marion Glasscoe, ed., *The Medieval Mystical Tradition in England* (Exeter, 1980), pp. 99-119.
64. See the useful modernisation of Suso in Frances M.M. Comper, ed., *The Book of the Craft of Dying* (London, 1917), pp. 103-124.

RESUME

Ce travail examine un *traité de la mort* anglais du 16ᵉ siècle, *A Dayly Exercyse and Experyence of Death*, de Richard Whitford de la maison des Brigittins de Syon, Isleworth. Imprimé un peu avant 1540, il fut composé vingt ans auparavant à la requête de l'abbesse de Syon en vue de l'édification des religieuses.

Whitford jouissait comme savant du respect des géants de son époque, Erasme et More. Son large savoir lui vaut une place éminente dans la lignée intellectuelle qui s'était très rapidement établie à Syon. Sa carrière démontre un intérêt tout particulier pour les problèmes de l'éducation, séculière d'abord, puis spirituelle. Après être entré en religion, Whitford composa plusieurs traités, d'aucuns sur la vie monacale, d'autres pour le bénéfice des laïques. Il semble que Syon ait encouragé ce genre d'ouvrages; d'autres membres de la communauté, notamment Thomas Betson, William Bonde et John Fewterer, avaient fait publier divers manuels vers la fin du 16ᵉ siècle.

Pour l'impression, un *Exercice Quotidien*, composé à l'origine pour les religieuses, fut partiellement adapté par Whitford lui-même pour un public plus vaste.

Comme *ars moriendi*, il combine une approche traditionnelle et des traits intéressants et inusités quant au contenu, au style et à la structure. Whitford n'a rien du pédant; il sait tempérer la rigueur de l'Ordre par sa connaissance de la faiblesse humaine.

★

LA JOIE DE MOURIR SELON SAINT BERNARD DE CLAIRVAUX

Jean Leclercq

I. Bernard témoin d'une tradition et d'un milieu

Le titre de cet exposé n'était pas prévu. Il s'est imposé à mesure que je relisais les textes dans lesquels saint Bernard s'est exprimé sur la mort, telle que lui et son milieu la concevaient, l'expérimentaient et, si l'on ose ce paradoxe, la "vivaient". Pour que l'enquête eût de la rigueur, elle devait se limiter à une époque et, en celle-ci, à un témoin et à son influence. Mais pour exceptionnel que soit son génie, saint Bernard, en ce domaine comme en tant d'autres, ne représente pas que lui seul. Il est enraciné dans une tradition spirituelle et culturelle, celle du monachisme, et il l'enrichit à son tour, dans l'immense foule de ceux qui peuplèrent ses fondations, et grâce à ceux qui copièrent et lurent ses oeuvres, attestées par une diffusion manuscrite dont on peut maintenant établir qu'elle fut la plus vaste du XIIᵉ siècle.

En sa génération et celles qui la précédèrent immédiatement, des recherches récentes, menées indépendamment les unes des autres, ont amené à constater que, dans les cloîtres, la mort était présentée comme "précieuse" parce qu'elle était "heureuse", attendue sans peur, accompagnée de sérénité et même de beauté, rendue contemporaine de celle du Christ dont on relisait la passion lors du "passage" d'un moine de cette existence terrestre à celle de la résurrection.[1] Ces témoignages ne manquaient cependant pas de réalisme: on y relève, par exemple, une notation psychologique étonnamment précise au sujet de Hugues de Marchiennes: sa dernière maladie s'accompagna d'une grave souffrance intérieure:

> Dans l'amertume de son âme, il se rappelait ses années passées, et comme pour cela sa mémoire était exceptionnelle, l'épreuve en était plus pressante. Il se représentait tout ce qu'il avait fait de bien et de mal; ce qui multipliait sa douleur et annulait toute grandeur.

JEAN LECLERCQ

Cette ultime humiliation ne l'empêcha pas de finir en "exultant", lui qui en vérité désirait s'en aller et vivre avec le Christ.[2] Aspiration vers Dieu, suivie, lorsqù'elle va être enfin satisfaite, d'un endormissement paisible, allant jusqu'à s'accompagner de plaisanteries: *ioculando mori*, écrit-on d'un autre contemporain de saint Bernard, Gossuin d'Anchin.[3] La contribution spécifique de saint Bernard sur ce point comme sur d'autres consiste, non à fixer les attitudes spirituelles du monachisme, mais à en élaborer la théologie. A cause du nombre élevé de textes de la Bible où se trouvaient le mot "mourir", ses dérivés et ses équivalents – comme *dissolvi* – , tous employés avec diverses significations, réelles ou symboliques, le vocabulaire de la mort est abondant dans saint Bernard. Moins que celui de la vie. Pour lui aussi il peut s'appliquer à la disparition de la foi – *mors fidei* – , de la mort même – *mors mortis* – , et à bien d'autres faits que la fin de la vie terrestre. Les thèmes de la mort et de l'après-mort ne l'obsèdent pas. Il n'a écrit ni un traité ni un sermon sur eux. Il en parle le plus souvent à propos d'autre chose; quand il le fait, c'est avec peu d'images, sans s'attarder à décrire des détails concrets et des circonstances. La mort est certes, pour lui, tout d'abord, un phénomène humain, une expérience que tous ont à faire; mais il s'attache de préférence à discerner le sens et la valeur de cet événement, qui, en lui, éveille plus d'idées que de phantasmes.

Son enseignement à ce sujet, il l'a exposé à propos de deux sortes de cas. Les premiers sont constitués par ces morts réussies que sont celles des saints; l'Eglise les présente comme des modèles, comme saint Pierre et saint Paul,[4] saint Clément,[5] ces privilégiés qui recurent la grâce du martyre, et déjà, sous le régime de l'Ancienne Alliance, les Macchabées.[6] Le vieillard Siméon meurt "avec une joie sûre et une sécurité joyeuse", comme en se jouant: voilà ce que signifient les mots *iucundus* et *iucunditas*. Quant à Jean Baptiste, en prison, c'est "joyeux" qu'il accueille la mort: cet adjectif est répété trois fois, avec insistance: *laetus, et tam laetus, mortem laetus accepit*, avec entraînement, *alacri animo*, et se réjouissant, *gaudens*.[7]

Mais ont-ils été imités? Une seconde espèce de modèles est proposé par saint Bernard: en certains de ses contemporains, l'idéal a été réalisé. A propos de la mort de tous, deux versets de Psaumes reviennent comme des thèmes qui sont parfois mis en contrepoint: pour les pécheurs, la mort est ce qu'il y a de pire: *Mors peccatorum pessima* (Ps 33, 22). Mais pour les saints et les justes elle est d'un grand prix: *pretiosa* (Ps 115, 15). C'est à ce second texte, certainement, que va la préférence de Bernard: il insiste davantage sur la joie que sur la tristesse. Il s'est complu à détailler les raisons pour lesquelles la mort a tant de prix: c'est surtout cette valeur, cette richesse de contenu qui l'intéresse. A-t-il aussi dit quelque chose sur ce qui se passe, au moment de cet événement, dans celui qui le vit et dans son entourage? Le mourant est-il dans la crainte ou dans la joyeuse espérance? Comment réagissent les témoins? Y a-t-il cohérence entre l'expérience du mourant, l'interprétation qu'en donne son milieu, et les idées de Bernard et la tradition qu'il représente et explicite? Laissons à quelques textes le soin de répondre.

II. La mort de la mort.

Le Livre aux Chevaliers du Temple, à la louange de la milice nouvelle comporte deux parties, répondant aux questions que se posaient leurs destinataires au sujet de leur activité et de leur prière. La seconde, la plus développée, leur propose des méditations sur les mystères qui se sont accomplies sur les Lieux saints où ils font leur service. Et, certainement, Bernard avait en vue bien d'autres lecteurs qui, de fait, ne manquèrent pas.[8] Or, le chapitre le plus long de cet exposé concerne le Saint-Sépulcre[9]: c'est un encouragement au "labeur" de la vie, en considération de la "douceur" qu'apporte à la faiblesse humaine "le repos de la dormition", la sécurité de la mort. Et aussitôt éclatent des formules denses et triomphantes, pleines de jeux de sonorités qu'aucune traduction ne peut rendre.

> La mort du Christ est pour moi une règle de vie, sa mort est mon rachat de la mort. Sa vie instruit ma vie, sa mort détruit ma mort. Sa vie certes est laborieuse, mais sa mort est précieuse; toutes deux sont également nécessaires.

Il n'y a point, pour ainsi dire, d'anthropologie de la mort sans une christologie. Et en Jésus, ce que contemple saint Bernard, plus que l'histoire, c'est le mystère. Or, à propos de cette mort unique, exemple et origine de toute mort chrétienne, le mot qui revient aussitôt, et qui sera fréquent, est celui de sécurité. Pourquoi cela? Le mystère de la mort n'est présent ni dans le Christ, ni dans le chrétien, sans la réalité de sa résurrection. Avant que ne finisse notre existence, bien plus: dès son origine, il y a en nous une mort qui est le péché. Mais le Christ, qui ne l'avait point, a souffert notre mort humaine pour nous en sauver; en condamnant la mort à mort, il nous a libérés du péché, il nous a remis nos péchés. S'il a pu ainsi "mettre en fuite la mort par sa mort", c'est parce que celle-ci a été en lui volontaire, spontanée, acte de liberté totale: il est mort par amour, par pitié, par désir de pardonner, par "miséricorde". Il nous a fait ce don de la part de Dieu son Père, en nous communiquant l'Esprit qui met en nous sa charité. Il a été capable de mourir parce qu'il était homme, de se libérer de la mort parce qu'il était Dieu. Auparavant il avait laissé retarder ce moment décisif afin d'avoir le temps de nous montrer comment vit l'Homme-Dieu.

Ainsi tout du Christ a eu une valeur pour nous, tout a été salutaire, tout était nécessaire... Sa mort nous a délivrés de la mort, sa vie de l'erreur, sa grâce du péché... La mort du Christ est la mort de ma mort, car il est mort pour que je vive. Comment ne vivrait-il pas désormais, celui pour qui la Vie est morte?

Notre résurrection est différée, pour que nous passions par la mort, mais celle-ci ne nous domine pas pour toujours: elle demeure seulement pour un temps. Du moins la douceur même de ces "joyeux mystères" – *iucunda sacramenta* – est-elle source de joie au milieu du "labeur", de la "fatigue" de la vie dure. Ainsi se réalise l'antique prophétie d'Isaïe:

En ce jour-là – *in die illa* – la tige de Jessé se dressera comme un étendard parmi les nations. Les peuples l'imploreront, et son sépulchre sera glorieux (*Is.* 11, 10).

Ainsi se concilie l'autorité de ce qui est ancien et – notons cette formule que nous retrouverons – la joie de la nouveauté, *de novitate iucunditas*.

Il fallait résumer cet hymne enthousiaste à la mort de la mort, car sans cette foi intense, lucide, si parfaitement intégrée dans le donné humain, on n'entend rien de ce que saint Bernard et ses lecteurs ont pensé de la mort.

III. La chevalerie face à la mort.

Dans la première partie de ce même traité, Bernard présente aux Templiers une justification de leur activité militaire en Terre Sainte. Or, dès le début, il place chacun d'eux devant la perspective de la mort, non pas celle de ses ennemis, lorsqu'ils deviennent ses victimes, mais la sienne, en face de laquelle ils éprouvent "sécurité".[10]

Soldat sans peur, sûr de tout côté ... Il ne craint pas même la mort, puisqu'il désire mourir: que craindrait-il en effet, vivant ou mort, puisque pour lui 'vivre c'est le Christ, et mourir est un gain'(*Phil.* 1, 21).

La mort de tout chrétien est, comme le dit le Psaume 115, 15, "précieuse", qu'elle ait lieu "dans un lit ou à la guerre". Mais dans le second cas, elle est encore "plus précieuse", accompagnée de plus de ''sécurité'', à condition que soit saint le combat qu'on mène.

Bernard, réformateur infatigable, saisit cette occasion d'établir un contraste entre deux chevaleries, celle du Christ, pour les Templiers, et celle du siècle: en celle-ci, on met à mort ou on est mis à mort sans profit; il y a alors homicide. Qu'elle soit donnée ou reçue, cette mort est ''criminelle''. Car sa valeur dépend des motifs qui l'inspirent: résulte-t-elle d'un acte exercé au service et par amour du Christ et de ses membres, ou d'une recherche de puissance ou de gloire inutile? Dans ce dernier cas, même si triomphe la force meurtrière, elle ne conduit qu'à une ''malheureuse victoire'', *infelix victoria*. La satire des ornements efféminés dont tant de chevaliers s'affublent intervient ici pour appeler les chevaliers à purifier leurs motifs.

Au milieu de tant de luttes locales, dont les pauvres étaient les victimes, Bernard exhorte ceux qui ont le pouvoir de tuer à vérifier leurs intentions: c'est là le moyen de limiter la violence, qui est partout[11]. Par cette méditation initiale, il replace chaque chevalier – chrétien ou séculier – devant le mystère de la mort. Loin d'encourager les combattants à tuer, il leur rappelle qu'ils sont aussi exposés à être tués: dans les deux cas, que ce soit pour de bonnes raisons. Le chevalier du Christ, lui, tue en toute sécurité, mais il est encore plus en sûreté – plus sûr de son désintéressement – lorsqu'il est tué: *securus interimit, interit securior*, sachant qu'il ne périt pas, mais parvient: *non periisse, sed pervenisse*. Toute la suite montre l'Ordre du Temple comme une force de paix intérimaire: ses membres ne rêvent pas de conquête, ils reviendront quand la Terre Sainte sera libérée. En attendant, qu'ils méditent les mystères de la vie du Christ, dont le plus important fut la mise à mort de la mort.

IV. *Moines devant la mort.*

Considérons maintenant quelques exemples de décès, survenus à Clairvaux, à l'occasion desquels le mystère de la mort fut, pour ainsi dire, personnalisé.

1. *Gérard ou la mort en chantant.*

Le premier texte auquel on pense est ce sermon fameux sur le Cantique des cantiques, le 26,[11] qui contient une lamentation provoquée chez Bernard par la mort de son frère Gérard[12]. C'est, en réalité, un exposé, et même une sorte de traité, sur l'amitié plutôt que sur la mort. C'est une complainte non sur le trépas de Gérard, mais sur l'existence de Bernard désormais séparé de lui: ''Je pleure à cause de toi, mais non sur toi'', *Plango, etsi non super te, tamen propter te*. Ce qui est ''amer'', c'est, pour Bernard, la séparation; ce qui est ''horrible'' est ce ''divorce'' apporté, entre deux amis, par la mort qui, à cause de cela, mérite d'être qualifiée de ''furieuse'' et d'''austère''. En effet, ''nous nous sommes aimés!'' ''Notre amour'', qui fut ''mutuel'', notre ''attachement intime'' avait créé entre nous une "présence" de l'un à l'autre. Le mot "ami" est ici employé jusqu'à sept fois, accompagné, selon un procédé cher à Bernard, de toute une série de termes dont le préfixe est un dérivé de *cum*, "avec", et signifie la communion: *concordia, communis, consortium, colloquium, consors, socialis conversatio*. En vérité, les deux frères ne faisaient qu'un seul coeur, un seul esprit: plus qu'une communauté de sang, il existait entre eux unité d'âme: non *consanguinitas, sed unanimitas*. Gérard était pour Bernard ce que dit parfaitement une formule biblique: l'homme d'un seul esprit avec lui, *homo unanimis*. Voilà ce à quoi met une fin la mort; d'elle, à cause de cela, Bernard, en une formule forte, assure qu'il a horreur, pour lui et pour les siens: *mortem horreo meam et meorum*.

Mais aussitôt, il commence à exalter, en contraste extrême, la joie que Gérard éprouva à mourir. Il avait toujours désiré "être dissous pour être avec le Christ" (*Phil.* 1, 23), "s'envoler vers les embrassements" du Christ, s'en aller pour se dépouiller de sa condition terrestre: *cupit exire, ut se possit avvun, bref le "repos" définitif. Au moment où ce bienfait lui est accordé, insultant la mort, il exulte en elle: *hominem in morte exsultantem, insultantem morti*. Jamais autant qu'en ce passage, pourtant bref, Bernard n'a chanté toute la joie qu'il y a à mourir: Gérard meurt en chantant et en chantant il meurt: *Iam cantando moritur homo et moriendo cantat*. Point de détails sur ses derniers instants; rien que le bonheur de l'esprit: la mort n'est pas un aiguillon, mais un moment de jubilation – *non stimulus, sed iubilus* – , de "liesse", de "gloire". C'est une porte de sortie, large et heureuse – *latum laetumque exitum* – vers la gloire. Gérard n'est pas seulement plein de "sécurité", mais d'allégresse et de louange: *laetabundes et laudans*. En souriant – *exhilarata facie* – il rend grâces à Dieu et il "chante": il réussit – Bernard en fait l'aveu, *fateor* – à "transformer mon deuil en un chant". Cette hilarité dans la mort est communicative, contagieuse; elle pénètre le milieu.

2. Humbert ou l'amitié transformé.

Plus tard, en 1148, Bernard reprend ce thème du contraste entre la joie de celui qui meurt dans le Seigneur et la peine de l'ami qu'il laisse séparé de lui. Il le fait à propos d'un autre de ses moines, Humbert.[13] Celui-ci était parvenu à l'âge de la "décrépitude". Il avait connu des "labeurs" et des "croix". Aussi Bernard répète-t-il ce qu'il a dit au sujet de Gérard: "Si j'éprouve de la peine, ce n'est pas pour toi – *Non super te doleo* – , car Dieu t'a accordé ce que ton âme désirait… Notre amitié, ajoute-t-il, était d'autant plus agréable qu'elle était plus ancienne". Ici Bernard, vieillissant lui-même, laisse échapper un émouvant aveu: à chaque fois que s'en va l'un de ses moines, il commence à mourir: "Je meurs en chacun d'eux, *ego morior in singulis*".

Sur le milieu, l'impression que produit chaque décès n'est rien d'autre que celle d'une séparation:

Ce n'est pas sur lui qu'il faut pleurer, c'est sur moi, sur vous tous et sur cette maison: il n'y a pas d'autre tristesse pour nous que d'être privés de ses conseils, et de son exemple.

De même, ''le Sauveur portait sa croix, comme un voleur porte la corde par laquelle il va être pendu'': quelle image! Et cependant, il consolait les femmes qui se lamentaient sur lui. Car la mort est une ouverture sur ''la joie et la liesse pour l'éternité''. Avec tendresse, Bernard évoque la ''charité'' qu'Humbert manifestait envers tous. Il prend occasion de la confiance ainsi créée pour donner à ses moines un avertissement qui en dit long sur l'atmosphère habituelle qui régnait à Clairvaux. La joie n'y était pas réservée aux jours de trépas; quotidiennement, on plaisantait beaucoup, trop même, et l'on savait qu'Humbert avait jadis ressenti cette tentation:

> Pour le reste, mes frères, voici ce que j'ai à vous dire: si vous suiviez son exemple, vous ne tomberiez pas aussi facilement dans les pensées vaines et les conversations oiseuses, dans les plaisanteries et les sottises, car en tout cela vous perdez beaucoup de votre vie et de votre temps... Je sais bien qu'il est dur au bavard de supporter le silence, à l'esprit vagabond de demeurer stable... Or l'homme qui est ici enseveli, dans ses débuts – je l'ai su – a dû lutter beaucoup contre la même tendance, qu'il a vaincue enfin: cette bonne habitude lui était devenue si naturelle qu'il n'aurait pu laisser son esprit s'envoler vers de telles inepties...

3. Malachie ou la mort comme fête.

Vers la fin de la même année durant laquelle était parti Humbert, le 2 novembre 1148, un nouveau deuil marquait Clairvaux et son abbé: celui de Malachie, archevêque d'Armagh, en Irlande, qui se rendait à Rome. L'un des derniers ouvrages rédigés par Bernard fut sa *Vie*. La partie finale de celle-ci constitue son ultime témoignage sur la mort, peu avant la sienne propre.[14] Malachie était mort en moine, entouré de tous les rites claustraux.[15] Mais comme il était irlandais, Bernard, d'emblée, caractérise l'événement comme un exercice de la *peregrinatio*, de la *migratio* si chère à la tradition celtique. Ici encore, les thèmes dominants sont ceux du désir, qui commence à être assouvi: ''*non fraudabor desiderii mei, qui partem iam teneo*''; de la confiance en la divine ''miséricorde'', du repos et de l'espérance: ''Je n'ai pas peu d'espoir, en cette journée – *in die illa* – durant laquelle tant de bienfaits sont obtenus des vivants pour les morts''. On approchait, en effet, de ce jour-là – *die ipse* – pendant lequel, à l'occasion de la Toussaint, on prie pour les défunts. Bien des moines avaient désiré mourir un jour de fête, et l'avaient obtenu.[16] Cette grâce n'allait pas être refusé à Malachie.

Ses derniers moments furent tout le contraire d'une agonie:

> Quand il allait recevoir le viatique, son visage n'était ni pâle, ni amaigri.

Pas de rides sur son front, ses yeux n'étaient pas enfoncés, ses narines
n'étaient point serrées; il n'avait ni les lèvres tendus, ni les dents usées,
ni le cou frêle, ni les épaules courbées, ni le corps épuisé. Son corps
était plein de grâce et son visage de gloire.

Toute la communauté accourt, et c'est la fête:

C'est la solennité lumineuse de Tous les Saints. Une antique formule
de l'Ecriture déclare que la musique n'est pas de mise dans le deuil.
Et cependant, malgré nous, nous chantons. Nous pleurons en chantant,
nous chantons en pleurant. Malachie, lui, bien qu'il ne chante pas, ne
pleure pas non plus. Pourquoi pleurerait-il, lui qui approche de la joie?
A nous le deuil: seul Malachie est en fête: *festum facit*. Le jour de sa
mort est un jour de fête: *dies festus*. Son corps lui fait défaut, la voix
lui manque; il lui reste de l'esprit pour une jubilante célébration: *ut
mentis iubile sollemnizet*. En pleine nuit, voici, pour lui, que se lève le jour,
que les ténèbres s'illuminent. Pourquoi cette 'sécurité'? 'J'ai aimé Dieu
et je vous ai aimés: la charité ne passera jamais'.

Voici donc notre "ami rapatrié". "Il s'est endormi heureusement:
vraie dormition. Son visage pacifié fut le signe de son paisible départ.
Il a gardé la même vivacité, la même sérénité qu'on observe sur ceux
qui dorment." Mais quel effet tout cela a-t-il sur le milieu? "Ce n'est
pas lui qui a changé, il nous a transformés: nos gémissements cessent,
notre tristesse devient joie, notre chant exclut toute plainte... La foi
l'emporte, le courage triomphe." En "finale", Bernard reprend et
entremêle tous les thèmes qui rendent la mort "précieuse": sommeil,
porte de vie, amitié, victoire, joie, désir surtout: "Je ne lui envie pas
ces biens, je les désire pour moi."
Aux faits rapportés dans la *Vie*, un sermon de Bernard lors du
passage de Malachie de ce monde à l'autre – de son "transit", *In
transitu*, au sens précis du terme – ajoute une autre circonstance[17]: au
moment de son décès, on venait de procéder au transfert, d'un
cimetière ancien en un nouveau, des corps des défunts de Clairvaux.
Il s'était alors "délecté" à écouter les chants, avant de "s'endormir
lui-même d'un sommeil très doux, très heureux". Bernard adresse
alors une invective à la mort, mais c'est pour avoir l'occasion de
réaffirmer la solution que le Christ lui a apportée: par sa propre mort,
il l'a vaincue. Désormais, pour les bien-aimés de Dieu, elle est sommeil
et rafraîchissement. Si elle reste pour les pécheurs ce qu'il y a de
pire – *pessima* –, elle est "précieuse" pour les justes: ils n'éprouvent
que "sécurité". "Il n'y a plus de quoi avoir peur et trembler: vers

ce rafraîchissement courons avec toute la cupidité et le désir le plus ardent dont est capable notre esprit.''

Même ton de victoire dans un autre sermon pour le jour de la mort de Malachie, qui, en réalité, est celui de sa fête[18]:

Il avait été maître et vainqueur de lui-même; qu'il ait maintenant pitié de nous qui, au milieu de nos misères, débordons du souvenir d'une douceur surabondante.

Souffrance et bonheur du chrétien! Bernard réutilise ici une paranomase qu'il avait déjà appliquée à Malachie, vers la fin de la *Vie: Mors tua, mortis portus et porta vitae*, ''Ta mort, c'est, pour la mort, un port d'arrivée; pour la vie, une porte d'entrée''. Ainsi demeure-t-il fidèle au symbolisme de la ''pérégrination'', par lequel s'ouvre ce sermon, et à celui de la ''migration''.

4. Bernard ou l'anticipation.

Enfin, voici un témoignage des plus surprenants, qui n'a point fini d'étonner les historiens: c'est un bulletin de santé écrit de sa main même, par Bernard sur son lit de mort. Dans sa correspondance, il avait parlé plus de vingt fois de sa mort, que son mauvais état de santé lui faisait croire parfois imminente. Il l'avait désirée, mais avait accepté avec sérénité de vivre encore, après lui avoir échappé. Au cours de ses voyages, il avait exprimé un voeu: qu'elle lui soit accordée à Clairvaux au milieu des siens. Ce souhait fut réalisé. Après son retour d'une dernière expédition en Lotharingie, au printemps de 1153, il eut encore le temps, la force physique, la vivacité d'esprit de rédiger la lettre 310, la dernière de cette collection d'épîtres qu'il avait lui-même préparée.[19] Elle est adressée à Arnaud, abbé de Bonneval.

La tradition manuscrite l'avait toujours fait considérer comme authentique. Puis des doutes furent soulevés: un moribond était-il en état de donner des détails cliniques si réalistes et si précis sur ses symptômes? Mais, tout récemment, un nouvel examen du texte et de ses sources bibliques a confirmé que la lettre est bien de lui.[20] De fait, on y retrouve, non seulement ses qualités de style et de pensée, mais sa belle humeur, depuis le jeu de mots du début – *in caritate et non in voluptate* – jusqu'à la légère ironie de la fin faisant allusion à une lettre, attendue, qui n'était pas venue: ''J'aurais préféré te répondre que t'écrire''. Même dans la description de ses malaises, il plaisante: ''S'il me reste quelque plaisir, c'est celui de ne rien manger''. Il s'amuse à personnifier son estomac: ''Il exige d'être soulagé par un peu de liquide... Ce peu même qu'il veut bien accepter, ce n'est pas sans une terrible douleur qu'il l'absorbe, mais il en craint une bien pire encore s'il restait à vide.'' Le manque de sommeil, l'enflure des jambes et des pieds caractérisent aussi sa ''chair infirme.'' Et cependant, son esprit est vivace, ''prompt.'' ''Je suis fou de le dire,'' ajoute-t-il avec humour, citant S. Paul au sujet de "l'homme intérieur".

Tout cela prépare une fin imminente: "Il est temps que je parte! Priez notre Sauveur, qui ne veut pas la mort du pécheur – selon les paroles d'Ezéchiel (33, 11) – , de ne pas différer mon voyage, mais de le prendre sous sa garde". Or cette formule du prophète, à chaque fois que Bernard l'a employée ailleurs, c'est en relation avec la résurrection du Christ: il l'a même fait prononcer par le Seigneur lui-même. Voilà ce que le Ressuscité lui suggère une fois de plus. Admirons cet art consommé dans le maniement de l'allusion significative. Une autre très subtile réminiscence, à la fois du tendon d'Achille et de la blessure du serpent prédite à Eve (*Gen.* 3, 15), annonce très discrètement une dernière attaque possible du démon: "Puisque sa tête est écrasée par Mère Eglise, il lui tend une embûche cruelle au talon".[21] "Par vos prières, dit Bernard à Arnauld, chargez-vous de protéger mon talon nu de mérites. Ainsi le serpent qui me guette ne saura où planter son croc. J'ai moi-même écrit cette lettre, malade comme je suis, pour qu'à la main bien connue tu reconnaisses mon affection."

Fidélité dans l'amitié, humilité, invincible confiance, joie, humour même: tout Bernard est là, tel qu'il avait été tout au long de son existence, tel qu'il va être en sa mort, qu'il sait toute proche. On possède bien peu d'exemples, en histoire littéraire, d'un écrivain qui anticipe ainsi, pour ainsi dire, sa propre mort: il la joue d'avance, en fait une sorte de répétition générale, dit ce qu'il éprouve en son esprit et en son organisme, dans l'avant-mort qui la précède immédiatement. Après avoir été le témoin du départ de plusieurs, Bernard l'était du sien. Non sans douleurs, mais dans une foi joyeuse.

Pour acquérir une vue complète de ce qu'était la mort dans la société monastique selon saint Bernard, il y aurait à examiner tous ses textes, même ceux où il n'en parle que brièvement, ou par des allusions qui peuvent être révélatrices. En ceux qui ont été interrogés ici, le ton d'exaltation, et d'exultation, risquait de devenir fatigant, mais non ennuyeux, car il était varié. Mais n'oublions pas que ces quelques passages sont dispersés au cours d'une oeuvre vaste où ils n'occupent guère plus de place que n'en avait, semble-t-il, la pensée de la mort.

Deux thèmes ont émergé, qu'il convient de mettre en lumière pour conclure. Le premier est celui de la lumière: *Dies illa*: le grand jour n'est pas celui d'un jugement qui inspirerait de la crainte. Ce n'est pas un *dies irae*. C'est celui de la lumière définitive, qui commence à poindre à l'aurore, après que la nuit même, par la résurrection du Christ, a été éclairée, transformée en un temps de bonheur.[22] Les mots latins qui veulent dire "le jour se lève" – *diescere, dies fit* – avaient été appliqués, dans la tradition chrétienne, à cet événement, à cet instant de gloire,[23] et à ceux qui, déjà, y ont participé totalement. Ainsi fait Bernard, à propos de Malachie: "Grand luminaire, lumière brillant dans les ténèbres... Etoile du matin, plus claire que les autres, parce que plus proche du jour, plus semblable au Soleil... Aurore qui devient jour sur notre terre: *O aurora diescens super terram*".[24]

Une autre idée qu'affectionne Bernard est celle de la surprise que causera la découverte d'une réalité entièrement neuve; l'une des trois raisons pour lesquelles la mort est précieuse est cette "joie de la nouveauté": *iucunditas de novitate.*[25] Cet émerveillement, cet étonnement joyeux – *gaudium de novitate*[26] – se perpétuera en une "éternelle curiosité".[27]

Enfin, de tout cet ensemble de convictions, Bernard a su tirer des conséquences pratiques. A un sous-diacre de la curie romaine, qui avait promis de se faire moine, Bernard rappelle ce fait en jouant sur les mots qui veulent dire "se souvenir", *memoria*, puis "délai", *mora*, enfin "mourir", *mori*. Le deuxième, *mora*, fait aussitôt penser à l'heure de la mort, *hora mortis*[28]:

Je veux que si tu ne peux l'éviter, du moins tu ne la craignes pas. Ainsi fait le juste, qui ne s'en garde, mais qui ne s'en effraie pas: *etsi non cavet, tamen non pavet*... Bonne est la mort par laquelle on meurt au péché. L'autre, qui fait sortir de cette vie, sera l'entrée dans une existence meilleure.

L'important est, comme le disait le nom d'un monastère cistercien, Morimond, de "mourir au monde": *Mori mundo.* Bernard prend plaisir à passer – et à faire passer son correspondant, ses lecteurs – d'un de ces registres ou niveaux à un autre: de la mort dans le péché, qui est ce qu'il y a de "pire", à la mort au péché, qui conduit à une joyeuse fin de vie: "Elle est bonne, la mort, à cause du repos; meilleure, à cause de la nouveauté; très bonne, à cause de la sécurité". Il développe ici, une fois de plus, ces trois bienfaits. L'insistance sur le second paraît constituer l'apport le plus original de Bernard: joie de l'étonnement devant la nouveauté, inséparable de la sécurité due à l'éternité: *iucunditas de novitate ac de aeternitate securitas.*

NOTES

1. Textes cités dans Henri Platelle, "La Mort Précieuse. La mort des moines d'après quelques sources des Pays-Bas du Sud", dans *Revue Mabillon* LX (1982), pp. 151-174; J. Leclercq, "La mort d'après la tradition monastique du moyen âge", dans *Studia Missionalia* XXXI, (1982): *Sens de la mort,* pp. 71-77; "Poèmes à la louange de S. Gossuin d'Anchin", dans *Analecta Bollandiana* C (1982), pp. 417-433.
2. Platelle, *art.cit.,* pp. 168-170.
3. *Poèmes à la louange...* , pp. 426-94.
4. *Sermo in sollemnitate Apostolorum Petri et Pauli,* 2, 5-6, S. *Bernardi opera,* V, pp. 195-196. Désormais les écrits de S. Bernard seront cités selon l'édition S. *Bernardi opera* (abrégé en S. *Bern. op.*), 8 vol., Rome 1957-1977.
5. S. *Bern. op.,*V, 412-414.
6. *Epist.* 98, S. *Bern.op.,* VII, pp. 248-251

JEAN LECLERCQ

7. *Ibid.*, pp. 251-252.

8. Sur l'abondante tradition manuscrite, aux XIIe et XIIIe siècles: *S. Bern. op.*,
   III, pp. 208-209. Les manuscrits datant d'époques postérieures sont nombreux
   aussi.

9. *Ibid.*, pp. 251-252.

10. *Ibid.*, pp. 229-237.

11. *Studies in Medieval Cistercian History*, II, ed. by John R. Sommerfeldt (Kalamazoo,
    1976), pp. 1-39. "L'attitude spirituelle de saint Bernard devant la guerre", dans
    Collectanea Cisterciensa XXXVI (1974), pp. 195-225.

12. *S. Bern. op.*, I, pp. 169-181.

13. *In obitu domni Humberti, S. Bern. op.*, V, pp. 440-447. La mort d'Humbert survint
    en septembre 1148, ou le 7 décembre de la même année, selon *Bernard de Clairvaux*,
    Paris, 1953, p. 608.

14. *Vita S. Malachiae*, n. 71-75, *S. Bern. op.*, III, pp. 375-378.

15. Ces rites ont été décrits par Louis Gougaud, *Anciennes coutumes claustrales* (Ligugé,
    1930), pp. 69-95.

16. Platelle, *op. cit.* p. 165; *Pierre le Vénérable* (Saint Wandrille, 1946), pp. 12-14: *Mourir
    un jour de fête.*

17. *In transitu S. Malachiae, S. Bern. op* ., V, pp. 417-423.

18. *De S. Malachiae, S. Bern. op* ., VI, 1, pp. 50-55.

19. *S. Bern. op.*, VIII, p. 230.

20. Denis Farkasfalvy, *The Authenticity of St. Bernard's Letter from his Deathbed*, dans
    Analecta Cisterciensa XXXVI (1980), pp. 264-267.

21. *Super Ps. Qui habitat*, 6, 7, *S. Bern. op.*, IV, 410.

22. *Sup. Cant.*, 26, 11, *S.Bern op.*, I, p. 178.

23. Geoffroy d'Auxerre, un moment "notaire" de saint Bernard, écrira également,
    pour distinguer le *dies defunctionis* et le *dies consummationis*, que le premier est le
    commencement du second: la vie éternelle *discit iusto cum moritur, amplius cum
    resurgit*: Ferruccio Gastaldelli, *Spiritualità e missione del vescovo in un sermone inedito
    di Goffredo di Auxerre su San Gregorio*, dans *Salesianum* XLIII (1981). p. 122. *Ibid.*,
    note 6, références sur l'histoire du mot *discere.*

24. *De S.Malachia, S. Bern. op.*, VI, 1, p. 55.

25. *Sent.*, III, 86, *S. Bern. op.*, VI, 1, p. 124.

26. *De diversis*, 64, *S. Bern. op.*, VI, 1, p.298.

27. *"Curiositas,"* à paraître dans les *Mélanges Diaz y Diaz.*

28. *Ep.* 105, *S. Bern. op.*, VII, p. 264.

SUMMARY

1. Bernard in his writings represents a *milieu* whose conceptions influence him and
are influenced by him. In monastic circles death was already conceived as "precious",
a joyous event to be met without fear, with serenity, even in a jocular vein. Bernard
rarely treats the theme of bodily death, and when he does so he is concerned not with
descriptive detail but with the theological significance of the event, his interest centring
in the spiritual content of the "successful" death of the just: *Pretiosa in conspectu Domini
mors sanctorum eius* (Ps. 33, v.22).

2. In his treatise for the Templars Bernard treats the subject in the light of the mystery
of Christ's death. Serenity and repose are the face death presents, since for the Christian
Christ's death has killed death, and

3. this mystery becomes actual in the death of *Christian soldiers*. For the Templars death
in battle is even more "precious", productive of greater "security", as long as the battle
is righteous. Meditation upon the mystery of death should lead them to consider their
motives, and be a force for peace rather than destruction.

4(i) In his 26th sermon on the Song of Solomon Bernard speaks of the death of his
fellow-monk Gerard. Death of a friend is sad and terrible for those separated from him,

not for the friend himself. Gerard had desired death that he might have eternal rest in God and be united with Christ. Therefore he exulted in death and died smiling, and singing his joy so powerfully that the joy was communicated to Bernard himself.

(ii) In 1148 another of his community died, the elderly monk Hubert. Bernard repeats the message of his reflections upon the death of Gerard: *Non super te doleo*.... but confesses that the pain of separation is like a death for him. He also uses Hubert to preach a lesson: the temptation to overmuch banal hilarity was one Hubert had overcome. Let his fellow-monks see jocularity in perspective.

(iii)   Later that year Malachy O'Morghair, bishop of Armagh, also died at Clairvaux on his way to Rome. In his *Life of Malachy*, written not long before his own death, Bernard for once gives a full description of the event, but drawing attention to the fact that Malachy's bodily state was not the usual one of the dying man: his face was *not* pale and thin, his eyes *not* sunken, etc. Malachy received the grace of death on All Saints' Day, a great feast day for the church, and the whole community, though they wept for his passing, sang for joy at the joy and certainty he manifested; once again proving that if for sinners death is the ultimate horror, for the just it is desirable, since Christ's death has made it a haven of rest and refreshment, and the gateway to life.

(iv)   In letter 310 Bernard as he is dying describes with extraordinary precision, and not without his customary humour and irony, his condition as he approaches death, the body decrepit and in pain, the spirit joyous in its faith and certainty.

Conclusion: Two principal themes emerge. The first, the theme of light: *dies illa* is not a day of judgement to inspire fear, a *dies irae,* but the dawning of perpetual light and happiness. The second is that of surprise: joyous surprise at what the perpetual light will reveal, which is the eternal newness of God. This *iucundas de novitate* for the soul secure in its eternal destiny is one of the reasons why death is so highly to be prized. It is in the development of this theme that Bernard's most original contribution to the theme of death seems to lie.

207

THE EUGENE VINAVER MEMORIAL FUND
LIST OF CONTRIBUTORS

★

Roy Abbott, Esq., 36, Brook Gardens, Harwood, Bolton BL2 3JD.

Dr.D.J. Adams, Department of French Studies, The University, Manchester M13 9PL.

Peter Ainsworth, Esq., Department of French Studies, The University, Manchester M13 9PL.

Dr. Robert J. Alexander, English Department, Point Park College, Pittsburgh, Pa. 15222.

Ms. Estelle Ash, 56, Princes Street, Cardiff CF2 3SL.

G.M. Ashton, Esq., Y Mowut, Victoria Park, Cadoxton, Barry, South Glamorgan.

Professor and Mrs. L.J. Austin, 2, Park Lodge, Park Terrace, Cambridge CB1 1JJ.

M.M. Austin, Esq., 4, Radernie Place, St. Andrews, Fife KY16 8QR.

Miss J. Bardsley, 33, Colemeadow Road, Coleshill, Birmingham B46 1BL.

Dr. W.R.J. Barron, Department of English, The University, Manchester M13 9PL.

Mlle. Yvonne Batard, 3, rue Montparnasse, Paris 6.

Mrs. Kathleen Beavis, 14, Brook Road, Fallowfield, Manchester M14 6UH.

M. Beresford, Esq., Department of Russian, The University, Manchester M13 9PL.

Mrs. Anne Berrie, Department of French Studies, The University, Manchester M13 9PL.

Miss Madeleine Blaess, French Department, The University of Sheffield, Sheffield S10 2TN.

Mrs. Brian Blakey, 616, Marley Road, Burlington, Ontario, Canada L7T 3R7.

Dr. David Blamires, German Department, The University, Manchester M13 9PL.

Dr. F. Bogdanow, Department of French Studies, The University, Manchester M13 9PL.

The Bolton Anglo-French Circle, Bolton, Lancashire.

Mrs. Margaret Bonsell, 75, Woodthorne Road South, Tettenhall, Wolverhampton WV6 8SN.

A.R. Borders, Esq., 3, Oakhurst Avenue, Oswestry, Shropshire SY11 1BP.

Mrs. W.M.D. Borland, Department of Hispanic Studies, The University, Hull HU6 7RX.

D. Bradby, Esq., Darwin College, The University, Canterbury, Kent CT2 7NY.

Mrs. José E. Brazier, Old Orchard, The Ruffitt, Littledean, Glos.

Professor G. Brée, 2135 Royall Drive, Winston Salom, N.C. 27106, U.S.A.

Dr. Derek S. Brewer, Emmanuel College, Cambridge.

M. Michel Bronstein, 4, rue des Eaux, 75016 Paris.

Mrs. J. Brown, 453, Gisburn Road, Blacko, Nelson, Lancashire BB9 6LS.

Peter Brown, Esq., Faculty of Humanities, Darwin College, University of Kent, Canterbury CT2 7NY.

Dr. R. Bromwich, 4, Cilfondan, Carneddi, Bethesda, Bangor, Gwynneth LL57 3SL.

Dr. Glyn Burgess, Department of French, Modern Languages Building, P.O. Box 147, Liverpool L69 3BX.

Dr. Eva M. Butchart, Wern Ddu Isaf, Wern Ddu, Oswestry, Shropshire SY10 9BN.

Professor P.F. Butler, Via Sansedoni 7, Siena, Italy.

Dr M.M. Callander, French Department, The University, Birmingham 15.

Miss D.M. Capes, 31, Inglemire Lane, Hull HU6 7TD.

Professor Carleton W. Carroll, Department of Foreign Languages and Literatures, Oregon State University, Corvallis, Oregon 97331, U.S.A.

Professor C. Chadwick, Department of French, The University, Aberdeen.

Miss H.F. Clementson, 24, Willowmead Close, Mount Avenue, London W5 1PT.

Mrs. Ruth Harwood Cline, 5315, Oakland Road, Chevy Chase, MD 20015, U.S.A.

Emeritus Professor John Cohen, 15, Didsbury Park, Didsbury, Manchester M20 0LH.

Professor R.J. Cormier, 761, Millbrook Lane, Haverford, P.A. 19041, U.S.A.

J.E. Coulthurst, 5, North Drive, Ancaster, Grantham NG32 3RB.

Mrs. J.M. Coussmaker, 39, Grétry Street, Antwerp 2000, Belgium.

Miss I.R. Cragg, 128, Layton Road, Blackpool, Lancashire FY3 8ER.

Mr. A.D. Crow, Oriel College, Oxford.

Dr. Renée Curtis, French Department, Westfield College, Hampstead, London NW3

Mr. Graham Daniels, Department of French, The University, Manchester M13 9PL.

Mrs. A. Davidge, 2, Locks Lane, Wantage OX12 9DB.

R.A. Davies, 17, Denning Road, Wrexham, Clwyd.

Miss Ruth J. Dean, Apartment 10-C, 165 West 66th Street, New York, N.Y.10023, U.S.A.

M. Maurice Delbouille, 75, rue des Mauvaises-Vignes, B 4600 Chênée, Belgium.

M. Maurice Delcroix, rue Père Damien 59, 1140 Brussels, Belgium.

Mrs. D. Dey, 4, Anthill Close, Denmead, Portsmouth, Hants.

J.F. Dinsdale, Esq., Garthside, 5, Valkyrie Avenue, Whitstable, Kent.

Miss E.M.R. Ditmas, 12, Castle Close, Benson, Oxon OX9 6SN.

Professor A.H. Diverres, 23, Whiteshell Drive, Langland, Swansea SA3 4SY.

B. Cauvet Duhamel, 336, rue d'Entraigues, 37000 Tours, France.

G.R. Edwards, Esq., 33, Holmefield Road, Liverpool L19 3PE.

Mrs Revel Elliott, 17, Newland Street, Eynsham, Oxon.

Professor Dorothy Emmet, 11, Millington Road, Cambridge CB3 9HW.

Mrs. Edith M. Eriksson, 6, Ethelbert Crescent, Cliftonville, Kent CT9 2AY.

Mrs Olga Evans, 23, Durham Road, London N2 9DP.

Professor Eugene H. Falk, 348, Wesley Drive, Chapel Hill, N.C. 27514, U.S.A.

Dr. D.A. Farnie, Department of History, The University, Manchester M13 9PL.

Mrs. R. Fennell, 23, Simmondley New Road, Glossop, Derbyshire.

Dr.J.M. Ferrier (Mrs. W. Love), 4, The Grove, Hartford, Huntingdon, Cambridgeshire PE18 7YD.

Miss E. Pauline Ferry, 42, Birchington Road, London N8 8HP.

Mrs. Nora M. Malins Fisher, 86, Crewe Road, Nantwich, Cheshire CW5 6JD.

A.W. Fitch, Esq., 115 Lisburne Lane, Stockport, Cheshire SK2 5RQ.

Mrs. J. Forster, 30, Westmorland Road, Didsbury, Manchester M20 8TA.

Professor C. Foulon, Université de Haute Bretagne, 4, rue des Gantelles, 35000 Rennes, France.

Professor J.-P. Fourquet, 95, boulevard Pasteur, 94260 Fresnes, France.

Professor David C. Fowler, Department of English, University of Washington, Seattle, Washington 98195, U.S.A.

Clive Frankish, Esq., Department of French Studies, The University, Manchester M13 9PL.

Professor Wilson L. Frescoln, Villanova University, Villanova, Pennsylvania 19085, U.S.A.

Professor Lilian R. Furst, University of Texas at Dallas, P.O. Box 688, Richardson, Texas 75080, U.S.A.

Professor B. Gaines, Department of English, University of New Mexico, U.S.A.

Professor Jean Gaudon, 15, rue Sarrette, 75014 Paris, France.

Rt. Rev. G.K. Giggall, Fosbrooke House, 8, Clifton Drive, Lytham FY8 5RQ, Lancs.

Professor P. Ginestier, Department of French, The University, Hull HU6 7RX.

Mrs. C.E. Glitz, 117, Norman Road, Wrexham, North Wales.

Mrs C.W. Good, 10A, Nelson Road, Southsea, Hants PO5 2AR.

Mrs. Ida Gordon, 14, Middlepenny Road, Longbank, Renfrewshire.

Mrs. Beryl Goudswaard, 65, Fraser Crescent, Upper Hutt, N.Z.

Mr. and Mrs. E. Green, 26, Warwick Drive, Hale, Altrincham, Cheshire WA15 9DY.

Professor T.G. Griffith, Department of Italian, The University, Manchester M13 9PL.

M. Léon Grinberg, 4, Cours Albert-1ᵉʳ, 75008 Paris, France. .

Mrs. P.J. Grocock, The Hawthorns, 89, Westgate, Tickhill, Doncaster DN11 9NF.

Miss P.B. Grout, Department of Romance Studies, University College of Swansea, Singleton Park, Swansea SA2 8PP.

Mme. R. Guiette, 164, Deurnestraat (B. F2), 2510 Mortsel, Belgium.

Dr. G. and Mrs. D. Gwynne, Department of French Studies, The University, Manchester M13 9PL.

Dr. G. Gybbon-Monypenny, Department of Spanish, The University, Manchester M13 9PL.

Professor C.A. Hackett, Shawford Close, Shawford, Winchester, Hants SO21 2BL.

H.R. and Mrs W.I. Halliday, 13, Newcroft, Warton, Carnforth LA5 9QD.

P. Hampshire, Esq., Eliot College, Canterbury CT2 9LT.

Professor Norman and Mrs. Jacqueline Hampson, 305, Hull Road, York YO1 3LB.

John H. Harris, Esq., 16, Vicarage Lane, Chalk, Gravesend, Kent.

Dr. P.M. Harry, Royal Holloway College, University of London, Egham Hill, Egham, Surrey TW20 0EX.

Miss Joan Harvey, 10, Little Bottom, Station Road, Marlow, Bucks SL7 1NR.

Mrs. R. Hester, 12, Monmouth Close, Toddington, Dunstable, Beds LU5 6AQ.

J.A. Higgins, 34, Gwendoline Close, Thingwall, Wirral, Merseyside L61 1DL.

Miss C. Hill, Department of French Studies, The University, Manchester M13 9PL.

J. Hochland, Esq., 70, Brooklawn Drive, Manchester 20.

Mr. and Mrs. Fletcher Hodges, Jr., 5812 Kentucky Avenue, Pittsburgh, Pa. 15232, U.S.A.

Mrs. Catherine Hodgson, South Landing, Swallowfield, Reading, Berks RG7 1RE.

Professor A.J. Holden, French Department, 4 Buccleuch Place, Edinburgh EH8 9LW.

Professor T.E. Hope, Rydal House, 5, Grosvenor Terrace, Grosvenor Road, Leeds LS6 2DY.

†Professor Jules Horrent, 38, rue des Buissons, B 4000 Liège, Belgium.

Mr. and Mrs. W.D. Hough, 50, Westmorland Road, Urmston, Manchester M31 1HL.

Mrs. Margaret Howe, 8, Park Avenue, Chapeltown, Sheffield S30 4WH.

Miss Mary A. Huddart, Acrewalls, Deanscales, Cockermouth, Cumbria.

Mrs. A. Hulse, Arleigh, Wooddale, Great Baddow, Chelmsford, Essex CM2 8EZ.

Mrs. E.F. Humble, 22, The Hyde, Winchcombe, Glos GL54 5QR.

Mr. A. Hunt, Department of French, St. Salvator's College, University of St. Andrews, Fife KY16 9PH.

Miss C.G. Hunter, Selborne, 3, Akeman Close, Kirtlington, Oxford OX5 3HX.

Mrs. Hilary Hutchins, 89, Christchurch Road, Norwich NR2 3NG.

Miss Joan V. Hyde, 5, Clarendon Gardens, London.

Professor Tadahiro Ikegami, 3-11-14 Kugenuma-kaigan, Fujisawa-shi, Kanagawa-kin, 251 Japan.

J. Illingworth, Esq., 56, Braithwell Road, Maltby, Rotherham, Yorks.

Professor J.C. Ireson, Department of French, The University, Hull HU6 7RX.

Michael Irwin, Esq., University of Kent.

Mrs. Catherine Ives, Greenways, Frenze Road, Diss, Norfolk IP22 3PB.

Professor S.W. Jackman, History Department, The University, Victoria, B.C., Canada.

Dr. A.R.W. James, Department of French Studies, The University, Manchester M13 9PL.

Professor A.O.H. Jarman, 4, Henllys Road, Cyncoed, Cardiff.

A. Jasper, Esq., 22, Maria Square, Belmont, Bolton BL7 8AE.

Mrs. Eryl Jenkins, 51, Cherry Grove, Sketty, Swansea, West Glamorgan.

Professor Omer Jodogne, 24, rue de Brabant, 5000 Namur, Belgium.

Ms. Edna R. Johnston, 67, Elie Avenue, Barnhill, Dundee DD5 3SJ.

Mrs. Gwenllian V. Jones, 1, Brunel Avenue, High Cross, Newport, Gwent NP1 0DN.

M. Henri Jourdan le Rieu, 42440 Noirétable, France.

Miss B. Kalpakdjian, 5, Clifton Court, Buckingham Road West, Heaton Mersey, Stockport SK4 4DB.

Ms. Shirley P. Keays, Wyndham Trees, 100, Selby Lane, Keyworth, Notts NG12 5AJ.

Professor R.E. Keller, Department of German, The University, Manchester M13 9PL.

Professor Douglas Kelly, Department of French and Italian, University of Wisconsin, Madison, Wisconsin 53706, U.S.A.

Mrs. Jean Kelly, 14, Scotstoun Park, South Queensferry, Scotland EH30 9PQ.

J. Kelly, Esq., Department of Language, University of York, Heslington, York YO1 5DD.

Dr. Angus Kennedy, Department of French, The University, Glasgow.

Dr. Elspeth Kennedy, St. Hilda's College, Oxford OX4 1DY.

Mr. and Mrs. K. King, 3, Waldon Avenue, Cheadle, Cheshire.

N.F. Kirkman, Esq., 25, Alcester Road, Sale, Cheshire M33 3GW.

R.S. Kirkman, Esq., Case postale 500, 1211 Geneva 22, Switzerland.

Professor R.C. Knight, Department of French, University College of Swansea, Singleton Park, Swansea SA2 8PP.

Professor L.C. Knights, 57, Jesus Lane, Cambridge CB5 8BS,

Professor James Laidlaw, Department of French, University of Aberdeen.

†Raymond Mostyn Lamb, Esq., 17, Coniston Road, Barrow-in-Furness, Cumbria LA14 5PL.

M. Jean Larmat, 1, avenue André Chénier, 06100 Nice, France.

R.G. Lascelles, Esq., Jodrell Bank, Macclesfield, Cheshire.

Miss H.C.R. Laurie, 4, Highfield Place, Glasgow G12 0LB.

Dr. A. Lavers, 45, Wellington Road, Hatch End, Pinner, Middlesex HA5 4NF.

L. Lawrence, Esq., 160 Lower Vicarage Road, Kennington, Ashford, Kent.

†Professor T.E. Lawrenson, Department of Theatre Studies, The University, Lancaster.

H.W. Lawton, Esq., 4, Timber Bank, Vigo Village, Meopham, Kent DA13 0RZ.

Mrs. J.R. Lawton, Wendon, Borth-y-Gest, Porthmadog, Gwynedd.

Félix Lecoy, Professeur au Collège de France, 84, boulevard Pasteur, Paris.

Professeur Pierre Le Gentil, Professeur hon. à la Sorbonne, Paris.

Professor M. Dominica Legge, 191A, Woodstock Road, Oxford.

Professor Roy F. Leslie and Mrs. Erika F. Leslie, Department of English, University of Victoria, Victoria, B.C. V8W 2Y2, Canada.

T.J. Lewis, Esq., Department of French Studies, The University, Manchester M13 9PL.

Mr. and Mrs. G. Lewney, 37, Belle Vue Road, Basing, Basingstoke, Hants RG24 0JP.

Lincoln College, Oxford 0X1 3DR.

Dr. J. Linskill, 23, Fawley Road, Liverpool 18.

Dr. A. Lodge, Department of French, The University, Aberdeen.

Mrs. Monica Lodge, School House, Ripon Grammar School, Ripon, N. Yorks HG4 2DJ.

Professeur Jeanne Lods, 84, rue Vergniaud, Paris.

Dr. C. Luttrell, Department of French, The University, Leicester.

Dr. Faith Lyons, Flat 3, 69, Marlborough Place, London.

Professor Ian McFarlane, Wadham College, Oxford.

Ms. Florence E. MacNeill, 17, Dalston Drive, Didsbury, Manchester M20 0LR.

Miss P.I. Maguire, The University, Hull,

Emeritus Professor J.C. Mahoney, 6, Tenth Avenue, Saint Lucia 4067, Queensland, Australia.

Richard Mansell-Jones, Esq., Founders Court, Lothbury, London EC2R 1HE.

Mr. and Mrs. W. Mansfield-Cooper, Fieldgate Cottage, 9, Station Road, Royston, Herts.

David Marks, Esq., 3, Paper Buildings, Temple, London EC4.

M. Paul Masse, 4 bis allée F. Schmitt, 92210 Saint-Cloud, France.

Dr. Margaret Mein, Westfield College, Kidderpore Avenue, Hampstead, London NW3 7ST.

Professor Geoffrey Mellor, Department of Modern Languages, The University, Salford.

Ms. Elizabeth Milestone, 55, Taylor Road, Wallington, Surrey.

Mr. D.M. Mitchell, Doordrift Lodge, Doordrift, Plumbstead 7800, Cape Town, R.S.A.

Mrs. S.S. Mitchell-Cameron, 40, Fanshawe Crescent, Ware, Herts SG12 0AS.

Mrs. Kathleen Morris, Six Bells, Pathlow, Stratford-upon-Avon.

Mrs. Joan I.S. Moss, 6, Chestnut Avenue, Southborough, Tunbridge Wells, Kent TN4 0BP.

Professor Odette de Mourgues, 1, Marion Close, Cambridge CB3 0HN.

Martin Moynihan, Esq., 5, The Green, Wimbledon Common, London SW19 5AZ.

Mrs Jean E. Murphy, 20, Milray Avenue, Wollstonecraft, N.S.W. 2065, Australia.

†Professor Helaine Newstead, Graduate School, The City University of New York, 33 West 42 Street, New York, N.Y. 10036, U.S.A.

Professor R. Niklaus, 17, Elm Grove Road, Topsham, Exeter EX3 0EQ.

Shunichi Noguchi, 1354 Kujo-cho, Yamato-Koriyama-shi, 639-11 Japan.

Professor Walter Oakeshott, The Old School House, Eynsham, Oxford.

J.A. Oakley, 75, Silhill Hall Road, Solihull, West Midlands B91 1JT.

R.A.C. Oliver and A.M. Oliver, Waingap, Crook, Kendal, Cumbria LA8 9HT.

A.W. Openshaw, Esq., 26, Cheltenham Crescent, Lee-on-Solent, Hants PO13 9HH.

J. O'Regan, Esq., 29, Wainwright Avenue, Denton, Manchester M34 2WW.

Dr. Eithne M. O'Sharkey, Department of French, The University, Dundee.

Dr. Yorio Otaka, 3-3-61, Suimeidai, Kawanishi, 666-01, Japan.

Dr. H.L. Owrid, Department of Audiology, The University, Manchester M13 9PL.

Dr. Michael Pakenham, Department of French and Italian, The University, Exeter.

Mrs. Margaret Parry, 22, Ridgeway, Tranmere Park, Guisely, Leeds LS20 8AJ.

Mrs. A.T. Paterson, 215, Boroughbridge Road, York.

Dr. Raymond Pearson, Department of History, New University of Coleraine, Coleraine, Northern Ireland.

Dr. Roger Pensom, Department of French and Italian, The University, Exeter.

† Professor C.E. Pickford, Department of French, The University, Hull HU6 7RX.

Dr. H. Popper, Department of German and Russian, University College of Swansea, Singleton Park, Swansea SA2 8PP.

Miss J.M. Porter, 9, Westgate, Bridgnorth, Shropshire WV16 5BL.

Mr. L.G. Pugh, 35, Wern Road, Skewen, West Glamorgan.

Mrs Phyllis Pybus, 1, Elm Court, Hyde Lea, Stafford.

Dr. M.D. Quainton, Department of French Studies, Lonsdale College, University of Lancaster, Bailrigg, Lancaster LA1 4YN.

Ms. Amanda Rainger, 10, St. Austell Road, London SE13 7EQ.

Dr. F.W. Ratcliffe, Light Alders Farm, Light Alders Lane, Disley, Cheshire SK12 2LW.

Professor Garnet Rees, 88, Newland Park, Hull, North Humberside HU5 2DS.

Gwilym O. Rees, Esq., 51, Westwood Lane, Leeds LS16 5NP.

†Professor T.B.W. Reid, 37, Blandford Avenue, Oxford OX2 8EB.

Dr. T.J. Reiss, 5194, Westbury Avenue, Montréal, Quebec, Canada H3W 2W3.

Mrs. F.J. Riddy, Flat 3.1.1., A.K. Davidson Hall, University of Stirling, Stirling FK9 4LA.

J.H. Riding, 45, Little Lane, Longridge, Nr. Preston PR3 3WS.

Mrs. R. Roberts, The Burgs, Berries Lane, Bayston Hill, Shrewsbury, Shropshire SY3 0AP.

Miss Judith Robinson, 2, Churchgate, Urmston, Manchester M31 1LE.

Dr. P.E.J. Robinson, Keynes College, The University, Canterbury, Kent.

Mrs. A. Roche, 1, Loen Crescent, Smithills, Bolton.

Mrs. P. Rodgers, 80, Marsh Lane, Shepley, Huddersfield HD8 8AS.

Dr. G.E. Rodgers, 34, Clayton Park Square, Jesmond, Newcastle-upon-Tyne NE2 4DP.

Dr. Winifred Rogers, 8, Abbot Road, Guildford, Surrey GU1 3TA.

Dr. Aubrey Rosenberg, Victoria College, University of Toronto, Toronto, Canada M5S 1K7.

Dr. Harold Rothera, Department of Education, University College of Swansea, Hendrefoilan, Swansea SA2 7NB.

Professor W. Rothwell, 11, Ramillies Avenue, Cheadle Hulme, Cheshire.

G.A. Runnalls, Esq., Department of French, The University, Edinburgh.

Dr. E.M. Rutson, St. Ann's College, Oxford.

Ms. Helen Salmon, 48, London Road, Shrewsbury, Shropshire.

Miss. C. Irene Salter, 8, Geoffrey Avenue, Neville's Cross, Durham.

F.W. Saunders, Esq., Department of French Studies, The University, Manchester M13 9PL.

D. Secrétan, Esq., Department of French Studies, The University, Manchester M13 9PL.

M. Sev, 50, rue Michel Ange, 75016 Paris, France.

Sewanee Mediaeval Colloquium, The University of the South, Sewanee, Tennessee 37375, U.S.A.

Professor J. Seznec, All Souls College, Oxford OX1 4AL.

Professor Robert Shackleton, All Souls College, Oxford OX1 4AL.

S.M. Sharman, 21, Bollinbarn Drive, Upton, Macclesfield, Cheshire.

Dr. Frank Shaw, Department of German, University of Bristol, 21, Woodland Road, Clifton, Bristol BS8 1TE.

Dr. David Shirt, Department of French, The University, Newcastle-upon-Tyne.

Mrs. Renée Short, House of Commons, London S.W.1.

T.H. Slater, Postfach 1511, 5483 Ahrweiler, Germany.

Miss Barbara A. Smith, 20, Monks Road, Windsor, Berks SL4 4PE.

G.W. Smith, Esq., Weinbergstrasse 96, Kilchberg 8802, Switzerland.

Dr. P.M. Smith, Department of French, The University, Hull HU6 7RX.

Society for the Study of Mediaeval Languages and Literature, Magdelen College, Oxford OX1 4AU.

Dr. S.E. de Souza, 3, Marine Parade, Seaford, E. Sussex BN25 2PL.

Mrs. E. Stansfield, 27, Priors Walk, Morpeth, Northumberland NE61 2RF.

Nina Howell Starr and Nathan Comfort Starr, 333 East 68 Street, New York, N.Y. 10021, U.S.A.

Mrs. Joyce M. Stoneley, 12, Winton Road, Ware, Herts SG12 7AX.

Lady Strabolgi, 115, Ebury Street, London SW1W 9QU.

Mrs. Nora Sugden, 22, Lodge Avenue, Willingdon, Eastbourne, Sussex BN22 OJD.

†Professor F.E. Sutcliffe, Department of French Studies, The University, Manchester M13 9PL.

Chris Swan, Esq., 54, Worcester Avenue, Birstall, Leicestershire.

Ms. Carolyn T. Swan, 5401, Weatherford Drive, Los Angeles, California 90008, U.S.A.

Professor Michael Swanton, Department of English, The University, Exeter.

Dr. Edward A. Synan, 59, Queen's Park Crescent, Toronto, Ontario, Canada M5S 2C4.

Professor and Mrs. F. Sweetser, 311, Hirst Court, Lake Bluff, Illinois 60044, U.S.A.

A.S. Tate, 78, Upton Court Road, Slough SL3 7LZ.

M. Antoine Tavera, 18, rue Saint-Saveur, Paris 75002.

Dr Jane H.M. Taylor, Department of French Studies, The University, Manchester M13 9PL.

W.B. Taylor, Esq., 112, Compstall Road, Romiley, Cheshire.

Sister Wendy B. Taylor, Carmelite Monastery, St. Vincent's Road, Fulwood, Preston, Lancashire PR2 4QA.

M. Jean-Claude Thiolier, Professeur à l'Université de Paris-Créteil, 11, rue de l'Estrapode, 75005 Paris, France.

Miss Brenda E. Thomas, 228, Stretford Road, Urmston, Manchester M31 1NB.

Dr. Peter E. Thompson, Waddon Thatch, Chudleigh, Newton Abbot, Devon.

Mrs. E.M. Thornton, 23, St. Vincent Avenue, Blackpool, Lancashire FY1 6RT.

H. Ellis Tomlinson, Esq., Chester House, 46, Victoria Road East, Thornton Cleveleys, Lancs FY5 5BT.

G.E. Tuaynor, Esq., 26, Auburn Road, Manchester 16.

Mrs. M.E. Tuddenham, 7, Trent Avenue, Huntington, York YO3 9SE.

Mrs. R. Turner, Department of German, The University, Manchester M13 9PL.

Miss Adeline P. Turton, 8, Broadway, Cheadle, Cheshire SK8 1NQ.

Mr. A. Unsworth, Flat 51, St. Peter's Way, Menston, Ilkley, West Yorks LS29 6NY.

Miss P.M. Vanes, 9, Withington Road, Helmsley, York YO6 5HE.

Professor Kenneth Varty, Department of French, The University, Glasgow.

The University of Victoria, P.O. Box 1700, Victoria, British Columbia, Canada V8W 2YZ.

A. Vinaver, Esq., 15, Norman Road, Canterbury, Kent.

Mrs. E. Vinaver, 149c, Island Wall, Whitstable, Kent.

M. Wladimir Vinaver, 13D, allée d'Honneur, 92330 Sceaux, France.

Dr. Carl Wachtl, P.O Box 1549, Evanston, Illinois 60204, U.S.A.

†Professor R.-L. Wagner, 2, rue Emile Faguet, Paris 14, France.

Dr. C.H. Wake, Darwin College, The University, Canterbury, Kent.

Professor R.M. Walker, Department of Spanish, Birkbeck College, Malet Street, London WC1E 7HX.

Professor J.M. Wallace-Hadrill, All Souls College, Oxford.

Ms. Martha Wallen, 1710, 5th Street West, Apartment 205, Menomonie, Wisconsin 54751, U.S.A.

Ronald N. Walpole, Esq., 1680, La Loma, Berkeley, California 94709, U.S.A.

J.F. Waring, Esq., 11, Hollies Rood, Wilpshire, Blackburn, Lancashire.

Mrs.Pamela M. Warrington, Lane Head House, Shepley, Huddersfield HD8 8BW.

Mme Jeanne Wathelet-Willem, Visé-Voie 56, B-4000 Liège, Belgium.

Mrs. Dylis E.C. Watson, 3, Windsor Terrace, Douglas, Isle of Man.

Richard C. West, Esq., 1922, Madison Street, Madison, W.I. 53711, U.S.A.

Dr. P.M. Wetherill, Department of French, The University, Manchester M13 9PL.

Dr. Muriel Whitaker,Department of English, University of Alberta, Edmonton, Canada T6G 2E5.

Miss Margaret A. Whitfield, Lower Pentmyn Cottage, Marshfield, Cardiff CF3 8TU.

Dr. Friederike Wiedemann, 23329, W. Mallard Court, Barrington, Illinois 60010, U.S.A.

Brother Wilfrid M.A., De La Salle College, Hopwood Hall, Middleton, Manchester.

A.M. Williams, Esq., 3, Avenue Road, Kings Lynn, Norfolk.

Mrs. Mary E.L. Williamson, 22, Longdale Lane, Ravenshead, Nottingham NG15 9AD.

Ms. Grace G. Wilson, 360, Central Park West, New York, N.Y. 10025, U.S.A.

Dr. Robert H. Wilson, Department of English, The University of Texas, Austin, Texas, U.S.A.

Professor R.A. Wisbey, Department of German, King's College, Strand, London WC2R 2LS.

Professor B. Woledge, 28A Dobbins Lane, Wendover, Aylesbury, Bucks.

Miss Florence Worsley, 4, Clifford Road, Poynton, Stockport, Cheshire SK12 1HY.

Emeritus Professor B.A. Wortley, 24, Gravel Lane, Wilmslow, Cheshire SK9 6LA.

Miss P.A. Wragg, 128, Hopefield Avenue, Frecheville, Sheffield S12 4XE.

Professor Barbara Wright, Department of French, New Arts Building, Trinity College, Dublin 2, Ireland.

Dr. M.L.M. Young, Department of French, The University, Manchester M13 9PL.

Miss Zara Zaddy, French Department, The University, Lancaster.

Dr. Melvin Zimmerman, Department of French Studies, Faculty of Arts, York University, 4700 Keele Street, Downsview, Ontario M3J 1P3, Canada.

Professor Michel Zink, 32, rue Ozenne, Toulouse 31000, France.

Dr. G. Zuntz, 1, Humberside Road, Cambridge CB4 1JD.

Dr. Atie Zuurdeeg, Department of French, Augustana College, Roch Island, Illinois 60201, U.S.A.

★